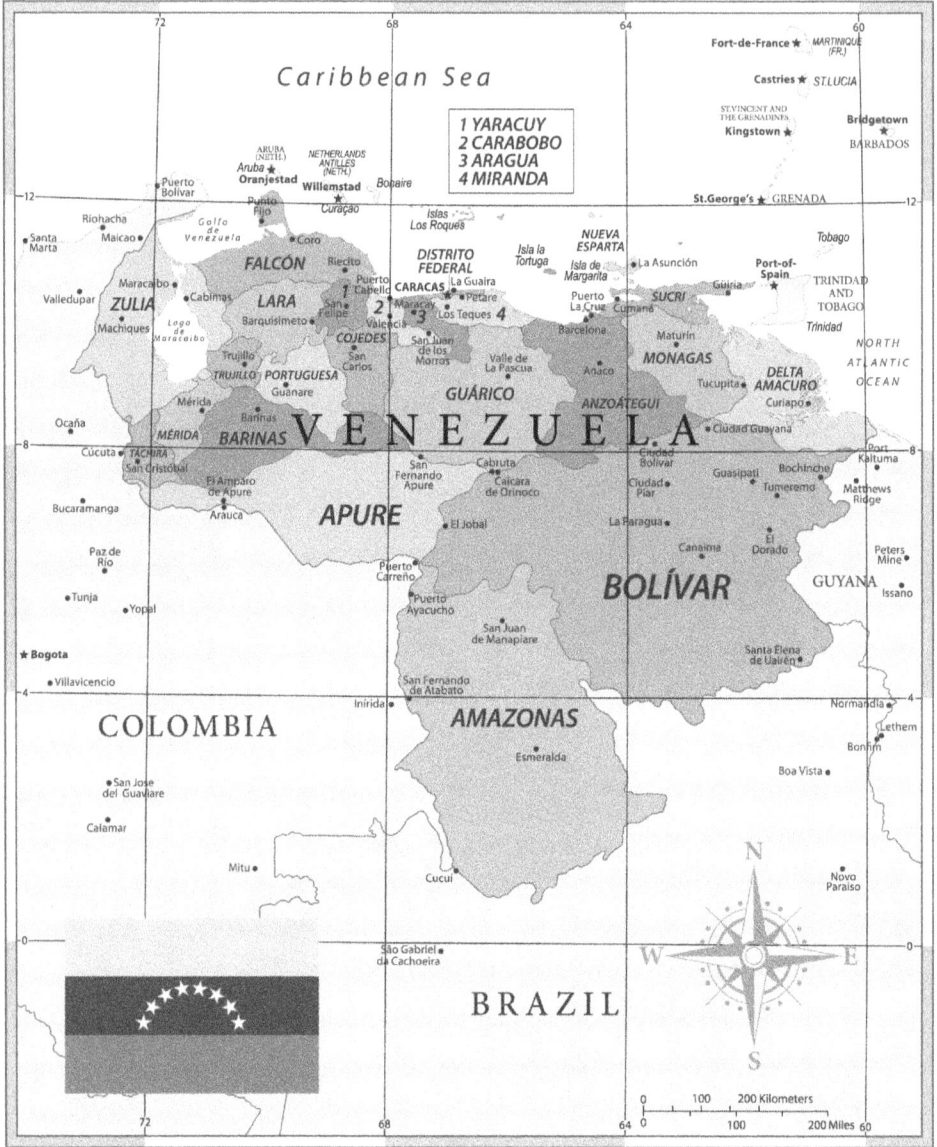

Caribbean Sea

Fort-de-France ★ MARTINIQUE (FR.)

Castries ★ ST.LUCIA

ST.VINCENT AND THE GRENADINES
Kingstown ★

Bridgetown ★
BARBADOS

| 1 YARACUY |
| 2 CARABOBO |
| 3 ARAGUA |
| 4 MIRANDA |

ARUBA (NETH.)
Aruba ★
Oranjestad

NETHERLANDS ANTILLES (NETH.)
Willemstad ★

Bonaire

St.George's ★ GRENADA

Puerto Bolívar

Punto Fijo

Islas Los Roques

NUEVA ESPARTA

Tobago

Riohacha

Golfo de Venezuela

Coro

Isla la Tortuga

Isla de Margarita

La Asunción

Port-of-Spain ★

TRINIDAD AND TOBAGO

Santa Marta

Maicao

FALCÓN

Riecito

DISTRITO FEDERAL

Güiria

Valledupar

Maracaibo

Cabimas

LARA

Puerto Cabello

CARACAS

La Guaira

Puerto La Cruz

Cumaná

SUCRI

Trinidad

ZULIA

Barquisimeto

San Felipe

1

Valencia

Maracay

2

Petare

Los Teques

3

4

Barcelona

NORTH

Machiques

Lago de Maracaibo

COJEDES

San Juan de los Morros

Maturín

MONAGAS

ATLANTIC OCEAN

Ocaña

Trujillo

TRUJILLO

San Carlos

PORTUGUESA

Valle de La Pascua

Anaco

Tucupita

DELTA AMACURO

Cúcuta

MÉRIDA

Mérida

Guanare

Barinas

V E N E Z U E L A

GUÁRICO

ANZOÁTEGUI

Curiapo

San Cristóbal

TÁCHIRA

BARINAS

San Fernando Apure

Cabruta

Ciudad Bolívar

Ciudad Guayana

Port Kaituma

El Amparo de Apure

Caicara de Orinoco

Ciudad Píar

Guasipati

Bochinche

Tumeremo

Matthews Ridge

Bucaramanga

APURE

Arauca

El Jobal

La Paragua

Paz de Río

Canaima

El Dorado

Peters Mine

Tunja

Yopal

Puerto Carreño

BOLÍVAR

GUYANA

Issano

Bogotá ★

Puerto Ayacucho

San Juan de Manapiare

Santa Elena de Uairén

Villavicencio

San Fernando de Atabato

Normandia

COLOMBIA

Inírida

AMAZONAS

Lethem

Bonfim

San José del Guaviare

Esmeralda

Boa Vista

Cálamar

Mitú

Cucuí

Novo Paraíso

São Gabriel da Cachoeira

BRAZIL

N

W

E

S

| 0 | | 100 | 200 Kilometers |
| 0 | | 100 | 200 Miles |

Communes and the Venezuelan State

SOCIAL MOVEMENTS IN THE AMERICAS

Series Editor: A. Ricardo López

This series reaches beyond conventional approaches and disciplinary boundaries to publish widely ranging studies in social movements—defined for this series, as the practice through which a multiplicity of actors transform, contest, challenge, consolidate, and reproduce society in variety of historical moments—from diverse perspectives. The fundamental premise of this series is that, if social movements have historically been constituted across nations, the study of them must be transnational as well. The main objective is threefold. First, the series de-emphasizes the nation-state as the primary framework for understanding social movements in the Americas. Second, the series constitutes a transnational and interdisciplinary intellectual community to explore the political, social, economic, cultural conditions through which social movements have played a fundamental role in shaping the experiences, categories, practices, and meanings of democracy. Third, the series reconsiders the origins of social change and democracy away from the U.S. and Europe. Social Movements in the Americas is dedicated to publishing translations of important scholarly work produced in Latin America.

Recent titles in the series:

Communes and the Venezuelan State

The Struggle for Participatory Democracy in a Time of Crisis

Anderson M. Bean

LEXINGTON BOOKS
Lanham • Boulder • New York • London

Published by Lexington Books
An imprint of The Rowman & Littlefield Publishing Group, Inc.
4501 Forbes Boulevard, Suite 200, Lanham, Maryland 20706
www.rowman.com

86-90 Paul Street, London EC2A 4NE, United Kingdom

British Library Cataloguing in Publication Information Available

Library of Congress Cataloging-in-Publication Data

Names: Bean, Anderson, 1983- author.
Title: Communes and the Venezuelan state : the struggle for participatory democracy
  in a time of crisis / Anderson Bean.
Description: Lanham : Lexington Books, [2022] | Series: Social movements in
  the Americas | Includes bibliographical references and index. | Summary: "In
  Communes and the Venezuelan State: The Struggle for Participatory Democracy in
  a Time of Crisis, Anderson Bean examines the communal movement in Venezuela,
  its origins, contradictory relationship to the state, and the challenges it faces amid
  Venezuela's largest economic and political crisis"— Provided by publisher.
Identifiers: LCCN 2021053811 (print) | LCCN 2021053812 (ebook) | ISBN
  9781793640840 (cloth) | ISBN 9781793640857 (epub) | ISBN 9781793640864 (paper)
Subjects: LCSH: Communal living—Venezuela. | Political participation—Venezuela. |
  Democracy—Venezuela. | Venezuela—Politics and government.
Classification: LCC HQ972.V4 .B43 2022 (print) | LCC HQ972.V4 (ebook) | DDC
  307.77/40987—dc23/eng/20211202
LC record available at https://lccn.loc.gov/2021053811
LC ebook record available at https://lccn.loc.gov/2021053812

For Phoenix

Contents

Acknowledgments

I could not have written this book without the generous support of many individuals. First and foremost, I would like to thank all the people who participated in this study, the communal council and communal organizers who were not only instrumental to the research of this project but also were equally as important as inspirations for this project. Without their cooperation this project could not have been completed. I would also like to thank my loving parents, Doug and Karen Bean, whose unwavering support made writing this book possible. I am also grateful for the many people who helped in a myriad of ways throughout the writing and research of this project. With those people in mind, I owe a special thanks to Mara Garcia Viloria, Yhon Pacheco, Aury Escobar de Rodas, Phoenix Carter, Hector Hernandez Albornoz, Sahar Haghighat, brian bean, Jason Smith, Cesar Romero, Sofia Viloria, Juan Garcia, Jhonattan Bueno, Melissa Gouge, and Andrea Pacheco. I want to extend a special thanks to Lester Kurtz, Peter Mandaville, and George Ciccariello-Maher for taking time out of their busy schedules to read and reread this manuscript and offer critical suggestions and feedback. I owe the greatest thanks to John Dale for his guidance, patience, valuable criticisms, and suggestions and for believing in me and this project; without him this project would never have been completed.

List of Abbreviations

Accion Democratica	AD
Alien Tort Claims Act	ACTA
Andean Community of Nations	CAN
Armed Forces of National Liberation	FALN
Bank of the South	BancoSur
Bolivarian Alliance for the Peoples of Our America	ALBA
Central University of Venezuela	UCV
Center for Economic Policy Research	CEPR
Center for Women's Studies	CEM
Comite de Organizacion Politica Electoral Independiente	COPEI
Common Southern Market	Mercosur
Communal Councils	CCs
Confederation of Workers of Venezuela	CTV
Constituent National Assembly	ANC
Councils of Good Government	JBGs
Fatherland for All	PPT
Fifth Republic Movement	MVR
Free Trade Agreement of the Americas	FTAA

Import Substitution Industrialization	ISI
Indigenous Federation of the State of Bolívar	FIB
International Monetary Fund	IMF
Landless Peasants Movement	MST
Local Public Planning Councils	CLPPS
Local Committees for Supply and Production	CLAP
Movement of the Revolutionary Left	MIR
Movimiento al Socialismo	MAS
National Assembly	AN
National Electoral Council	CNE
National Indigenous Council of Venezuela	CONIVE
National Union of Venezuelan Labor	UNT
National Women's Institute	Inamujer
The New Television Station of the South	TeleSUR
North American Free Trade Agreement	NAFTA
Participatory Budgeting	PB
People's Electoral Movement	MEP
Petroleum of Venezuela	PDVSA
Popular Education Center	PEC
Radio Caracas Television	RCTV
Rebel Zapatista Autonomous Municipalities	MAREZ
Revolutionary Bolivarian Movement 200	MBR-200
Regional Organization of the Indigenous Peoples of the Amazonian State	ORPIA
Special Economic Zone	SEZ
Structural Adjustment Program	SAP
United Socialist Party of Venezuela	PSUV
Union Republicana Democratica	URD
Union of South American Nations	UNASUR
Venezuelan Communist Party	PCV

World Trade Organization	WTO
Venezuelan Communist Party	PCV
Venezuelan Federation of Chambers of Commerce	Fedecámeras
Venezuelan Program of Education-Action in Human Rights	PROVEA
Zapatista Army of National Liberation	EZLN

Introduction

I was told there was a direct bus from Caracas to Chabasquen. What was supposed to be a simple six-hour bus trip, turned into a twelve-hour journey up the Cordillera de Mérida mountain range. The trip consisted of two bus rides, a van ride, a car ride, and finally a bumpy truck ride where we had no other choice but to stand up in the back of a truck, locking arms with other passengers to keep from falling onto the dusty dirt road below us, all the while with our eyes closed to avoid the dust from entering our eyes. Chabasquen, a small village in Northwestern Venezuela high in the Cordillera de Mérida mountain range, is the host to the *Gran Asamblea Comuna del Corredor Político Territorial Fabricio Ojeda* (henceforth the *Gran Asamblea*), a gathering of twelve communes in the Venezuelan states of Portuguesa and Lara. Communes are grassroots organs of self-administration and popular power that bring together community organizations that have emerged in mostly poor neighborhoods around issues of water, electricity, health, and more recently around the production of textiles and agricultural products. The *Gran Asemblea* in Chabasquen brings together twelve such communes from two different states in order to coordinate on projects that affect the territories of these communities.

As Chabasquen sits high in the Cordillera de Mérida mountain range, a northeastern extension of the Andes Mountains, one of the first things I notice as we arrive at the assembly is that the temperature is noticeably cooler, at least 15 degrees, than the more tropical climate of Caracas. As soon as we jumped off the truck, with our brown shirts covered in dust, we were all welcomed by a jubilant crowd of over a few thousand communal organizers. The assembly was festive and familial. Children were running around with cotton candy, live music was blaring from the speakers, and most everyone had red shirts, the color worn by supporters of the late President Hugo Chávez.

Tables lined the walkway approaching the outdoor stage with products produced by the various communes in attendance. The tables were filled with
fruits, vegetables, coffee, flour, sugar, salt, pineapples, bananas, corn, white,
purple, and yellow maize, all produced in the communes. One table was col-
lecting a variety of communal products to donate to people from a nearby
town whose houses were destroyed by a recent flood.

We were quickly ushered on stage to seats just behind the podium and
introduced to the crowd as international visitors (I was traveling with three
Venezuelans and a woman from San Cristóbal de las Casas, México). The
stage was surrounded with banners that read *Comuna o Nada* (the commune
or nothing), *Territorio Liberado y Comunalizado Ejerciendo la Soberana
Popular* (Communalized and Liberated Territory Exercising Popular Sovereignty), *Ni un Paso Atras* (not a single step backwards), as well as banners
from each of the twelve communes represented in the assembly.

From the stage there was poetry readings; spoken word; traditional folk
music; renditions of popular folk songs by the late Ali Primera, the most
recognized Venezuelan folk singer, poet and activist; and various types of
dance performances. There were musicians of all ages, including a young
nine-year-old girl singing *Joropo* (Venezuela's national popular folk musical
style and dance), children and adults dancing the Salsa and the *Merengue*. At
one point I was swept from my seat on stage by an older woman to join her on
the dance floor. Around lunchtime, free lunch plates piled with black beans,
fried plantains, rice, and shredded beef (a traditional Venezuelan meal) was
passed around to all attendees.

Interspersed between the festivities were political discussions about various ways to consolidate popular power, increase production, and better organize the distribution of products, and was entertainment from members of the
communes. Many spoke of cooperation and better ways for the communes
to coordinate. Speakers frequently referenced *El Golpe de Timón*, Hugo
Chávez's 2012 speech announcing a leap forward in the Bolivarian Process
to what is referred to as the "communal state." Some speakers spoke of the
need to increase production of black beans, while others opined that the only
way to take power and control of the state was to take control of production
and put it under the self-management of the communes. Independence was
another common theme from the stage, many making the argument that true
independence comes when workers control the means of production. Most
speakers concluding their speech with the oft-repeated phrase "*Comuna o
Nada*" (the commune or nothing), another reference to *Golpe de Timón*.

If you were to read about Venezuela in the mainstream press you may
not hear about large gatherings of grassroots organs of self-administration,
or participatory democratic structures like the communal councils and
communes described above. Venezuela is currently struggling with its
fair share of problems, particularly in the last few years, as it has faced its

largest existential crisis to date, with problems ranging from high inflation, violence, governance, and long queues for and shortages of a wide range of staple goods like beans, milk, chicken, flour, diapers, and tampons (these issues will be discussed in detail in chapters 5 and 6). However, there is much more to the story than what is regularly reported. This book tells the story of a movement that has not garnered much attention in the mainstream press. It is a movement where, despite its many challenges, obstacles, and sometimes outright messiness, regular workers and ordinary citizens are fighting for more direct control over the political decision-making process though the construction of participatory democratic structures, the creation of various forms of self-governance, and by directly managing public policies and projects that affect their daily lives. This movement is complicated by the contradictions of the Venezuelan government, which has vacillated between at times promoting and facilitating the communal movement and at different times being an obstacle and source of resistance to the movement.

To begin this story, we must begin with what is called the Bolivarian Revolution (sometimes called the Bolivarian process or Bolivarian movement). This is the name given to the social and political process that officially began with the election of Chávez but has roots in grassroots movements that preceded and now have succeeded Chávez. The Bolivarian process is made up of three key components. The first is the re-writing of the constitution, which was approved in a popular referendum in December of 1999. The new constitution added two branches of government, changed the country's name, introduced popular referenda and local planning councils, recognized Venezuela's large indigenous population, recognized housework as an economic activity, and in some ways strengthened presidential power. Many commentators argue that Venezuela has the world's most progressive constitution in the sense that it provides for broad citizen participation and comprehensive human rights protections.[1] Title III includes more than one hundred articles directly addressing a wide range of civil and human rights. Human rights were a central component in the constitution and often went far beyond what most constitutions incorporate and often beyond liberal notions of human rights.[2] Not only are civil and political rights included but also social and economic rights, such as the right to employment, education, healthcare, and dignified housing. These rights are seen as fundamental and an obligation of the state.

The second component is the redistribution of oil profits through various social programs, called "missions." Social missions are social programs implemented early in the Chávez administration that are primarily funded by oil profits. These missions span from education (Mission *Robinson*, an adult literacy program), food (Mission *Mercal*, which provides access to basic foods at a discounted price), healthcare (Mission *Barrio Adentro*, which provides free healthcare services to under-served and impoverished communities), land reform (Mission *Zamora*, which redistributes land to the poor), indigenous rights (Mission *Guaicapuro*, which restores communal land rights to indigenous communities), to housing (*La Gran Mision Vivienda* Venezuela, a low-cost housing program). Partly because of the redistribution of oil wealth through social programs like these, poverty was reduced by 37.6 percent, and extreme poverty dropped by 57.8 percent from the election of Chávez in 1999 until 2011.[3]

The third and perhaps most transformative component of the Bolivarian process is the transfer of power from traditional nodes of power to the popular sectors through the creation of new forms of popular assemblies and experiments with worker's control, communal councils, and communes. The latter two specifically are the focus of this book and the topic to which we now turn.

The communal movement in Venezuela is made up of communal councils—which are neighborhood-based bodies of self-governance and self-administration—and communes—which are made up of collections of communal councils. These two networks of popular power function to circumvent representative democracy and traditional sites of constituted power in order to create sites of participatory democracy and to transfer direct political power and decision making to the people directly affected by these decisions and to social sectors that have been traditionally excluded from sites of power, particularly the poor and people of color.

This book examines both the ways in which workers and peasants, through these networks of popular power, exercise agency over their own development, and the significant challenges, both internal and external, the movement faces as it operates largely within a market economy and a capitalist state. Moreover, this book explores the tensions between the "official" Bolivarian Process represented by the Maduro government and ordinary citizens, workers, and peasants and their different conceptions of democracy and visions of the Bolivarian Process. The stories from below that are explored here allow us to see a more complicated picture of the Bolivarian Process that rejects the old Cold War framework of two distinct sides in the struggle, one being the Maduro government and the stereotype that he and the Bolivarian Process are one and the same, and on the other side an opposition to Maduro that is in support of the project of neoliberalism in the service of Western imperialism. This book makes clear how democracy is a constant struggle from below, and precisely because of this, it cannot be merely understood in two categories as described above.

My case study focuses primarily on communes and communal councils in Venezuela. The council movement in Venezuela is both an example of a network of popular power as well as a case of counter-hegemonic globalization from below. My primary research question is: To what extent do networks of popular power exercise agency over their own social, cultural, and economic development? As I explore this question, I will also answer a series of related questions regarding the significance of popular power to Venezuela's future and the relevance of these networks historically: 1) What are the communes' and councils' relationship to the state, what are their origins, and do they have the potential to transform the capitalist state? 2) Do workers only have agency at the point of production, or do councils that organize at the neighborhood level also have revolutionary potential to transform society? And what power do communal councils have beyond Venezuela?

In answering these questions, I used three qualitative methods. First, I conducted qualitative interviews with council and commune organizers, participants, and representatives, two Venezuelan authors of books on communes and representatives of the Ministry of Communes. Second, I conducted focus groups with council and communal organizers. Lastly, I conducted participant observations at communal council and commune activities and assemblies.

This introduction will be organized as follows. The first section will discuss some of the key themes of the book, agency, popular power, participatory democracy, and democratic self-governance. This section briefly discusses the literature around these topics and where my research falls within this research. The second section is an overview of some of the key findings and conclusions that I draw from the data. The third section discusses the three research methods used in this study to collect data. The final section gives a brief overview of the organization of the book and its six chapters.

AGENCY, CHANGE, AND
DEMOCRATIC SELF-GOVERNANCE

Sociologists have long grappled with the question of how society changes. One important societal change is the democratization of society. Democratization can take a number of forms including transitions from authoritarian to representative democracies, increased participation in representative democracies, or in the form of councils as a bottom-up alternative to the representative model. This book examines the intersection between democratization and social movements and the ways in which the success or failure of an expansion of democracy from below is contingent on the activity and influence of social movements.

Over the past century, workers and communities have fought to gain more control over their workplaces, communities, and the decisions that affect their lives. Workers have gained varying degrees of power by occupying factories, forming workers' and communal councils, and operating self-managed enterprises. Worker and communal councils have emerged at various geographic locations and historical moments as a genuine expression of workers' interests. Different forms of workers' control have sprung up in a myriad of places in the world and in many different historical contexts. Some of the most prominent examples include Paris 1871, Russia 1917–1918, Hungary 1956, France 1968, Chile 1972–1973, Portugal 1974–1975, Iran 1979, and Poland 1980–1981, just to name a few.[4, 5, 6, 7] Ordinary people have also organized themselves around the slogan of popular power. Some historical examples include: The 1968 general strikes in France,[8] the Water Wars in Cochabamba, Bolivia,[9] the Portuguese Revolution,[10] Chile under the Popular Unity Government in 1970–1973,[11] the 2001 rebellion in Argentina,[12] and the 2006 teachers' strike in the Mexican city of Oaxaca,[13] to name a few.

Movements to create councils and movements for popular power offer a critique and alternative to parliamentary, liberal notions of democracy and traditional nodes of power. While liberal democracy is based on the delegation to representatives who are only accountable to those they represent during the time of elections, social movements stress a system of direct or participatory democracy. By opening new channels of access to the political system, social movements contribute to the creation of public space that is separate from traditional political institutions and can also contribute to a transfer of power over states.[14, 15]

Another major theme in this book is agency, and in what ways workers, peasants, and those in the informal sector are able to exercise agency in the neoliberal era. In the Marxist literature, because of workers' unique position in the production of society's wealth, workers' agency and the potential for workers' power was theorized to reside at the point of production or, in other words, at the workplace. This literature suggests that the labor movement is especially positioned to increase democracy. Over the past few decades, however, we have seen the labor movement experience a drastic decline in unionization rates. This is not to say that the labor movement cannot experience resurgence, but in this decline other competing movements have emerged to pursue different projects and mobilize people around different interests. One important movement examined in this book is the communal movement in Venezuela. The expansion of communes in Venezuela demonstrates an alternative form of workers' power where citizens wield power, not at the point of production in the traditional Marxist literature, but at the community level. Though some of the communes have more recently taken over abandoned factories and other sites of production, for the most part they exercise their power not in their workplaces but in their neighborhoods. This book examines the ways in which ordinary Venezuelans, through the construction of communes, are able to exercise a significant degree of agency, but also how this agency is limited by certain structural constraints including the limited control the communes have over the economy as a whole.

KEY FINDINGS

The main argument presented in this book is that the construction of networks of communes and communal councils in Venezuela has achieved three important things. First, it has restructured how power is distributed and decisions are made for many Venezuelans. Second, it presents an alternative form of development to the neoliberal model. And lastly, it has enabled workers and peasants in the country to exercise a significant degree of agency in the face of neoliberal globalization. The communal movement has been able to achieve these three things primarily through four specific characteristics.

The first is participatory democracy. Participatory democracy in the communes enables citizens to be active participants in the process and decision making over the area in which they live or work. Members of the communes play a significant role in developing projects that benefit the entire community. Moreover, direct participatory democracy in the communes remedies some of the exclusionary aspects of representative democracy. This is apparent in the citizens' assemblies, where historically excluded sectors of society, the poor, indigenous, and other marginalized groups are prominent.

Second is endogenous development, a socioeconomic model of development that is driven from within or from the inside the nation state or local communities, rather than development from without or from the outside. This model focuses on development based on the country's developmental needs rather than by the demand of goods on the international market. Also distinct from the top-down centralized model of import substitution industrialization, popular in Latin America from the 1940s to 1980s, endogenous development enables communes to make decisions internally based on the needs of the community, enhancing community control over their own resources.

Third is the communal control over production, which not only allows for community members themselves to decide what is produced, how it is produced and how it is distributed, but also gives workers in these production sites the power to make decisions about their own working conditions, compensation, work hours, and vacation time.

And lastly is the communal market, which gives workers further control over their own development in that it enables communes to produce directly based on the needs of the community rather than the market dictating what should be produced, how it is distributed and the prices of those goods, and services produced. Communal markets are distinct from capitalist markets in that cooperative participatory planning methods are employed for the production and distribution of goods. These four primary characteristics of the communal movement all function to deepen direct democratic community control over the resources and development of local communities. Furthermore, the networks between communes and communal councils deepens self-determination and direct democratic control of even larger geographic and political spaces.

Though the successes that the communes have achieved so far are impressive, it is important to also mention a series of various serious obstacles that they confront. The challenges are varied and come from both within and without the process. First are the limitations that come with communal production and distribution in the midst of a capitalist economy, both domestically and in the global market economy. Second is the explicit challenges from the right-wing opposition, whether that is hoarding, speculation, or outright violence. And finally, the verticalist structure of the United Socialist Party of Venezuela (PSUV) and the hostility to some of the more radical currents of Chavismo (the left-wing political ideology based on the ideas of Hugo Chávez) that has at various key moments impeded the transfer of power to workers and the popular sectors of society. Though the communal movement was legitimated and legalized through a series of communal laws passed and promoted by the Bolivarian government, a growing level of bureaucracy within the government is often one of the largest obstacles to the growth and success of the movement. Many in the government, both at the local and national level, resist conceding power to these grassroots expressions of popular power. Even Chavista officials, who speak with radical rhetoric about socialism and popular power, often undermine the communal movement, as they see it as an encroachment on their power and legitimacy. The survival and spread of the communes require a confrontation with these three obstacles and the further building of popular power from below, and a deepening of the Bolivarian process as a whole.

METHODS/DATA

My field work in two separate trips spanned over two years, between 2015 and 2016. In 2015 I did field work in Venezuela for five months, then again in 2016 for an additional six weeks. In total I was in Venezuela doing research for seven months. I also conducted follow-up interviews in 2020 via Zoom.

My research was based on three qualitative methods of data collection: qualitative interviews, focus groups, and participant observation. During my seven months in Venezuela, I conducted twenty-four in-depth, formal, and informal interviews and focus groups. The interviews included twenty communal council or commune organizers or what are called *voceros*, two representatives from the ministry of communes, and two academics who have written books on the communes. The interviews spanned from forty-five minutes to just over two hours, with the majority around an hour and twenty minutes. Of the twenty-four interviews, eighteen were one-on-one interviews and six were focus groups with anywhere from two to seven people. My interview subjects represented twenty different communes and communal councils from a combination of urban, rural, and indigenous areas and in five different states and the federal district (Caracas, Carabobo, Lara, Miranda, Portuguesa, and Zulia). I also tried to achieve gender parity among interview respondents and of the twenty-four total interviews, ten ended up being with women.

My interviews were semi-structured in that for the most part I started with the interview questions but the conversation often went in many different directions and my follow-up questions varied depending on the respondent's answers. Questions also changed slightly depending on if the respondent was a *vocero(a)*, a representative from the ministry, or an author. The benefit from doing semi-structured interviews was that it gave me, the researcher, the freedom to tailor the questions to the different people I was talking to, to different contexts and situations, and the freedom to ask follow-up questions based on the respondents' responses.

In addition to interviews and focus groups, I also conducted participant observation. I visited twenty different communes and communal councils, and just like with the interviews, they represented urban, rural, and indigenous areas in five different states and in the federal district. I went to communal assemblies, communal council assemblies, the *Gran Asamblea* mentioned above, which was an assembly that brought together twelve different communes from two different states, and I was given tours of various communal projects including communal controlled factories (as in the case of El Sur Existe) as well as communal controlled stores and markets. In total I took about one hundred pages of field notes.

ORGANIZATION OF STUDY

Chapter 2 gives a detailed look at communal councils and communes. This chapter explores what the councils and communes are, how they function, how they are created, how decisions are made, how they coordinate with other communes, what type of projects they develop, and what role they play in the Bolivarian process. In order to answer these questions, I give three case studies of three different communes. The first is *Comuna El Sur Existe,* a mixed commune that consists of twelve urban and seven rural communal councils located in Carabobo Venezuela. The second is *Comuna Jose Pío Tamayo*, an urban commune in Barquisimeto. The third is *Comuna El Maizal,* a rural commune that consists of twenty-two communal councils located in the state of Lara.

In chapter 3, I engage with the literature in political sociology with an emphasis on democracy studies. Political sociologists have written about a variety of forms of democracy that have been pursued by social movements. This section focuses primarily on the major debates as they pertain to five different forms of democracy, representative, participatory, worker and communal councils, and popular power. I explore the following questions in turn: What are the conditions in which councils emerge, why have councils been short-lived, what are their theoretical foundations, and are all councils revolutionary or do some work within and support the capitalist representative model of democracy?

The second section in chapter 3 examines the role social movements play in promoting and struggling for expansions of democracy, whether by increasing participation or in forming workers' or communal councils. This section analyzes the role of social movements in democratization as well as the ways in which social movements can expand people's power over the decisions that affect their lives either through their explicit program of democratization or as by-products of their action. Finally, I discuss social movements as a form of democracy from below. This type of democracy is distinguished from Western and liberal notions of democracy called "democracy from above".

Chapter 4 explores the dynamic between the Venezuelan state, which has, at times, committed itself to a discourse on grassroots political participation and civil society that has responded to this call in ways that often exceed and challenge the expectations of the government. The Bolivarian process has raised Venezuelans' expectations of the state, and its very success depends on both the actions of grassroots activists and the Chavista government. While the government has opened up spaces for grassroots organization, what social-movement actors in Venezuela see as radical transformation still requires direct confrontation with those in political power. The Bolivarian process is not something that can be decreed from above, but must involve struggle, organization, and ordinary people's ability to act independently of the state.

Chapter 4 is divided into four parts. The first part gives a brief history of popular organization and the left in Venezuela from 1958 to the *Caracazo*. Part two analyzes the economic and social crises leading up to Hugo Chávez's election in an attempt to understand the broader context of resistance and social movements in which he came to power. Part three analyzes the relationship between civil society and the state by looking at the 2002 coup, the creation of the 1999 constitution, the radicalization of Chávez, and the activity of popular movements. Part four focuses on participatory democracy as a form of popular power.

Chapter 5 discusses the communes as networks of popular power and as a form of globalization from below. This chapter makes the argument that workers through these networks of popular power have some agency over their own development. I look specifically at four characteristics of the communes in which workers exercise, to various degrees, agency and self-determination, and how these four characteristics are distinctly different from neoliberal forms of development. The four characteristics are as follows: participatory democracy, endogenous development, communal control of production, and communal markets. The next section discusses the communal movement's connections with other transnational social movements and the importance of solidarity between movements. Chapter 5 concludes with a discussion of some of the limitations and challenges (both internal and external) that the communes face, and ultimately that the fate of the communes themselves is inextricably connected to the fate of the Bolivarian process in general.

The final chapter, chapter 6 analyzes the current economic and political crisis in Venezuela and how it has impacted the communal movement. This chapter analyzes two separate but related geopolitical trends and the ways in which they have impacted and shaped the communal movement and what implications it has for the future of the communes. The first is the economic crisis, precipitated by a downturn in global commodity prices, that has gripped Venezuela since roughly 2012. The second is the regional decline of the Pink Tide. After over a decade of left and center-left electoral victories in Latin America (Venezuela 1998, Brazil 2003, Argentina 2003, Uruguay 2005, Bolivia 2006, Honduras 2006, Ecuador 2007, Paraguay 2008, Nicaragua 2007), the Latin American left is now in retreat. Over the last few years Pink Tide governments have suffered a series of setbacks and are now facing new challenges by a resurgent right-wing.

The future of the communes is very much connected to the future of the Bolivarian process. If the Bolivarian process fails, the communal movement will likely also fail. Venezuela is facing its largest existential crisis to date, with problems ranging from high inflation, violence, governance, and declining wages and purchasing power. The crisis and the broader regional decline of Pink Tide in the region have produced major challenges to the communal movement and its prospects to achieve its ultimate goal of constructing a communal state. This chapter analyzes the causes of the crisis and places the communes in their geopolitical context. Finally, this chapter analyzes the ways in which the crisis and the decline of the left in the region have changed the terrain where the communal struggle takes place, and what implications this has for the future of the communal movement.

NOTES

1. Gregory Wilpert, *Changing Venezuela by Taking Power* (London: Verso, 2007).

2. Anderson Bean, "Venezuela, Human Rights and Participatory Democracy," *Critical Sociology* 42, no. 6 (September 1, 2016): 827–843.

3. Jeffery Webber, "What is Hugo Chávez's Legacy?" *Socialistworker.org*, March 8, 2013, http://socialistworker.org/2013/03/08/what-is-hugo-chavezs-legacy.

4. Colin Barker, ed., *Revolutionary Rehearsals* (Chicago: Haymarket Books, 1987, 2002).

5. Sheila Cohen, "The Red Mole: Workers' Councils as a Means of Revolutionary Transformation," in *From Ours to Master and to Own*, ed. Immanuel Ness and Dario Azzellini (Chicago: Haymarket Books, 2011).

6. Donny Gluckstein, "Workers' Councils in Europe: A Century of Experience," in *From Ours to Master and to Own*, ed. Immanuel Ness and Dario Azzellini (Chicago: Haymarket Books, 2011).

7. Immanuel Ness and Dario Azzellini, *From Ours to Master and to Own* (Chicago: Haymarket Books, 2011).

8. Joel Geier, "Year of Revolutionary Hope," *International Socialist Review*, 59 (May–June 2008).

9. Oscar Olivera and Tom Lewis, *Cochabamba! Water War in Bolivia* (New York: South End Press, 2008).

10. John Hammond, *Building Popular Power: Workers' and Neighborhood Movements in the Portuguese Revolution* (New York: Monthly Review Press, 1988).

11. Peter Winn, *Weavers of Revolution: The Yarur Workers and Chile's Road to Socialism* (Oxford: Oxford University Press, 1989).

12. Marina Sitrin, ed., *Horizontalism: Voices of Popular Power in Argentina* (Chico, CA: AK Press, 2006).

13. Chris Harman, "Latin America: The Return of Popular Power," *International Socialism* 114, (2007).

14. Donatella della Porta, *Can Democracy Be Saved?* (Malden, ME: Polity Press, 2013).

15. Charles Tilly, *European Revolutions 1492–1992* (Oxford/Cambridge: Blackwell, 1993).

Chapter One

Communes in Theory and Practice

Today there are 47,000 communal councils and over 3,000 communes. This has grown significantly since the passage of the Organic Law of the Communes, which legitimated this level of popular power. For a point of comparison, there were only twelve communes in 2013, compared to 3,000 in 2020. Not only have the number of communes been on the rise in recent years but also the percent of communal councils that have been integrated into the communes. By 2016, 13,000, just over one fourth, communal councils in the country were integrated into communes.

The communes have not only grown quantitatively but also qualitatively. The first communes focused primarily on infrastructural projects, focusing on water, roads, parks, and so on. By 2016 many communes had shifted their focus to production. The shift to production was a response to a number of socioeconomic factors.

First, Venezuela is a country whose oil reserves make up 95 percent of its total export earnings, and the oil and gas sector is about 25 percent of its gross domestic product (OPEC 2016). In the summer of 2014, for a number of reasons the price of oil began to drop. By the beginning of 2016 the price of a barrel of oil dropped by more than 70 percent.[1] Oil prices fell to $33 a barrel, the lowest rate in more than thirteen years.[2] Venezuela needs oil prices to reach $111 a barrel to break even on their national budget. The fall of oil revenue resulted in a decline in the ability of the government to import raw materials and foodstuffs to maintain the social programs and subsidies on regulated goods, which could previously be sold at a loss. One response of the government to the sudden decline in revenue was to print more money. The injection of enormous amounts of money into the economy, the prioritization of the payment of foreign debt over importing goods, and an increase of corruption all led to massive inflation.[3] Some estimates put the country's inflation rate at around 270 percent by mid-2016.[4] The drop in oil prices coupled with high rates of inflation has led to high levels of capital flight, with one estimate that capital flight has taken $250 billion out of the country in the last few years.[5] In addition to some capital sectors migrating from Venezuela, there are also other commercial sectors of concentrated capital that are moving from agricultural sector to the financial sector. So, what we see is a decrease in agricultural production. These two processes opened a space that the communes began to fill. In 2015 alone, the communes produced over 60,000 hectares of agricultural production, including corn, rice, beans, coffee, cereals, and so on. To put this in perspective, according to the Ministry of Agriculture, 66,000 hectares is equivalent to one month of national consumption. In other words, the communes in 2015 were producing one twelfth of the agricultural products that Venezuelans consume per year. By 2016, according to the Ministry of Communes, communal agriculture production exceeded 100,000 hectares. Although production in the agricultural sector has certainly been the most significant, communes also have increased production in other sectors, like textiles.

In addition to the shift from infrastructural projects to production, another qualitative shift with regards to the communes was the creation of *mercados comunales*, or communal markets. Communal markets were created in the second half of 2015 as a response to the economic crisis and as an alternative to the traditional distribution and exchange of goods dictated by the free market. One strategy of the right-wing opposition has been to engage in economic activities that destabilize the economy in order to undermine the Bolivarian process. These activities are known in Venezuela as the "economic war." The economic war will be discussed in more detail in chapter 5, but it is important to know that some of the strategies the opposition uses to undermine the economy are currency speculation and the creation of manufactured shortages. The business class has hoarded regulated goods and sold them on the black market at exorbitant prices or sold them across the border in Colombia. They have also simply hoarded goods to manufacture shortages to undermine the government.

As a response to the economic war, speculation, hoarding, and more generally the vicissitudes of the market, the government created communal markets as a strategy to try to break the economic dependence of the private sector. An alliance between the government and the communes was established for the creation of communal markets, which integrate state national distribution with the communal production. By 2016 there were already over 1,000 communal markets in the country. Communal markets are spaces for direct distribution, from producer to consumer, without intermediation. This is a space where the communes are bypassing the free market and private or state intermediaries to distribute products produced by the communed directly to the consumers. Each weekend in several territories in the country, communal products go directly to communal markets. This is a space where different communal producers can bring their products to distribute, and the transportation of the goods to the market is also owned by the communes. The dates and times of where the food will be distributed is announced beforehand, and anyone is welcome to come buy the products that are sold at regulated prices.

Producing for the free market can create all sorts of problems. First as we see with the fluctuation of oil prices, the rise and drop in prices can create crises, often leading to limited access to basic goods. Also, producing for the free market, despite being produced in a commune, can reproduce the same patterns of accumulation, and exploitation as production in the state or private sphere. Producing for the communal market, as a system of direct distribution of goods based on need, in theory is supposed to avoid some of the limitations of the free market. Since the creation of the communal market, much of the production from the communes is still bought and sold by private companies and the state, but the percent that is being distributed through the communal markets has increased significantly.

WHAT IS A COMMUNAL COUNCIL, A COMMUNE, AND HOW DO THEY WORK?

Communal Councils

Although, as mentioned earlier, various types of popular organizations and neighborhood associations predated the Chávez era and many date back to the 1989 *Caracazo*, it was not until the 2006 Law of Community Councils that many of these organizations were legitimated by the state. The 2006 law was then reaffirmed and updated in a second law of Communal Councils in 2009. The law calls for the creation of new councils and for the legitimization of existing neighborhood-based organizations in order to create non-representative structures of direct democracy. These organizations are grassroots neighborhood-based bodies that bring together community organizations that have emerged in mostly poor neighborhoods around issues of water, electricity, health, education, and media.[6,7,8]

Communal councils (CCs) are similar to workers councils except that they are organized at a community level instead of at the workplace. These councils are permanent governing structures that play a significant role in encouraging the incorporation of broader social sectors into the political decision-making process. They enable previously excluded sectors of society to directly manage public policy and projects that affect their daily lives. Although CCs are functioning in various areas around the country, they are concentrated in underprivileged communities. They often take over activities that were previously the responsibility of the local, state, or national government. The Communal Council Law recommends that in urban areas each council should contain 200–400 families, in rural areas at least twenty families, and at least ten families in indigenous communities.[9] The councils decide their own geographic boundaries, and all decisions are made in neighborhood assemblies. The assemblies are open to the whole community and decisions are made by majority vote in which every citizen over the age of fifteen can vote. A minimum of 30 percent of residents must be present for a vote on any decision. Though participation in assemblies is uneven from one CC to the next, on average participation in communal council assemblies is around 40 percent. Council decisions are binding. If a majority of CCs make a decision, then the mayor and local officials must abide by it.[10] Some of the projects that CCs have overseen include the establishment of over 300 communal banks, street pavings, sports fields, medical centers, and sewage and water systems.[11]

Funding for communal councils comes mostly from municipal, state, and city governments, but they can also get funds from their own fundraising and donations. They are encouraged to play a direct economic role, such as creating cooperatives or taking over idle factories. But money does not only go into the councils; it can also flow out. Councils often award grants for community projects and give loans to cooperatives or other activities.[12, 13, 14]

Communes

The communal councils are the basic level of a number of levels of popular power in Venezuela. In 2007, Hugo Chávez called for the creation of the communal state, which is supposed to replace the bourgeois capitalist state. In order to replace the capitalist state and achieve the communal state, various levels of communal popular power were to be established.[14] The first, at the neighborhood level, are the communal councils, second are the communes, followed by the communal cities, and then eventually the communal state. Each of these communal organizations are to be structures of bottom-up self-administration. At the base is the communal council, organized at the neighborhood level, then communes are larger bodies of popular power that are made up of a collection of communal councils, then the communal city is made up of a collection of communes, and so on. At this point in the Bolivarian process, the highest stage that has been achieved is the commune, though we have seen the collaboration of large groups of communes giving us a glimpse of what the communal city can look like.

The stated aim of the commune movement as a whole is to replace the state's representative political structures. Communes are made up of groups of communal councils in a specific geographic territory, and the decisions in the communes are made in the council assemblies. The councils decide the geography of these communes. While the councils develop more local short-term projects, the communes develop medium- and long-term projects, often affecting larger geographic areas.[16, 17]

In order for a group of CCs to create a commune they must first do a census of the territory and write a foundational letter that gives a static description of all the details and demographics of the territory as well as the functional description or stated goals and priorities of the territory. For example, the static description includes information like the geographic territory, inhabitants, number of CCs, and the limits of the commune. And then they have the function description, which describes the stated purpose of the commune, its plan and how social relationships integrate together. The letter has to be based on the history of the CCs. Before the foundational letter is submitted it is discussed and approved in a citizens' assembly with all the CCs that make up the commune, to ensure that everyone agrees with the letter before it is submitted. A vote is taken at the assembly, and at least 70 percent of the members of the community have to vote for the letter in order for it to pass. The letter is then taken to the Ministry of Communes to be approved. The Ministry then enters the commune into the Integrated System of Popular Power (SIPP), and the commune is given a code that represents their commune. Currently there are over 3,000 communes in the country.

The geographical boundaries of the various instances of popular power do not follow formal political divisions. A commune, for example, can include CCs from different cities, counties, or even states and are not confined to existing political boundaries. The geography of each of the communes and which particular councils make up each commune are decided by the councils themselves. Their territorial boundaries are typically organized to reflect similarities in geographic or economic criteria or in contiguous territories where both communities benefit from collaboration or joint projects, rather than through formal political delineations of the territories.

THREE CASE STUDIES

To get a good understanding of how communes function and what they look like on a practical level, the following section, based on my interviews and observations, focuses on three specific communes, *Comuna El Sur Existe*, *Comuna El Maizal*, and *Comuna Pío Tamayo*. These three communes were chosen for two reasons. First, while there are many communes that are not functioning very well, it is important to look at those that are functioning well to see the potential of communes and the potential that working people have through networks of popular power in actively participating in their own development more broadly. The second reason I chose these three communes was to take a look at three different types of communes, one being urban (*Comuna Pío Tamayo*), another being rural (*El Maizal*), and the last being an urban/rural hybrid (*Comuna El Sur Existe*). I will begin with the latter.

Comuna El Sur Existe

In 2007, three years before the Organic Law of the Communes recognized communes as a legitimate form of popular power organization, a group of people in Valencia started a social, cultural, and sports project. Despite some early successes, they were limited by the space they had in order to carry out their projects. In their community there was 207 hectares of land that was once used as a stable to train racehorses. With the passage of the Communal Law in 2010, they were able to take control of part of this land as well as an old, abandoned building. This land and the abandoned building became what is now the commune *El Sur Existe* (The South Exists).

The name comes from a poem by Uruguayan poet, playwright, novelist, and essayist Mario Benedetti. The poem is an indictment on the imperial policies of the global North and of the United States more generally. It is also a commentary of the way in which the global South is often depicted as just an object in which the global North acts upon. The poem argues that the global South are not objects but rather subjects, with agency, who make their own history despite, and in the face of imperial aggression from the North. The final stanza of the poem reads:

> The North is the one who orders
> But down here, down
> Near the rootsIs where memory
> Omits no memory
> And there are those
> Who defy death for
> And die for
> And thus together achieve
> What is impossibleThat the whole world
> would know
> That the South,
> That the South also exists.[18]

According to the *comuneros* in Commune *El Sur Existe*, the commune is the expression of this sentiment. In the face of imperial aggression and neo-liberal globalization, the commune has created networks of popular power, instruments of direct self-management, to meet the needs of their communities. Using the resources and creativity that these local communities have, communes are creating something inspiring so that possibly the "whole world would know that the South also exists."

The commune *El Sur Existe* lies just over one hundred miles east of Caracas in the industrial and manufacturing city of Valencia, Carabobo. Located in a valley surrounded by the mountain range *Cordillera de la Costa*, Valencia is the third largest city in Venezuela. Most communes in Venezuela fit under three categories: rural, urban, or indigenous. *El Sur Existe* is a mixed commune that consists of twelve urban and seven rural communal councils.

El Sur Existe is involved in a number of projects and endeavors, but what seem to be the three most central to the commune are a small textile factory, a grocery store, and a paper store. In 2013, the commune took over an abandoned building and turned it into a textile factory. Among the products produced in the factory, school uniforms is its primary focus. They produce over 5,000 school uniforms per year. The second project is the grocery store. The store distributes products produced not only in their commune but also neighboring communes in the state of Carabobo. The store sells milk, eggs, cheese, meat, and yogurt that is produced in the communes. The products are sold at regulated, solidarity prices. The third project of the commune is the paper store. Like the grocery store, all products are mostly produced in the communes and are sold at regulated, solidarity prices. For example, the school uniforms that are produced in the factory in *El Sur Existe* are sold at solidarity prices in the paper store. Other products sold in the store include paper, notebooks, pens, pencils, and other school supplies. In addition to these projects, the commune also works with the national orchestra and teaches music to students in the area, runs a baseball training program, and controls the Aldea Boliviariana University. In the university, the students are in the classroom part of the day and work the land for the rest of the day, inspired by the Robinsonian (an educational theory created by the national liberation hero Símon Rodriguez) idea of learning while you practice. The commune is also currently trying to gain control of what remains of the 207 hectares in order to grow food.

Comuna Jose Pío Tomayo

All decisions in both the communal councils and the communes are made in popular (or citizen) assemblies. Decisions are made by a simple majority, and according to the Law of the Communes, 30 percent of the members of the commune must be present to vote. Each communal council elects spokespeople to represent their council in the commune, and typically a spokesperson from each communal council must be present for a vote in the commune. Assemblies are typically held once a week or more frequently if necessary.

The needs and goals of the commune and the projects aimed to achieve these goals are decided by the communes themselves. The commune conducts participatory diagnostics of the community and decides in the assemblies what the community needs most and what projects they want to carry out. In the case of *Comuna Pío Tomayo*, the commune did a diagnostic of what the community needed, and in an assembly of over 1,000 people they decided that the most pressing issue was housing.

Communal projects can either be something that they create on their own or they can choose to work with an existing social program, or what in Venezuela are called "social missions." Social missions are social programs implemented early in the Chávez administration that are primarily funded by oil profits. These missions span from education (Mission Robinson, an adult literacy program), food (Mission Mercal, which provides access to basic foods at a discounted price), healthcare (Mission Barrio Adentro, which provides free healthcare services to under-served and impoverished communities), land reform (Mission Zamora, which redistributes land to the poor), indigenous rights (Mission Guaicaipuro, which restores communal land rights to indigenous communities), to housing (*La Gran Mision Vivienda Venezuela*, a low-cost housing program).

Pío Tamayo (named after a Venezuelan Marxist and poet who also was one of the founders of the Communist Party in Cuba), recognizing the need for safe, affordable housing, decided to work with *Gran Mision Vivienda* to build and restore houses in the community for those who needed it. Initially proposed by Hugo Chávez in a nationally televised TV program in 2011 as a response to the country's housing crisis, *Gran Mision Vivienda* has become the country's largest housing program. Since its launch in 2012, over one million houses have been built for low-income Venezuelans. The mission sustains three different types of housing projects: new houses (building a house from scratch), substitution (when the materials from the old house are used in the construction of a new house), and recuperation (when an existing house is renovated, retrofitted, or remodeled to meet operational standards).

After the commune decided to work with *Gran Mision Vivienda* to build and restore houses, they began to organize workshops on the three dimensions (new, substitution, and recuperation). With the government funding provided to the commune through the *Gran Mision Vivienda* program, over 315 homes were built or restored in *Pío Tamayo*. The actual construction of some of the larger housing complexes that have parking lots, cultural centers, basketball courts, and so on, are contracted out to public or private companies, but most of the more simpler houses and much of the substitution and recuperation are self-constructed by the commune members themselves. Communal members receive training in construction and are supervised during the construction of the foundation of the houses.

Other projects that the *Pío Tamayo* commune are involved in include: the worker's takeover of an abandoned beer factory, the buying and selling of pigs, and the distribution of communal products from other communes. Just after Chávez was restored to power after the 2002 coup, a Brazilian transnational beer company called Brahma (now a subsidiary of Anheuser Busch) shuttered its door and fled the country. Because of the poor water system in the area and the communities' need for a reliable source of potable water, workers took control of the factory and turned it into an industrial water production plant. The plant now produces and distributes water for local consumption. Despite court orders to remove the workers, they continue to fight for the expropriation of the factory and to be placed under direct democratic control of the commune.

The company, now run by the commune, has been renamed The Company of Direct Communal Social Property Proletarians Unite (*Empresa de Propiedad Social Directa Comunal Proletarios Unios*) and employs eighty-five communal members whose salaries are paid by company profits. Profits that do not go toward salaries are used for what is called "reinvestment social funds." This money is used for healthcare, education, and training, whether that be funding to attend workshops, encuentros, or congresses. And what is left of the profits is used to buy and sell pigs.

The purpose of the buying and selling of pigs is to increase food production for the community. Currently the commune has 120 pigs and will be using those pigs for food. Pork is a staple food in many Venezuelan dishes, most importantly a traditional Christmas dish. The idea to use profits from the worker-controlled water-processing plant was not only a means to feed the community but also, as I was told by one communal organizer, a way to ensure that every family in the community would have pork for their traditional Christmas dinner.

Comuna El Maizal

The origins of *Communa Maizal* are typical to the origins of many other communes across the country, particularly in rural areas. El Maizal sits on 2,000 hectares of land, in the rural outskirts of Barquisimeto, Lara. Much of the land currently controlled by the commune was previously owned by the wealthy Alvarado family. In late 2008, community members made proposals to the Chávez administration to expropriate the land and put it under collective control of the community on grounds that the land originally belonged to the people in the area until a group of wealthy families illegally took the land from them. In the proposals, the people in El Maizal made clear that they were going to use the land to produce. Not too long later, on his famous weekly television show *Alo Presidente*, Chávez announced that the land in El Maizal would be expropriated and given back to the people and that the land could no longer be divided into sectors for private production. The goal of this expropriation was to stimulate agricultural production by transferring vast plots of idle land from private ownership to local famers. The recovery of the land must be accompanied by collective production by the community.

So, in March of 2009, the commune *El Maizal* was founded. Now the commune is made up of twenty-two rural communal councils (encompassing over 3,500 families and over 8,000 people) and produces a variety of agricultural products, including corn, black beans, coffee, and beef. Financial resources garnered from agricultural production are used in the community for healthcare, food for communal schools, and infrastructure. In addition to agricultural production, El Maizal also has a social production enterprise, which provides gas for its twenty-two communal councils.

Of the 2,000 hectares of land controlled by the commune, only 800 is used for production; the remaining 1,200 hectares are a national reserve, protected by the commune. Five hundred hectares of land are dedicated to the production of maize, beans, and coffee, with the remaining 300 hectares used for cows and the production of beef. The maize that is produced in the commune is sold to the state, and the coffee is sold to both the state and private companies.

The *El Maizal* commune is comprised of land from two states. The commune sits on the border of southern Lara and northern Portuguesa. With just over 250 registered communes, Lara has the highest concentration of communes in the country. The high concentration of communes in Lara is no accident. Lara has a rich history of militant *campesino* struggle dating back to the 1960s.

Communal Coordination

As mentioned earlier, the stated goal of the various levels of popular power is to not only transfer political power and decision making to popular sectors of society in the short term but also to eventually replace the capitalist bourgeois state with the communal state in the long term. The plan, laid out by Chávez, would begin with the first level of popular power, then communal councils, then the communes, then to the communal cities and eventually the communal state. Although the third level of popular power, the communal cities, has yet to be constructed, there are various ways that communes have begun to coordinate on various projects and create structures that allow for the collaboration between communes. This section will discuss a few of these structures of collaboration.

At the most basic level, many communes collaborate on various projects that impact the geographic territory that encompass both (or in some cases more than two) communes. *Pío Tamayo* commune mentioned above is involved in two such projects. First, *Pío Tamayo* has coordinated with a neighboring commune (*Comuna Socialista Maria Colmenarez*) on a housing project. Using the resources that were allocated to *Pío Tamayo* to build houses, the two communes decided to collaborate and build houses for families in both communes. Together, the two communes collaborated to construct eleven houses.

Pío Tamayo also collaborates with *Comuna El Maizal. El Maizal* is a rural commune and one of the most productive communes in the state of Lara. *Pío Tamayo* is an urban commune that does not have the same space as *El Maizal* to grow food but does have the capacity to distribute products produced by other more productive communes like *El Maizal*. On several occasions Pío Tamayo has collaborated with El Maizal to distribute their products to consumers or buyers.

More important than instances of ad hoc collaboration between neighboring communes are the more formal structures of communal collaboration that provide spaces for larger and more encompassing bodies of popular power. In the state of Carabobo there is a formal structure called the *Bloque Gran Comunal*. This structure was created through collaboration between various communes in the area who decided in their citizens' assemblies to create a formal structure that took on more long-term projects and projects that encompass larger geographical areas. This is a space where thirty-six communes from the state of Carabobo coordinate larger and more long-term projects that affect families in those territories. *Bloque Gran Comunal* meets almost once a week to discuss and organize matters that relate to their territories. With anywhere between 200–400 families represented in each communal council and three to thirty communal councils represented in each commune, the *Bloque Gran Communal* is likely a self-governing organ of direct democracy and popular power that encompasses a territory that includes over 100,000 people.

One other important block of communes is the *Gran Asamblea Comuna del Corredor Político Territorial Fabricio Ojeda* (henceforth the *Gran Asamblea*), which comprises twelve communes, including urban, rural, and mixed communes, and 159 communal councils in the states of Lara and Portuguesa. The *Gran Asamblea* meets four times a year on a quarterly basis. At these gatherings communal spokespeople discuss more long-term projects in which the communes can coordinate as well as decisions that were made in the citizen's assemblies of the communes. The *Gran Asamblea* and the *Bloque Gran Comunal* mentioned above are in between two instances of popular power; they are collections of communes but not yet legitimated as communal cities. Because of their legal status, the finances used to fund projects carried out by these two bodies come from the communes and communal councils. They may also use funds they may have earned through productive projects.

Most decisions in the corridor are made in the CCs, where the decisions are made in their respective citizens' assemblies. Decisions are then taken to the communal parliaments in each commune to be discussed and debated.

Then the corridor (which represents the twelve communes in the *Gran Asamblea*) discusses the decision in its own parliament. After the parliament of the corridor makes its recommendations, those decisions are then taken back the CCs. In short, decisions are made, discussed, and debated in a circular pattern where each level of popular power is able to discuss and make recommendations on the decisions made that affect the territory of all the communes and CCs represented in the corridor.

Large blocks of communes like the two mentioned above are not just bodies that collaborate on infrastructural or productive projects that affect their territories but also spaces where larger strategic discussions take place. Larger questions of political economy and debates about how the communal movement should orient itself to the state are also common topics. In my field work, I heard discussions on strategies to combat the economic war, how to orient to the upcoming midterm elections, how to consolidate popular power, strategies to increase production and better organize the distribution of products, and better ways for the communes to coordinate. One particularly common theme was the communal state and how to best achieve it. There tends to be a general agreement about how taking power and control of the state is best achieved through the self-management of production and true independence comes when workers control the means of production, but how to get to this point is the subject of debate.

NOTES

1. Clifford Krauss, "Oil Prices: What's Behind the Drop? Simple Economics," *New York Times*, March 30, 2016, https://www.nytimes.com/2015/01/13/business/energy-environment/oil-prices.html.

2. Virginia Lopez, "Venezuela's Economic Crisis Worsens as Oil Prices Fall," *Al Jazeera*, January 8, 2016, http://www.aljazeera.com/news/2016/01/venezuela-economic-crisis-worsens-oil-prices-fall-160108105010345.html.

3. Juan Manuare and Carlos E. Juarena, "Venezuela: A Balance Sheet of 2016 and Perspectives for 2017," *In Defence of Marxism*, February 27, 2017, https://www.marxist.com/venezuela-a-balance-sheet-of-2016-and-perspectives-for-2017.htm.

4. .Virginia Lopez, "Venezuela's Economic Crisis Worsens as Oil Prices Fall," *Al Jazeera*, January 8, 2016, http://www.aljazeera.com/news/2016/01/venezuela-economic-crisis-worsens-oil-prices-fall-160108105010345.html.

5. Heirbert Barreto, "Fuga de Capitales y Desfalco en Venezuela (1999–2013) Datos Para una Auditoria, Ponencia de Heibet Barreto," *Aporrea*, June 9, 2015, http://www.aporrea.org/contraloria/n271878.html.

6. Dario Azzellini, "Venezuela's Solidarity Economy: Collective Ownership, Expropriation, and Workers Self-Management," *The Journal of Labor and Society* 12 (2009): 171–191.

7. Steve Ellner, *Rethinking Venezuelan Politics: Class, Conflict, and the Chávez Phenomena* (Boulder, CO: Lynne Rienner, 2008)

8. Frederico Fuentes, "Venezuela: New Moves to Build People's Power," *Green Left Weekly* 831 (2010).

9. Josh Lerner, "Communal Councils in Venezuela: Can 200 Families Revolutionize Democracy?" *Z Magazine*, March 6, 2007.

10. Gregory Wilpert, *Changing Venezuela by Taking Power* (London: Verso, 2007).

11. Josh Lerner, "Communal Councils in Venezuela: Can 200 Families Revolutionize Democracy?" *Z Magazine*, March 6, 2007.

12. Ibid.

13. Dario Azzellini, "Venezuela's Solidarity Economy: Collective Ownership, Expropriation, and Workers Self-Management," *The Journal of Labor and Society* 12 (2009): 171–191.

14. Steve Ellner, *Rethinking Venezuelan Politics: Class, Conflict, and the Chávez Phenomena* (Boulder, CO: Lynne Rienner, 2008).

15. Dario Azzellini, "Venezuela's Solidarity Economy: Collective Ownership, Expropriation, and Workers Self-Management," *The Journal of Labor and Society* 12 (2009): 171–191.

16. Ibid.

17. Ewan Robertson, "Independent National Communard Council Created in Venezuela," *Venezuelaanalysis.com*, June 6, 2014, https://venezuelanalysis.com/news/10727.

18. Mario Benedetti, "El Sur Tambien Existe," *Monthly Review*, February 8, 2007.

Chapter Two

Theorizing Participatory Democracy, Popular Power, and Counter-Hegemonic Globalization from Below

Each January, 50,000 Brazilians in the harbor town of Porto Alegre gather in dozens of assemblies across the city to collectively decide how to allocate and distribute their $200 million budget. Decisions about housing, public transport, social housing, literacy, schooling, sewage, and so on are made in assemblies constituted by the people of Porto Alegre. In more recent years, this form of participatory budgeting spread to 100 cities in the country. Six hundred miles southeast of Porto Alegre, the workers of the Brukman textile factory in Balvanera Argentina are both the stockholders and managers of the company. Brukman is one of at least 160 Argentine factories that are currently being owned and organized as a cooperative by their employees. In the northern part of the continent, Venezuelans have organized themselves in thousands of communal councils. These councils make binding decisions about matters that affect the daily lives of Venezuelans. Issues include water, health, education, and media. These examples of popular power offer a glimpse of alternatives to corporate-driven globalization.

Popular power can best be understood as the capacity of workers, the marginalized, and oppressed to collectively control the political, social, and economic conditions in which they live. As Edgardo Lander writes, "popular power has to do with people's capacity to take the reins."[1] The building of popular power is the creation of relations of power contrary to the logic of capital. Central to the idea of popular power is the way it refers to people taking power themselves, whether in their workplaces, communities, or neighborhoods. As Dario Azzelini writes:

> Neither can popular power, by its own logic, be awarded from above. Popular power cannot be conceived of by the state, nor can it be conceived of without the state. The question of sovereignty, or control of resources, puts on the table the question of the relation between state power and popular power.[2]

Popular power can thus be seen as an alternative site of power or counter-power to parliamentarism, state power, or other traditional nodes of power. It is a form of direct democracy that can be exercised in various ways, including in workers' councils, communal councils, neighborhood associations, popular assemblies, and different forms of workers' control.

Popular power, whether in the form of councils or otherwise, must be understood as not only related to social movements and resistance from below but as inextricably intertwined. In his letter from a Birmingham jail, Dr. Martin Luther King Jr. famously wrote that "freedom is never voluntarily given by the oppressor; it must be demanded by the oppressed." The same is true with power. Self-determination and popular power are never granted to the powerless without pressure from below. One important form of resistance of the oppressed is social movements. Charles Tilly defines social movements as "a series of contentious performances, displays and campaigns, by which ordinary people make collective claims on others."[3] For Sidney Tarrow, social movements are "sequences of contentious politics based on underlying social networks on resident collective action frames and on the capacity to maintain sustained challenges against powerful opponents."[4] Contentious politics, as defined by Tilly,[5] are "interactions in which actors make claims bearing on someone else's interests," often by the use of disruptive techniques with the intention to make some specific change. Implied in both definitions is that social movement activity takes place outside of traditional channels of politics. Social movements are a vehicle for ordinary people's participation in politics when traditional channels are closed. Though at times social movements do often engage with and influence traditional channels of politics.

But if movements are an expression of resistance, why do we experience periods with little movement activity? Surely it is not due to a lack of grievances. Under what conditions do social movements emerge and flourish? What conditions are conducive for democratization? What is the relationship between democratization and social movements? What role do movements have in the development of different forms of popular power? With these questions in mind, this chapter analyzes three overarching and interrelated themes: participation and workers' control as an expression of workers' (or people's) power, the role of social movements in democratization, and social movements as a form of resistance to representative democracy.

Political sociologists have written about a variety of forms of democracy that have been pursued by social movements. Some of those include strong democracy,[6] discursive democracy,[7] communicative democracy,[8] welfare democracy,[9] associative democracy,[10] agonistic pluralism,[11] workers' councils,[12, 13, 14, 15] communal councils,[16, 17, 18] participatory democracy,[19, 20, 21, 22, 23] representative democracy,[24, 25, 26] and popular power.[27, 28, 29, 30, 31, 32] To best understand the emergence, successes, and failures of workers' power, it is helpful to familiarize ourselves with the major debates as they pertain to the latter five forms of democracy (representative, participatory, workers' and communal councils, and popular power). In the first section of this chapter, I explore the following questions in turn: What are the conditions in which councils emerge, why have councils been short-lived, what are their theoretical foundations, and are all councils revolutionary or do some work within and support the capitalist representative model of democracy?

In section two I then examine the role social movements play in promoting and struggling for expansions of democracy, whether by increasing participation or in forming workers' or communal councils. I analyze the role of social movements in democratization as well as the ways in which social movements can expand people's power over the decisions that affect their lives either through their explicit program of democratization or as by-products of their action. In the final section of this chapter, I discuss social movements as a form of democracy from below. This type of democracy is distinguished from Western and liberal notions of democracy called "democracy from above."

REPRESENTATIVE VS. PARTICIPATORY DEMOCRACY

Representative Democracy

The term "democracy" is derived from the Greek *demos* (the people) and *kratos* (rule). The notion of democracy as the rule of the people rests on the idea that the general public should participate in the decision-making process that affects their daily lives. Democracy for most people in the world is synonymous with some form of representative system.[33] The central idea in representative democracies is that people have power because they elect representatives, and those representatives are held accountable to voters for their decisions through elections. The rule of the people is exercised through the periodic activity of voting in elections, not the day-to-day activities of governance.[34, 35] Theorists of representative democracy do argue that there is a role for citizen participation in a democracy, but the role is limited to the activities intended to influence the selection of representatives or the decisions they make. Participation is confined to activities within the framework of consent to be the governed.

Representative democracy is commonly accepted as the most conventional form of democracy, the version taught, for example, in schools and government agencies. This view refers to democracy as a type of political system and is used to classify nation states and distinguish them from authoritarian states, military dictatorships, and monarchies. In contrast to the latter, liberal democracies have a free press, free and fair elections, a multi-party system, equal rights, the rule of law, courts free of political control, and tolerate opposition.[36, 37]

Theorists of representative democracy argue that in large, complex societies the election of a small number of representatives who are granted decision-making powers is the most efficient way to administer things.[38, 39] They argue that other versions like participatory or direct democracy are impractical in such large and complex systems. Robert Dahl, for example, argues that participatory or direct democracy "has never existed in historical times . . . and try as hard as I may I can discover no way by which it could be made to exist in the foreseeable future."[40]

By the end of the twentieth century, the limitations of representative democracy started to become more apparent. Though the majority of nation states maintained a representative democratic system, various movements for alternative forms of democracy began to emerge. Participatory budgeting in Brazil,[41] worker-controlled factories in Argentina, [42] communal councils in Venezuela, and the Occupy movement all offered both critiques of representative democracy and, perhaps more importantly, offered alternatives. Some scholars have written about what is called the "democratic deficit,"[43, 44] and others about the "death" of democracy.[45] The democratic deficit comes from waning trust in democratic institutions as they become less responsive and more disconnected to the citizens they are supposed to represent. This trend in the West can be seen in the decline in both voter turnout rates and in the number of people joining political parties.[46, 47] Della Porta points out that in seventeen of the nineteen countries where we have data, the percent of the population who identify with a party is in decline.[48] The number of citizens who claim attachment to parties dropped in almost all European countries between 1972–1995.[49]

The shortcomings of representative democracy and the corresponding decline in its appeal to many working people across the globe can be attributed to a number of factors. The first is the extensive sum of money that is spent on campaigning and lobbying. Disproportionate funding from big business and other elite institutions ensure that the interests of elites supersede that of the electorate. The second and not unrelated factor is the concentration of economic power. As economic power becomes increasingly concentrated and powerful, its influence on representative politics increases.

Powerful economic interests are increasingly able to make their desires felt in the legislative process. Laxer suggests that contemporary democracy is becoming more of a plutocracy in the way that the power of wealth and money play an increasing role in determining political outcomes.[50] This is accomplished in a variety of ways, including the calculated use of corporate media, the aforementioned funding of powerful lobbies, and various methods of manipulating the electorate. Representatives depend more on lobbies than their constituents during election cycles, resulting in lobbies having a greater influence on policy than everyday voters. The media often relies on images and personalities rather than the debate on important issues. According to the Center for Responsive Politics, in 93 percent of United States House of Representative races and 94 percent of Senate races (in the United States), the candidate that spent the most money ended up winning. Most of the money that comes from political financing comes from corporate donations, political action committees, and wealthy individuals. The concept of "one person, one vote" is becoming harder to reconcile with representative democracy. Money, not people, tends to have more influence on the political process. The intention of the "rule of the people" was to guarantee that political decisions were inspired by and dictated by the interests of the people. When representatives make the decisions, there is no guarantee that political decisions will reflect the desires of the people. The effect is an increasing number of people alienated from electoral politics, a key institution to representative democracy.

Representative democracy has also been critiqued for being exclusionary.[51, 52] Historically, exclusion was achieved by limiting who is allowed to participate in democracy. Whether it is women, indigenous, aboriginal, black, or the property-less, restrictions have kept many different people from the entire democratic process. Even today in the United States, people in prison and convicted felons are excluded from participation in elections. Voter ID laws also disproportionately disenfranchise people of color.

In Latin America, the crisis of representative democracy, and the new forms of institutionalized direct democracy that responded to that crisis, was perhaps more acute. Peruzzotti and Selee suggest that the "central problem that is affecting the political dynamics of representative democracy in the region [is] the emergence of a growing gap between citizens and the political system."[53] Elected officials were becoming increasingly unresponsive to the public. As Maxwell A. Cameron et al. wrote:

> The elected governments often failed to provide physical or social security or economic well-being, and were plagued by levels of corruption, clientelism, and unaccountability that undermined legitimacy. Fundamental flaws persisted with regard to electoral procedures, adherence to constitutional provisions, and the separation, coordination, and balance of powers between

the executive and competing branches of the government, as well as the availability of opportunities for citizen participation in public affairs.[54]

Representative democracy in Latin America, perhaps most importantly,
failed to properly confront the negative impacts of neoliberalism. The election of Carlos Andres Perez in Venezuela and the subsequent popular rebellion to his failure to break from neoliberalism is but one example. In the
1988 presidential campaign, Carlos Andres Perez ran on an anti-neoliberal
platform. Just a few weeks after taking office, Perez implemented a harsh
neoliberal, IMF-imposed structural adjustment program (SAP). On the
morning of 27th of February, just ten days after Perez announced the SAP,
commuters who traveled to the city by bus noticed that the fares had doubled.
Venezuelans immediately began protesting in Caracas and by mid-morning
the protests had spread to all the country's major cities. This rebellion, later
called the *Caracazo,* was one of the first popular revolts to neoliberalism
in the region and an expression of the crisis of representative democracy's
failures to properly confront neoliberalism and the collective yearning for
something different. It was in this context that various new forms of direct
or participatory democracy began to take shape in Latin America.

Participatory Democracy

The concept of participatory democracy holds that citizens should be active
participants in the process of governing the country (or state, city, community, workplace, etc.). In this model, citizens must play a significant role in
developing government policy and prioritizing budgets and projects in a way
that benefits the entire community. The main principle behind participatory democracy is the constant participation, consultation, and discussion
by citizens in the political process. This conception of democracy is quite
different than the representative model where the extent of participation
among citizens is going to the voting booth once every two to four years.
The constant participation of citizens in the political process serves to better
ensure selfdetermination. Participatory democracy strives to create an active
political culture, opportunities for the incorporation of broader sectors of the
population into the political process, and a healthier civil society in general.

There are two prominent critiques of participatory democracy. The first is
that direct democracy can only function efficiently on small scales and is un-
tenable in larger communities.[55] The second is that governance should be left
to experts.[56] According to this critique, governance requires a certain level of
skill and experience and should not be entrusted to the everyday worker. The
first argument is made both by theorists who reject participatory democracy
outright[57] and by those who advocate participation only in small doses or as a
complement to, rather than an alternative to, representative democracy.[58] The

notion that participatory democracy will fail if practiced in large communities is an old one. Writing in 1748, Montesquieu said:

> As in a country of liberty, every man who is supposed a free agent ought to be his own governor, the legislative powers should reside in the whole body of the people. But since this is impossible in large states, and in small ones is subject to many inconveniences, it is fit the people should transact by their representative what they cannot transact by themselves.[59]

For Montesquieu, representative democracy grew out of the infeasibility of participatory democracy in larger communities. Technical and organizational difficulties are the most cited reasons for why participatory democracy could not work in larger areas. It would be difficult for people in countries with large populations to unite in assemblies or meetings to make decisions.

Selee and Peruzzotti make the case that participatory democracy is only effective in small communities where face-to-face interaction is possible and only to improve or enhance representative democracy.[60] They argue that instead of replacing representative institutions, participation can only work to enhance representation. Selee and Peruzzotti argue that there are four ways in which this is the case.[61] First, participatory mechanisms can replace clientelistic relations. Clientelistic situations where public goods are negotiated in uneven private interactions can be mitigated by adopting more participatory forms of intermediation. Second, participation can bring more voices into the political arena and increase incentives for low-income communities to participate in the decision-making process. Third, participatory institutions can encourage more deliberative processes of decision making. Through deliberation, Selee and Peruzzotti argue, citizens become the "true subjects of public decision making."[62] Fourth, the sum of the first three produces a more equitable distribution of resources. Selee and Peruzzotti are quick to point out that these benefits of participation are to "enhance accountability and outcomes of existing democratic regimes," not to replace them.[63] Not all forms of participatory democracy are seen as alternatives to the representative model, but as ways to improve and enhance it.

The second major critique of participatory or direct democracy is that the common person is not fit to govern. The notion that governance should be left to "experts" dates back for centuries. Plato and Aristotle, for example, were hostile to the idea of "non-experts" governing their own affairs. The complex task of governing requires specialized knowledge and should be left to political experts. Just as you want a mechanic to fix your car, a pilot to fly a plane, and a doctor to perform surgery, the argument goes that governing also requires specialized knowledge, skills, training, and temperament. Paul Ginsborg, characterizing the work of the great political theorist John Stuart

Mill, wrote that Mill "felt passionately that the working classes, men and women, were not yet ready or sufficiently educated for democracy."[64]

When the Founding Fathers wrote the U.S. constitution, they also had this idea in mind. The purpose of the constitution was to prevent non-experts from meddling in policy matters.[65] Alexander Hamilton wrote that if you were to have participatory democracy on a mass scale, "you must expect error, confusion, and instability."[66] John Adams warned that "men in general in every society, who are wholly destitute of property are also too little acquainted with public affairs to form a right judgment, and too dependent upon other men to have a will of their own."[67] As a way to secure both the wealth and power in the hands of a small minority, the participation of the majority was excluded from the political process.

Theorists of participatory democracy argue that not only are working people capable of governing their own affairs but that they are in fact better equipped to do so than representatives.[68, 69, 70] Rather than the notion that only an elite set of experts have the skill set and expertise to rule, to put it in the words of the Marxist theorist and historian C. L. R. James, "every cook can govern."[71] Proponents of this view make two arguments to support this idea. The first is that local actors are in a better position to make policy decisions that directly affect them because they have better knowledge of their own local needs. Moreover, when citizens are directly involved in the decision-making process, they become more invested in the projects and decisions in which they have determined.[72, 73]

Second, the specialized knowledge, skills, and training that one needs to govern are attained through the process of governing itself. Participatory democracy is praised by theorists as "schools of democracy" that function as an institutional space for citizenship learning and empowerment and a space for citizens to be better democrats.[74] Participatory democracy thus not only gives excluded sectors channels to voice their concerns but also educates them on how to best use that voice. The more citizens participate in the decision-making process, the more they are informed, educated, and empowered to administer their own affairs. [75, 76] Participation creates a cyclical process where participation trains and provides experience for citizens to be more informed, knowledgeable, and skilled democrats, thus reproducing and improving the efficiency of participation, which opens more spaces for more participation. Politics and participatory governance become its own university. It is by participating that people learn to participate.[77]

Jurgen Habermas, for example, argues that democratic settings and increased participation are likely to produce individuals with democratic dispositions and the capacities necessary for democracy.[78] By resolving political issues by means of democratic and participatory discourse, participants develop autonomy, the social capacities of judgment, and are better able to make critical decisions of their interests and needs. For Habermas, autonomy implies agency (the ability for one to have control over their own life), and "the ability to create, to bring new ideas, things and relations into being."[79]

Montambeault argues that participatory decision-making processes function as schools of democracy.[80] The first argument is the ways in which participants become better citizens at an individual level. On an individual level, participants learn the democratic skills necessary to govern. These might include learning how to organize and mobilize, communicate more effectively, listen to other perspectives, to formulate demands, and so on. Participatory decision making is more successful when participants have experience, and participation itself contributes to the education and learning process necessary.

Secondly, participation contributes to citizens becoming better positioned to pursue the interests and the common good of the community. By developing democratic attitudes toward the governance process, participants develop shared understandings of the political sphere, the world, and the common good.[81, 82] Shared understandings lead participants to engage in public thinking and envisioning a common future. Individual beliefs, values, and preferences, in this conception, are not static and unchanging but rather created and transformed through the participatory process. Through participation the issues and political preferences held by the individual are embedded in the interests of the community to which they belong.

Testing this theory, Francoise Montambeault analyzed the Brazilian participatory budgeting model (PB) as a school for democracy. She found that in all the cities in her study, PB created formal spaces for the voices of the excluded. Citizens were included in every step of the local democratic process. This included the decision-making process, policy implementation and monitoring. PB also contributed to making citizens "better democrats" but to varying successes. In two of the three cities studied, participants developed new understandings of politics and citizenship and learned how to better pursue the interests and the common good of their community. In the third city, Recife, PB still opened spaces for traditionally excluded, but politicized interests prevailed over the common good.[83]

Increasing the direct involvement of the traditionally excluded in the decision-making process also serves to introduce new, important issues that might otherwise not be considered. While representative democracy serves the interests of those who fund lobbyists or have the resources to make major contributions to political campaigns, participatory democracy should give more power to the powerless as they themselves are directly involved in the construction of values and issues. Participation opens up spaces for the traditionally excluded to debate, discuss, and formulate issues that are important to them and that directly affect their lives.[84]

The expansion of democracy, be it participatory or otherwise, was never a gift from above, but was achieved through relentless, protracted, and sometimes violent social struggles. Participatory democracy or democracy from below has emerged from resistance and social movements in the form of collective action. It is from these actions that different forms of democracy have developed. It is not simply the power of ideas created by great thinkers, but rather the self-activity of living humans as an ongoing process that safeguards or improves democracy.[85] Although early experiments in participatory democracy can be found in the West, classical Greece being one example[86] in our contemporary age the global South is taking a lead in its promotion and practice in participatory democracy. While Western notions of representative democracy are losing favor in many parts of the global south, citizens are reconfiguring democracy under their own terms. Since 1989, participatory budgeting in Porto Alegre, Brazil, has allowed residents to directly participate in the allocation of city funds. Budgeting decisions are made by dozens of assemblies made up of poor and middle-class men and women across the city. Currently, more than 50,000 residents participate in the budgeting process in a city of 1.5 million people.[87]

Responding to the economic crisis of 2001, workers in Argentina created hundreds of neighborhood assemblies. Argentines also began to take control of factories. The number of occupied and worker-controlled factories subsequently grew into the hundreds.[88] Building off factory occupations that took place during the Dirty War of the 1970s, workers cooperatively run the factories, decisions are made democratically by worker assemblies rather than professional managers, and profits are distributed equitably to all workers.[89]

Historically, social movements (particularly the labor movement) have put forward alternative conceptions of democracy from the liberal representative model. With an emphasis on positive and collective rights over individual and negative rights, participation over delegation to politicians, social movements have been at the forefront of experimenting with different democratic models.[90] Movements from the Occupy Movement to the Indignados in Spain to participatory budgeting in Brazil, demonstrate that participation remains central to movements today.

Participation, and more specifically participatory democracy, is but one component in a broader constellation of ways in which workers and everyday citizens exercise their own self determination and collectively control the social conditions under which they live. The Venezuelan Communes exhibit characteristics of popular power and democratic self-governance, two topics that will be discussed in more detail below.

POPULAR POWER AND PARTICIPATORY DEMOCRACY IN LATIN AMERICA

In Latin America, the literature on popular power and participatory democracy has been subject to vigorous debate, with a variety of different perspectives ranging from sympathetic depictions of the ways in which participation has enhanced democracy to those who argue that participation has only failed to generate more democracy. Critics of participatory democracy argue that the expansion of participatory experiments is just another form of neoliberalism. They argue that participation is often used by governments to transfer responsibilities typically associated with the state to community organizations. In other words, participatory democracy is just another reduction of state influence and functions in the economy, another reduction of the role of the state in securing basic resources, just this time under the guise of "participation."[91, 92, 93, 94]

While this may be the case in some instances, I argue that popular power and participatory democracy, when driven from the popular sectors, can offer a genuine alternative form of development to neoliberal development. Critiques of the ways in which participatory democracy has been used by powerful states and international financial institutions to legitimate increasing inequalities are certainly useful, but scholars should not readily dismiss emerging forms of participation when many of them have emancipatory potential.

Baiocchi and Ganuza distinguish between a top-down form of "democracy from above" and a bottom-up form of "democratization from below."[95] They argue that despite the very genuine concerns about top-down forms of democratization from above, we should not throw the baby out with the bathwater and should focus on what they call the "utopian undercurrent" of participation, that is to say its emancipatory potential to give a voice to the voiceless and empower marginalized communities. I take a similar approach in putting forth the argument that networks of popular power, when driven from below, can significantly expand and deepen democracy, especially for traditionally excluded and marginalized sectors of society.[96]

Other critics of participatory democracy argue that it sows distrust, defection, and disorder.[97, 98, 99] Hanson, for example, argues that in certain political and institutional contexts participation generates mistrust in the community and concludes that participatory experiments are not always good for democracy.[100] I argue that in the instances where participation fails to live up to its promise, it is the political and institutional contexts that have placed barriers and limitations on the expansion of democracy, not that the problem is necessarily participatory experiments themselves.

Not surprisingly, scholars are also divided on Venezuela's experiments in popular power and participatory democracy. There are those who argue that the relationship between the Chavista state and networks of popular power prevent democracy to thrive.[101, 102] Margarita Lopez Maya questions the autonomy and democratic credentials of networks of popular power in Venezuela arguing that popular movements and organs of popular power were created and directly overseen by the state.[103] Hawkins and Hansen argue that earlier forms of popular power, the Bolivarian Circles, reinforced clientelistic relations between Chávez and civil society.[104] While the communes certainly retain some of the clientelism Hawkins and Hansen describe in their work, I look at the ways in which this new form of popular power has in many instances achieved a significant amount of autonomy from the state, breaking from clientelistic traditions long held in Venezuela.

Other scholars like Gabriel Hetland[105] and Sujatha Fernandes[106] (2010) are critical of the incompatibility thesis and argue that it is inadequate to understand contemporary Venezuela. Hetland shows that populist mobilization can set in motion processes that can indirectly generate participatory democracy.[107] Fernandes traces the history of urban social movements in Venezuela and examines the contradictions of movements for the expansion of participation that are supported by the state while at the same time fighting for autonomy from the state.[108] This article, in line with the work of Hetland[109] and Fernandes[110] does not merely celebrate or condemn participatory democracy in Venezuela but tries to offer a more nuanced account.

This book explores the various ways that networks of popular power have expanded democracy and autonomy in ways that was at times in contact with, and with the direct support of, the state and at times in contentious conflict with the state. I argue that the expansion of democracy and contact with the Chavista state is not simply an inverse relationship. My research shows the autonomy that many of these movements and organs of popular power have been able to achieve.

THEORIZING POPULAR POWER

The slogan of popular power has been raised in many historical cases, including the 1968 general strikes in France,[111] the Water Wars in Cochabamba, Bolivia,[112] the Portuguese Revolution,[113] Chile under the Popular Unity Government in 1970–1973,[114] the 2001 rebellion in Argentina,[115] and the 2006 teachers' strike in the Mexican city of Oaxaca,[116] to name a few. The following section will attempt to theorize the notion of "popular power."

Thomas Muhr defines popular power as "an expansion of the territorial distribution of power (in addition to municipal, federal state, and national power) in the construction of a direct democratic governance structure."[117] In another definition, Cairns and Sears define popular power as "the ability of vast numbers of people to control collectively the political, economic, and social conditions under which they live."[118] The legal definition of popular power in Venezuela's Law of Popular Power, states that:

> Popular power is the full exercise of sovereignty by the people in the political, economic, social, cultural, environmental, international, and any other sphere of the progression and development of society through their diverse forms of organization that build the communal state.[119]

Popular power can thus be seen as an alternative site of power or counter-power to parliamentarism, state power, or other traditional nodes of power. In other words, popular power is a form of direct or workers' democracy. Workers' councils, communal councils, neighborhood associations, popular assemblies, and different forms of workers' control are all examples of ways citizens can exercise popular power.

In Latin America, "popular power" has been theorized as an important component and a building block for the construction of socialism. As Argentine theorist Miguel Mazzeo writes, "popular power is not distinct from socialism, although it alludes to a singular form of conceiving and building it."[120] The singular form of conceiving socialism that Mazzeo refers to is through the construction of participatory and protagonistic democracy.[121] Building popular power amounts to the construction of different forms of participation, whether that be councils, participatory budgeting, or various forms of worker control and direct democratic self-governance. For Mazzeo, popular power is the process of constructing social relations that disrupt and are contrary to the logic of capital, as a way toward socialism.[122] The point that it is conceived as a process is important; as Azzelini argues, popular power is not a finished concept but is continually in development and renovation.[123]

In the case of Venezuela, as Venezuelan sociologist Edgardo Lander points out, the communal council has been defined as not only a body of popular power but the most important point in the transformative process in Venezuela.[124] Communes and communal councils play an important role in promoting the organization and participation of broader sectors of society. Hugo Chávez was also clear in his writings and speeches that the actualization of socialism has to be carried out through popular power:

> In order to advance toward socialism, we need a popular power capable of dismantling the networks of oppression, exploitation, and domination that linger in Venezuelan society, capable of configuring a new sociality out of daily life where fraternity and solidarity run in parallel with the permanent emergency of new ways of planning and producing the material life of our pueblo.[125]

What is important for Chávez, is that the communal council was to be seen as the first organizational form in the process of building popular power in Venezuela (Machado et al. 2018).

Zeguel also makes the connection between popular power and socialism in his definition of popular power: "[Popular power] is a prefigurative political strategy of socialism that constitutes itself as a concrete expression of popular sovereignty in a determined socio-political and sociocultural context."[126] Zeguel goes on to write: "Popular power is the end and the means for where democratic socialism is developed."[127] From the outset, Zeguel argues that popular power has the purpose of configuring the conditions for the construction of socialism.[128] Zeguel, like Mazzeo and Lander, points to examples of experiments in participatory democracy as driving forces of popular power in Venezuela.[129, 130, 131]

Popular power is often framed as "democracy from below" in contrast to traditional forms of power or "democracy from above." Cairns and Sears use the term democracy from below to "refer to more expansive processes of self-government that are based on the establishment of popular power in all areas of life."[132] Hal Draper suggests that while democracy from above stops at governmental forms, democracy from below works to transform human relations in all areas of society and toward the democratization of socioeconomic life in general. Fundamental to the idea of popular power is direct decision making by those who are affected by those decisions.[133] But more than a style of government or form of decision making, it is about participants controlling all aspects of their lives.[134]

Sociologist John L. Hammond contrasts popular power to centralism.[135] The centralist model "is viewed as a command structure in which people's participation consists largely in supporting decisions made in their name by a central authority."[136] The popular power model on the other hand argues that the state must be transformed by the activities of citizens. According to Hammond, true popular power comes through processes of struggle in which workers "come to control the means of production directly and collectively."[137] For Hammond,[138] like Draper,[139] popular power rejects representative governing structures and is predicated upon direct participation by all in both political and economic decisions. Popular power is something that is created by collective organization of popular struggles making demands against the ruling class and the state.

Movements for popular power offer a critique and alternative to parliamentary, liberal notions of democracy and traditional nodes of power. While liberal democracy is based on the delegation to representatives who are only accountable to those they represent during the time of elections, social movements stress a system of direct or participatory democracy. By opening new channels of access to the political system, social movements contribute to the creation of public space that is separate from traditional political institutions and can also contribute to a transfer of power over states. [140, 141] Two prominent forms of popular power, workers' councils and communal councils, will be discussed in further detail below.

COUNCILS AND DEMOCRATIC SELF-GOVERNANCE

Over the past century, workers and communities have fought to gain more control over their workplaces, communities, and the decisions that affect their lives. Workers have gained varying degrees of power by occupying factories, operating self-managed enterprises, and forming workers' and communal councils. Worker and communal councils have emerged at various geographic locations and historical moments as the genuine expression of workers' interests. Workers have organized themselves in councils in many cases without prior knowledge of councils that have preceded them. In this way councils can be seen as a natural tendency for rank-and-file workers.[142] The following section will examine the history and theory of councils from the Paris Commune of 1848 to the present.

Workers' Councils

A workers' council can be defined broadly as a form of political and economic organization in which a workplace is controlled collectively by the workers of that workplace. Councils represent the collective expression of the working class whereby workplaces are collectively controlled by the workers rather than the bosses. The workers themselves, through assemblies and the election of temporary and recallable delegates, make all the necessary decisions in that workplace. Delegates come from and are elected by the workers themselves; they generally make the same wages as the other workers and are meant to rotate frequently. Delegates are elected to pursue a mandate that was given to them by the workers, and if the mandate is betrayed, the delegate is recalled. There are no managers in the council; all decisions are made through the delegate system. Councils are also marked by their independence from official and institutional structures. Different forms of workers' control have sprung up in a myriad of places in the world and in many different historical contexts. Some of the most prominent examples include Paris 1871, Russia 1917–1918, Hungary 1956, France 1968, Chile 1972–1973, Portugal 1974–1975, Iran 1979, and Poland 1980–1981, just to name a few.[143, 144, 145, 146]

Councils have sprung up in a variety of different geographic locations, types of states, in both more and less developed countries as well as in both urban and rural sectors. In each of these examples, workers' councils form very similar democratic structures, regardless of whether the workers had much prior knowledge of previous council structures. Workplace-based, direct democratic structures repeatedly appear in unpredictable moments of working-class struggle. Councils are generated in the midst of worker uprisings regardless of the experience or awareness of the workers involved. One conclusion drawn from this is that the council structure is an organic expression of workers in a context that requires such organization.[147, 148]

How and When Do Workers' Councils Emerge?

The literature suggests that there are two necessary conditions for the emergence of workers' councils. The first condition is that councils emerge in times of major crisis, and the second is a high level of independent organization among workers.[149] Much of the research on workers' councils has found that they usually emerge in times of capital crisis, whether economic, political, or both.[150, 151, 152] Although councils have appeared at various junctures, they tend to go further and deeper in revolutionary periods.

Regarding the second condition for workers' councils, the existence of a strong, independent organization among workers, there is much debate about what types of organization are necessary, how they organize, and the level of spontaneity in their emergence. Comparing the successful establishment of Soviets in Russia and the failure of the German councils, Barker argues that the key to success in Russia was the existence of an effective revolutionary organization rooted in the working class.[153] At the time of the revolution the Bolsheviks had a few thousand members with a strong tradition in the laboring class. Barker contends that the Bolsheviks were ready when the objective factors presented the opportunity for councils to take power.[154] In the case of the German councils, Barker argues the Spartakists were born only in the moment of the 1918 revolution and were not as well established, nor did they have the coherent revolutionary strategies that the Bolsheviks did.[155] Wallis argues that the role of a revolutionary party is to give priority to workers' control at each stage of development, to provide self-protection, and to ensure the movement's cohesion.[156]

The conditions for the development of councils (social and economic upheaval, crisis, war, and the destruction of state structures) were present in both the post-WWI and post-WWII periods but they only appeared to a significant extent in the post-WWI period. Gluckstein locates the dearth of councils in the weakness of independent working-class organizations in the WWII period.[157] The repression of independent working-class activity by Stalinist Russia and Nazi Germany was one factor, but also the communist parties, who once promoted councils in the WWI period, now opposed them. Communist parties post WWII were oriented primarily to support Moscow and were discouraged to actively encourage the formation of workers' councils.

One example of this dynamic is the 1956 revolutionary workers' movement in Hungary. Workers in Hungary armed themselves and formed independent democratic councils that challenged extant traditional state institutions. In the end, the workers' movement was crushed by Stalin's successors and dismissed as "counter-revolutionary" and under the influence of Western financing. The suppression of the democratic councils was supported by communist parties internationally.[158]

On the question of organization, there is an important debate on the extent to which workers' council structures emerge "spontaneously" without conscious preparation or as a result of conscious organization. The debate is often framed as the spontaneity vs. organization debate. In times of crisis and heightened class conflict, workers form identical committee-based, delegateled, directly democratic structures. These structures are created by the requirements of the situation and are generated to meet the immediate organizational needs of workers. Because the generation of councils can be seen as a natural expression out of the concrete needs of workers, some theorists argue that their organization is spontaneous.[159] Councils, according to Cohen, are not premeditated or the result of conscious preparation.[160] She argues that because all accounts of workers' councils are almost identical in structure, they emerge because real material conditions require that type of organization among workers rather than being "plucked from thin air." The specific council structure arises and is shaped by the capitalist labor process and capitalist production.[161]

Hallas on the other hand, although acknowledging spontaneity, emphasizes the importance of conscious organization. [162] He argues that from the position of organizations, any action or event carried out by workers not part of a formal organization appears to be spontaneous, but from the point of view of the workers, their actions are conscious and deliberate. Hallas argues that:

> Spontaneity and organization are not alternatives; they are different aspects of the process by which increasing numbers of workers can become conscious of the reality of their situation and of their power to change it. The growth of that process depends on a dialogue, on organized militants who listen as well as argue, who understand the limitations of a party as well as its strengths and who are able to find connections between the actual consciousness of their fellows and the politics necessary to realize the aspirations buried in that consciousness.[163]

For Hallas, workers do act spontaneously, but organization provides the cohesion and coordination necessary for a workers' movement to sustain itself and be successful in the end.[164]

Why Have Councils Been Short-lived?

Though the appearance of the workers' councils on the world stage was of great importance, their existence was brief. The question of why historic examples of workers' councils have been short-lived is an important one in the literature. Are the internal dynamics of councils and the nature of workers' power in general more inefficient and rife with internal institutional problems than traditional workplace organization? Or do the problems with councils come from outside the council itself, from either the state or party officials or having to operate within the capitalist marketplace? Ness and Azzellini contend that the challenges of worker control come more from without rather than from within.[165] Places of worker-controlled production operating in the dominant capitalist culture must interact with sectors of capitalist society and on a capitalist playing field. Many workplaces are occupied after capitalist entrepreneurs abandon their firm because of obsolete production methods or because of eroded distribution markets. The recently occupied workplace thus faces additional hurdles by taking over enterprises with obsolete technology or that are non-profitable because of market failures. It is in this context that worker-run industries must compete in the capitalist marketplace against domestic and foreign enterprises.[166] Additionally, worker-run industries, despite their democratic nature, must produce for the market, undermining the democratic elements of the worker council itself. Decisions that in theory are made by the council are often influenced by the capitalist marketplace in which it operates. For example, the market dictates what is to be produced and the prices for commodities, influencing decisions in the council.

In addition to operating within a market system, worker-run industries also face attacks from the state or other outside forces. Wallis argues that in the thirteen cases of workers-control in his study, each of them was destroyed by the threat or use of force.[167] In the case of Russia, the Soviets were destroyed in counter-revolution led by the White Army in the Civil War. In Spain, workers' control was suppressed when Nazi and Italian Fascist forces intervened in their Civil War on the side of Franco, and in Chile, the government returned seized factories to their previous owners in exchange for military guarantees to protect elections.

In the case of Russia, Harman locates the failures of the Soviets in the decimation of the working class and the decline in industrial and agricultural production that resulted from the Civil War.[168] Fourteen capitalist countries sent forces to Russian to fight alongside the White Army to crush the Soviet system. The Red Army ended up winning the war but not without significant losses. By 1920, industrial output was just 18 percent of the pre-war figure, and labor productivity was just one third of what it was before the war. The working class was reduced to 43 percent of its former numbers.[169] The workers who once ran the factories were the most likely to fight on the front-line in the war and the most likely to suffer the most casualties. The decima-tion of production and the decimation of the working class led to decline in genuine workers' power. The class that made up the Soviets ceased to exist in any meaningful sense after the war, hindering any chance of sustaining genuine workers' democracy.[170]

Theoretical Foundations

The theoretical foundation for workers' control is rooted in Marxism or more specifically in late nineteenthand early twentieth-century socialist theory. Marx argued that workers are the most revolutionary and democratic force in society. As Marxist theorist Hal Draper points out, it is not that workers are more clever, more humanitarian, or that they are better human beings because they are workers but that:

> The special "advantage" of the working class springs from inherent drives of its *class* position in society, its ineradicable interests as a group, its condi-tions of life; and its "advantage" comes into play only insofar as this class organizes itself (as it is inevitably driven to do) and transforms the thinking of its individual components in the course of class experiences.[171]

The workings of capitalist production have created a new laboring class both through the development of industry, which increases the working class in number, and through the socialization of production, which concentrates workers in workplaces. Capitalist production led to increasingly large and concentrated production units. Other oppressed groups that existed before the modern working class (for example, peasants or farmers) were atomized, separated, and relied on individual effort to survive. In contrast, to meet the needs of capitalism, workers were thrown together in crowds and organized in assembly lines, work teams, and shifts in a way that they never had been before. Capitalism not only organized workers in workplaces, teaching work-ers the principles of working together and solidarity, but also subjected work-ers to similar stresses on the job. Their collective grievances, their inherent organization as a class, and their overwhelming majority in numbers gives the working class a different kind of economic power. Workers exercise this power primarily through their ability to withhold their labor and shut off the source of wealth in society.[172, 173]

If the working class is a revolutionary class, then the worker council rep-resents the collective expression of workers' interests. Marx, writing about the Paris Commune, acknowledged the revolutionary potential of workers' councils. About the commune, he wrote, "It was essentially a working-class government, the product of the struggle of the producing against the appro-priating class, the political form at last discovered under which to work out the economical emancipation of labor."[174] Lenin's analysis of the 1905 Petrograd Soviet also suggests that councils can be the basis for a new, worker-run society.[175] Cohen argues that the councils that emerged in Russia in 1917 also embodied the features of a potential workers' state. She contends that these bodies also had the potential to lead the conquest of power, eventually leading to what Engels called the "withering away" of the state.[176]

Are All Councils Revolutionary?

Some forms of workers' councils directly challenge capitalist hegemony while others operate within the capitalist logic of profit. Examples like the Soviets in Russia and the councils during the Paris commune offer a glimpse of an alternative to capitalism. These councils emerge not out of any state or party but out of the grassroots conditions of working life.[177] Because the workers' councils mentioned above actively challenge capitalist logic of production and profitability they must be distinguished from councils and other forms of participation that work within and support the capitalist representative model. The national policy councils and national policy conferences in Brazil, although important in expanding participation to the traditionally excluded, are neither a challenge to capitalist hegemony nor can they be seen as organs for a fundamentally different type of society. The national policy councils are permanent bodies that work within the structure of the executive branch, and half of its representatives are from the government and half from civil society.[178] Thamy Pogrebinshci argues that these bodies are genuinely participatory but "strengthen formal political representation and potentially reinforce the functions and activities of traditional political institutions, such as the legislature and political parties."[179]

Consultative councils in Mexico are another example. The consultative councils in Mexico play an ancillary role to established institutions. They consult in the formulation of policies, evaluate policies, and make recommendations for specific issues to government agencies. [180]

Self-management councils in Tito's Yugoslavia, despite existing in a very different type of state as the Brazilian and Mexican examples above, also played a supportive role to ruling class institutions. These councils were largely instruments of the ruling bureaucracy rather than genuine organs of democratic control from below. Yugoslav councils were quite unique in their acceptance and promotion of official state ideology, which was a marketoriented approach to modernization. For the first few decades of selfmanagement the trade unions were an essential ally of the pro-market faction of Yugoslav leadership.[181] Councils demanded deregulation and lower taxes. Workers' councils acted more as "collective entrepreneurs . . . than organs of workers' control over management."[182] Additionally, unlike the Russian Soviets, workers did not have full control over the surplus value produced in their workplaces. In the end, the councils' reliance on the marketplace on determining remuneration resulted in workplace insecurity and declining standards of living. Music argues that "the self-management councils, as the principal structures, could not serve as democratic organs for exercising dissent, since their primary purpose was to play a managerial function in the operation of firms, not to serve as political organs of the working class."[183]

The difference between councils that challenge capitalism and those that work within it is that in the former the councils control the means of production and collectively make binding decisions in their workplaces, while in the latter the councils serve a more advisory and non-binding role supporting or supplementing traditional political institutions.

POPULAR POWER AND COUNTERHEGEMONIC GLOBALIZATION FROM BELOW

The concept of globalization from below derives from the study of social change. One important impetus for social change is social movements. Scholars have been interested in the ways humans band together in an organized fashion to encourage (or discourage) social change. Social movements connect people who share similar political goals. In this case, globalization from below has the goal of "making the global system safe for decent societies." Douglas Kellner defines globalization from below as "the ways in which marginalized individuals and social movements resist globalization and/or use its institutions and instruments to further democratization and social justice."[184] Kellner's definition is very useful in the way that he conceptualizes globalization from below as two different (yet overlapping) phenomena. On the one hand it is a reaction, a movement that exists solely to resist the inequities of corporate globalization, but on the other it looks at the ways people at the grassroots level have taken advantage of the openings and possibilities created by globalization to build an alternative globalization based on democracy and social justice. Not only have activists taken advantage of openings and possibilities but they have also played a role in creating them.

Some examples of globalization from below that sociologists have studied include transnational social movements,[185] deglobalization,[186] the World Social Forum,[187] the Zapatista movement,[188, 189] the Free Burma Movement,[190] the Global Justice Movement,[191] and the Bolivian Water Wars,[192] among others. These authors are interested in the ways in which counterhegemonic social movements have played a role in shaping our global world and challenging hegemonic neoliberal globalization from above.

Evans defines counter-hegemonic globalization as "a globally organized effort to replace the neoliberal global regime with one that maximizes democratic political control and makes the equitable development of human capabilities and environment stewardship its priorities."[193] Evans begins with the assumption that neoliberal globalization is unsustainable.[194] Neoliberalism has come to be uncontested by dominant elites, but outside of elite circles, dominant economic institutions, and government officials, widespread disillusionment of the failures of neoliberalism prevail. Disillusionment stems from neoliberalism's failure to protect individuals and groups from the market, whether it be crises, inequality, or decreasing access to health and education. Moreover, neoliberal governance has failed to even protect the assets of capitalists themselves.

What is important for Evans, however, is that while neoliberalism has failed to protect people from the vicissitudes of the market, it has created the conditions and opened up the space for counterhegemonic social movements that challenge globalization from above.[195] Evans argues that neoliberalism has in many ways expanded the possibilities for social movements to organize at the global level.[196] Advances in technological tools as well as the social and organizational resources that have expanded under neoliberal globalization have given social movements the tools that enable them to organize in ways that were unthinkable one hundred years ago.

Scholars on transnational activism, in particular Chase-Dunn, Morosin, and Alvarez, argue that Latin American social movements resisting neoliberalism are part of broader transnational efforts involving other movements in the semi-periphery.[197, 198] The case of the communes in Venezuela supports this thesis but goes one step further. The emergence and proliferation of communes and communal councils are not just an expression of resistance to neoliberal, corporate-led globalization but also the creation of a new form of development and democratic self-governance. The communal struggle is marked not simply by what it is fighting against (neoliberal development), but what it is fighting for (an alternative model of development that is predicated on community led, self-administration, and managed endogenous development). In other words, the Venezuelan communal movement does not just contribute to a transnational movement struggling against neoliberal development but also contributes a model of an alternative type of development to fight for. Communal councils have already incorporated traditionally excluded sectors of society into political decision-making processes, but the question remains, do these networks of popular power have the potential to fundamentally transform the capitalist state in the era of globalization?

The study of globalization from below is generally interested in transnational networks and movements. The communes and communal councils in Venezuela should be understood as a response and a reaction to neoliberal globalization. Community organizations in Venezuela and the precursors to communal councils emerged from the *caracazo*, which was a response to

IMF imposed neoliberal globalization. Many civil society organizations and social movements in Venezuela organized transnationally in various campaigns, including the rejection of the Free Trade Agreement of the Americas (FTAA). The communal councils and communes also have a transnational component. One example is the collaboration between various indigenous communal councils in Venezuela and the Zapatistas in Chiapas, Mexico. These connections will be further elaborated in chapter 5.

Sociologists have long grappled with the question of how society changes. One important societal change is the democratization of society. Democratization can take a number of forms, including transitions from authoritarian to representative democracies, increased participation in representative democracies, or in the form of councils as a bottom-up alternative to the representative model. This chapter examined the intersection between democratization and social movements and the ways in which the success or failure of an expansion of democracy from below is contingent on the activity and influence of social movements.

In the Marxist literature, because of workers' unique position in the production of society's wealth, the potential for workers' power was theorized to reside at the point of production, in other words at the workplace. This literature suggests that the labor movement is especially positioned to increase democracy. Over the past few decades, however, we have seen the labor movement experience great decline in unionization rates. This is not to say that the labor movement cannot experience resurgence, but in this decline other competing movements have emerged to pursue different projects and mobilize people around different interests. One important movement examined in this book is the communal council movement in Venezuela. The expansion of communal councils in Venezuela demonstrates an alternative form of workers' power where citizens wield power, not at the point of production in the traditional Marxist literature, but at the community level. Though some of the communes have more recently taken over abandoned factories and other sites of production, for the most part they exercise their power not in their workplaces but in their neighborhoods.

Marx and Engels wrote in the Communist Manifesto that "the history of all hitherto existing society is the history of class struggle."[199] Though not all social movements promote democracy, and in some cases are antidemocratic in nature, social movements as a form of resistance and an expression of the oppressed are important catalysts in history. While social movements and class struggle, as Marx and Engels wrote, are the motors of history and play a significant role in the democratization of society, democratization also creates the conditions that are conducive for the mobilization of social movements.[200] It is through this dialectic between movements and various forms of participation and popular power that we can begin to understand the democratization of society.

NOTES

1. Edgardo Lander, "El Estado y Los Tensiones de la Participacion Popular en Venezuela," *Observatorio Social de America Latina* 8 no. 22 (2007).

2. Dario Azzelini, *Communes and Worker's Control in Venezuela: Building 21st Centruy So cialism from Below* (Leiden, Netherlands: Brill, 2016).

3. Charles Tilly, *Social Movements, 1768–2004* (Boulder, CO: Paradigm Publishers, 2004): 3.

4. Sidney Tarrow, *Power in Movement* (Cambridge, UK: Cambridge University Press, 1994): 7.

5. Charles Tilly, *Contentious Performances* (Cambridge, UK: Cambridge University Press, 2008): 5.

6. Benjamin Barber, *Strong Democracy* (Berkeley: University of California Press, 2003).

7. John Dryzek, "Discursive Democracy vs. Liberal Constitutionalism" in *Democratic Innovation: Deliberation, Representation and Association*, ed. Michael Saward (London and New York: Routledge, 2000).

8. Iris M. Young, "Communication and the Other: Beyond Deliberative Democracy," in *Democracy and Difference: Contesting the Boundaries of the Political*, ed. Seyla Benhabib (Princeton, NJ: Princeton University Press, 1996).

9. Tony Fitzpatrick, "The Two Paradoxes of Welfare Democracy," *International Journal of Social Welfare* 11 (2002).

10. Piotr Perczynski, "Active Citizenship and Associative Democracy," in *Democratic Innovation: Deliberation, Representation and Association*, ed. Michael Saward (London and New York: Routledge, 2000).

11. Chantal Mouffe, *The Democratic Paradox* (London: Verso, 2000).

12. Colin Barker, ed., *Revolutionary Rehearsals* (Chicago: Haymarket Books, 1987, 2002).

13. Sheila Cohen, "The Red Mole: Workers' Councils as a Means of Revolutionary Transformation," in *From Ours to Master and to Own*, ed. Immanuel Ness and Dario Azzellini (Chicago: Haymarket Books, 2011).

14. Donny Gluckstein, "Workers' Councils in Europe: A Century of Experience," in *From Ours to Master and to Own*, ed. Immanuel Ness and Dario Azzellini (Chicago: Haymarket Books, 2011).

15. Immanuel Ness and Dario Azzellini, *From Ours to Master and to Own* (Chicago: Haymarket Books, 2011).

16. Dario Azzellini, "Venezuela's Solidarity Economy: Collective Ownership, Expropriation, and Workers Self-Management," *The Journal of Labor and Society* 12 (2009): 171–191.

17. Steve Ellner, "A New Model with Rough Edges: Venezuela's Community Councils," *NACLA Report on the Americas* 42, no. 3 (2009): 11–14.

18. Frederico Fuentes, "Venezuela: New Moves to Build People's Power," *Green Left Weekly* 831 (2010).

19. James Cairns and Alan Sears, *The Democratic Imagination: Envisioning Popular Power in the Twenty-First Century* (Toronto: University of Toronto Press, 2012).

20. Donatella della Porta, *Can Democracy Be Saved?* (Malden, ME: Polity Press, 2013).

21. Carole Pateman, *Participation and Democratic Theory* (Cambridge, UK: Cambridge University Press, 1970).

22. Francesca Polleta, *Freedom is an Endless Meeting: Democracy in American Social Movements* (Chicago: University of Chicago Press, 2002).

23. Sherry Arnstein, "A Ladder of Citizen Participation," *Journal of the American Institute of Planners* 35, no. 4 (1969).

24. Anthony Arblaster, *Democracy, 3rd ed.* (Buckingham, UK: Open University Press, 2002).

25. Robert Dahl, *Democracy and its Critics* (New Haven, CT: Yale University Press, 1989).

26. Albert Weale, *Democracy, 2nd ed.* (New York: Palgrave Macmillan 2007).

27. John Hammond, *Building Popular Power: Workers' and Neighborhood Movements in the Portuguese Revolution* (New York: Monthly Review Press, 1988).

28. Peter Winn, *Weavers of Revolution: The Yarur Workers and Chile's Road to Socialism* (Oxford, UK: Oxford University Press, 1989).

29. Marina Sitrin, ed., *Horizontalism: Voices of Popular Power in Argentina* (Chico, CA: AK Press, 2006).

30. Chris Harman, "Latin America: The Return of Popular Power." *International Socialism* 114, (2007).

31. Joel Geier, "Year of Revolutionary Hope," *International Socialist Review* 59 (May–June 2008).

32. Oscar Olivera and Tom Lewis, *Cochabamba! Water War in Bolivia* (New York: South End Press, 2008).

33. Anthony Arblaster, *Democracy, 3rd ed.* (Buckingham, UK: Open University Press, 2002).

34. James Cairns and Alan Sears, *The Democratic Imagination: Envisioning Popular Power in the Twenty-First Century* (Toronto: University of Toronto Press, 2012).

35. Helena Catt, *Democracy in Practice* (London: Routledge, 1999).

36. James Cairns and Alan Sears, *The Democratic Imagination: Envisioning Popular Power in the Twenty-First Century* (Toronto: University of Toronto Press, 2012).

37. Gerhard Lenski, *Power and Privilege* (New York: McGraw-Hill, 1966).

38. Robert Dahl, *Democracy and its Critics* (New Haven, CT: Yale University Press, 1989).

39. Albert Weale, *Democracy, 2nd ed.* (New York: Palgrave Macmillan, 2007).

40. Robert Dahl, *Democracy and its Critics* (New Haven, CT: Yale University Press, 1989): 323, quoted in James Cairns and Alan Sears, *The Democratic Imagination: Envisioning Popular Power in the Twenty-First Century* (Toronto: University of Toronto Press, 2012): 12.

41. David Lewit, "Porto Alegre's budget of, by, and for the people," *Yesmagazine.org*, December 31, 2002, https://www.yesmagazine.org/issues/what-would-democracy-look-like/ 562.

42. Marina Sitrin, ed., *Horizontalism: Voices of Popular Power in Argentina* (Chico, CA: AK Press, 2006).

43. Pippa Norris, *Democratic Deficit: Critical Citizens Revisited* (Cambridge, UK: Cambridge University Press, 2011).

44. Thomas D. Zweifel, *Democratic Deficit: Institutions and Regulation in the European Union, Switzerland, and the United States in Comparative Perspective* (Lanham, MD: Lexington Books, 2002).

45. John Keane, *The Life and Death of Democracy* (London: Simon and Schuster, 2009).

46. James Cairns and Alan Sears, *The Democratic Imagination: Envisioning Popular Power in the Twenty-First Century* (Toronto: University of Toronto Press, 2012).

47. Donatella della Porta, *Can Democracy Be Saved?* (Malden, ME: Polity Press, 2013).

48. Ibid.

49. Ibid.

50. James Laxer, *Democracy* (Toronto: Groundwood Books, 2009): 102.

51. James Cairns and Alan Sears, *The Democratic Imagination: Envisioning Popular Power in the Twenty-First Century* (Toronto: University of Toronto Press, 2012).

52. Paul Foot, *The Vote: How it Was Won and How it was Undermined* (London: Viking, 2005).

53. Andrew Selee and Enrique Peruzzotti, *Participatory Innovation and Representitive Democracy in Latin America* (Washington, DC: Woodrow Wilson Center Press, 2009): 2.

54. Maxwell Cameron, Eric Hershberg, and Kennth E. Sharpe, eds, *New Institutions for Participatory Democracy in Latin America: Voices and Consequence* (New York: Palgrave MacMillan, 2012): 3.

55. Andrew Selee and Enrique Peruzzotti, *Participatory Innovation and Representative Democracy in Latin America* (Washington, DC: Woodrow Wilson Center Press, 2009).

56. Joseph Schumpeter, *Capitalism, Socialism, and Democracy* (New York: Harper & Brothers, 1942).

57. Ibid.

58. Andrew Selee and Enrique Peruzzotti, *Participatory Innovation and Representative Democracy in Latin America* (Washington, DC: Woodrow Wilson Center Press, 2009).

59. Charles Montesquieu, *The Spirit of the Laws* (New York: Cosimo Classics, 1748, 2010): 155.

60. Andrew Selee and Enrique Peruzzotti, *Participatory Innovation and Representitive Democracy in Latin America* (Washington, DC: Woodrow Wilson Center Press, 2009).

61. Ibid.

62. Ibid: 6.

63. Ibid: 6.

64. Paul Ginsborg, *Democracy: Crisis and Renewal* (London: Profile Books, 2008): 6.

65. Anthony Arblaster, *Democracy, 3rd ed.* (Buckingham, UK: Open University Press, 2002).

66. Ibid., quoted in James Cairns and Alan Sears, *The Democratic Imagination: Envisioning Popular Power in the Twenty-First Century* (Toronto: University of Toronto Press, 2012): 39.

67. Quoted in Paul Le Blanc, "What Do Socialists Say About Democracy?" *International Socialist Review* 74 (2009).

68. John Ackerman, "Co-governance for Accountability: Beyond Exit and Voice," *World Development* 32, no. 3 (2003): 447–463.

69. Benjamin Barber, *Strong Democracy* (Berkeley: University of California Press, 2003).

70. Carole Pateman, *Participation and Democratic Theory* (Cambridge, UK: Cambridge University Press, 1970).

71. C. L. R. James, "Every Cook Can Govern," *Correspondence* 2, no. 12 (1956).

72. John Ackerman, "Co-governance for Accountability: Beyond Exit and Voice," *World Development* 32, no. 3 (2003): 447–463.

73. Francoise Montambeault, "Learning to Be Better Democrats? The Role of Informal Practices in Brazilian Participatory Budgeting Experiences," in *New Institutions for Participatory Democracy in Latin America: Voices and Consequence*, eds. Maxwell A. Cameron, Eric Hershberg, and Kenneth E. Sharpe (London: Palgrave MacMillan, 2012).

74. Ibid.

75. Carole Pateman, *Participation and Democratic Theory* (Cambridge, UK: Cambridge University Press, 1970).

76. Donatella della Porta, *Can Democracy Be Saved?* (Malden, ME: Polity Press, 2013).

77. Ibid.

78. Jürgen Habermas, *The Structural Transformation of the Public Sphere: An Inquiry into a Category of Bourgeoise Society* (Cambridge, MA: MIT Press, 1991).

79. Ibid.

80. Francoise Montambeault, "Learning to Be Better Democrats? The Role of Informal Practices in Brazilian Participatory Budgeting Experiences," in *New Institutions for Participatory Democracy in Latin America: Voices and Consequence*, eds. Maxwell A. Cameron, Eric Hershberg, and Kenneth E. Sharpe (London: Palgrave MacMillan, 2012).

81. Ibid.

82. Carole Pateman, *Participation and Democratic Theory* (Cambridge, UK: Cambridge University Press, 1970).

83. Francoise Montambeault, "Learning to Be Better Democrats? The Role of Informal Practices in Brazilian Participatory Budgeting Experiences," in *New Institutions for Participatory Democracy in Latin America: Voices and Consequence*, eds. Maxwell A. Cameron, Eric Hershberg, and Kenneth E. Sharpe (London: Palgrave MacMillan, 2012).

84. Donatella della Porta, *Can Democracy Be Saved?* (Malden, ME: Polity Press, 2013).

85. James Cairns and Alan Sears, *The Democratic Imagination: Envisioning Popular Power in the Twenty-First Century* (Toronto: University of Toronto Press, 2012).

86. Cornelius Castoriadis, *The Imaginary Institution of Society* (Cambridge: MIT Press, 1975).

87. David Lewit, "Porto Alegre's budget of, by, and for the people," *Yesmagazine.org*, December 31, 2002, https://www.yesmagazine.org/issues/what-would-democracy-look-like/ 562.

88. Marina Sitrin, ed., *Horizontalism: Voices of Popular Power in Argentina* (Chico, CA: AK Press, 2006).

89. Peter Ranis Peter, "Factories Without Bosses: Argentina's Experience with Worker-run Enterprises," *Labor: Studies in Working-Class History of the Americas* 3, no. 1 (2006).

90. Donatella della Porta, *Can Democracy Be Saved?* (Malden, ME: Polity Press, 2013).

91. Valeria Guernos-Meza and Mike Geddes, "Local Governance and Participation under Neoliberalism: Comparative Perspectives," *International Journal of Urban and Regional Research* 34, no. 1 (2010): 115–129.

92. Caroline Lee, *Do-It-Yourself Democracy: The Rise of the Public Engagement Industry* (Oxford, UK: Oxford University Press, 2015).

93. Patricia Richards, *Pobladoras, Indigenas, and the State: Conflicts over Women's Rights in Chile* (Princeton, NJ: Princeton University Press, 2004).

94. Jon Shefner, *The Illusion of Civil Society: Democratization and Community Mobilization in Low-Income Mexico* (University Park, PA: Pennsylvania State University Press, 2008).

95. Gianpaulo Baiocchi and Ernesto Ganuza, *Popular Democracy: The Paradox of Participation*, (Stanford, CA: Stanford University Press, 2017).

96. Ibid.

97. Benjamin Goldfrank, *Deepening Democracy in Latin America: Participation, Decentralization, and the Left* (University Park, PA: Pennsylvania State University Press: 2012).

98. Rebecca Hanson, "Deepening Distrust: Why Participatory Experiments Are Not Always Good for Democracy," *The Sociological Quarterly* 59, no. 1 (2018): 145–167.

99. Robert Putnam and Robert Leonardi, *Making Democracy Work: Civic Traditions in Modern Italy* (Princeton, NJ: Princeton University Press, 1993).

100. Rebecca Hanson, "Deepening Distrust: Why Participatory Experiments Are Not Always Good for Democracy," *The Sociological Quarterly* 59, no. 1 (2018): 145–167.

101. Allan R. Brewer-Carias, *Dismantling Democracy in Venezuela: The Chávez Authoritarian Experiment* (Cambridge, UK: Cambridge University Press, 2010).

102. Uribarri Sanchez, "Venezuela, Turning Further Left?" in *Leftovers*, ed. Jorge Castenada and Marco Morales (New York: Routledge, 2008).

103. Margarita Lopez Maya, "Populism, 21st Century Socialism and Corruption in Venezuela," *Thesis Eleven* 149 (2018): 67–83.

104. Kirk A. Hawkins and David Hanson, "Dependent Civil Society: The Circulos Bolivarianos in Venezuela." *Latin American Research Review* 41 (2006): 102–132.

105. Gabriel Hetland, "The Crooked Line: From Populist Mobilization to Participatory Democracy in Chávez -Era Venezuela," *Qualitative Sociology* 37 (2014): 373–401.

106. Sujatha Fernandes, *Who Can Stop the Drums? Urban Social Movements in Chávez's Venezuela* (Durham, NC: Duke University Press, 2010).

107. Gabriel Hetland, "The Crooked Line: From Populist Mobilization to Participatory Democracy in Chávez -Era Venezuela," *Qualitative Sociology* 37 (2014): 373–401.

108. Sujatha Fernandes, *Who Can Stop the Drums? Urban Social Movements in Chávez's Venezuela* (Durham, NC: Duke University Press, 2010).

109. Gabriel Hetland, "The Crooked Line: From Populist Mobilization to Participatory Democracy in Chávez -Era Venezuela," *Qualitative Sociology* 37 (2014): 373–401.

110. Sujatha Fernandes, *Who Can Stop the Drums? Urban Social Movements in Chávez's Venezuela* (Durham, NC: Duke University Press, 2010).

111. Joel Geier, "Year of Revolutionary Hope," *International Socialist Review* 59 (May–June 2008).

112. Oscar Olivera and Tom Lewis, *Cochabamba! Water War in Bolivia* (New York: South End Press, 2008).

113. John Hammond, *Building Popular Power: Workers' and Neighborhood Movements in the Portuguese Revolution* (New York: Monthly Review Press, 1988).

114. Peter Winn, *Weavers of Revolution: The Yarur Workers and Chile's Road to Socialism* (Oxford, UK: Oxford University Press, 1989).

115. Marina Sitrin, ed., *Horizontalism: Voices of Popular Power in Argentina* (Chico, CA: AK Press, 2006).

116. Chris Harman, "Latin America: The Return of Popular Power." *International Socialism* 114, (2007).

117. Thomas Muhr, "TINA go home! ALBA and Re-theorizing Resistance to Global Capitalism," *Cosmos and History: The Journal of Natural and Social Philosophy* 6, no. 2 (2010): 37.

118. James Cairns and Alan Sears, *The Democratic Imagination: Envisioning Popular Power in the Twenty-First Century* (Toronto: University of Toronto Press, 2012): 76.

119. Ley Organica del Poder Popular. *Gazeta Oficial* 6.011, (December 21, 2010): 7.

120. Migueal Mazzeo, *El Sueño de una Cosa: Introducción al Poder Popular* (Caracas, Venezuela: El Perro y la Rana, 2007): 61.

121. Ibid.

122. Ibid.

123. Dario Azzellini, *Communes and Worker's Control in Venezuela: Building 21st Centruy Socialism from Below* (Leiden, Netherlands: Brill, 2016).

124. Edgardo Lander, "El Estado y Los Tensiones de la Participacion Popular en Venezuela, *Observatorio Social de America Latina* 8, no. 22 (2007).

125. Hugo Chávez, "Propuesta del Candidato de la Patria Comandante Hugo Chávez para la gestión Bolivariana Socialista 2013–2019," *Sistema de Información de Tendencias Educattivas en America Latina*, 2012, http://www.chavez.org.ve/Programa-Patria-2013-2019.pdf

126. M. Zeguel, "El Poder Popular como perspectiva estratégica de construcción de la Izquierda libertaria," *Rebelión*, December 21, 2013, https://rebelion.org/el-poder-popular-comoperspectiva-estrategica-de-construccion-de-la-izquierda-libertaria/.

127. Ibid.

128. Ibid.

129. Ibid.

130. Migueal Mazzeo, *El Sueño de una Cosa: Introducción al Poder Popular* (Caracas, Venezuela: El Perro y la Rana, 2007).

131. Edgardo Lander, "El Estado y Los Tensiones de la Participacion Popular en Venezuela," *Observatorio Social de America Latina* 8, no. 22 (2007).

132. James Cairns and Alan Sears, *The Democratic Imagination: Envisioning Popular Power in the Twenty-First Century* (Toronto: University of Toronto Press, 2012): 13.

133. Hal Draper, "Marx on Democratic Forms of Government," *Socialist Register* (1974).

134. James Cairns and Alan Sears, *The Democratic Imagination: Envisioning Popular Power in the Twenty-First Century* (Toronto: University of Toronto Press, 2012).

135. John Hammond, *Building Popular Power: Workers' and Neighborhood Movements in the Portuguese Revolution* (New York: Monthly Review Press, 1988).

136. Ibid: 19.

137. Ibid: 20.

138. Ibid.

139. Hal Draper, "Marx on Democratic Forms of Government," *Socialist Register* (1974).

140. Donatella della Porta, *Can Democracy Be Saved?* (Malden, ME: Polity Press, 2013).

141. Charles Tilly, *European Revolutions 1492–1992* (Oxford/Cambridge, UK: Blackwell, 1993).

142. Immanuel Ness and Dario Azzellini, *From Ours to Master and to Own* (Chicago: Haymarket Books, 2011).

143. Colin Barker, ed., *Revolutionary Rehearsals* (Chicago: Haymarket Books, 1987, 2002).

144. Shelia Cohen, "The Red Mole: Workers' Councils as a Means of Revolutionary Transformation," in *From Ours to Master and to Own*, ed. Immanuel Ness and Dario Azzellini (Chicago: Haymarket Books, 2011).

145. Donny Gluckstein, "Workers' Councils in Europe: A Century of Experience," in *From Ours to Master and to Own*, ed. Immanuel Ness and Dario Azzellini (Chicago: Haymarket Books, 2011).

146. Immanuel Ness and Dario Azzellini, *From Ours to Master and to Own* (Chicago: Haymarket Books, 2011).

147. Shelia Cohen, "The Red Mole: Workers' Councils as a Means of Revolutionary Transformation," in *From Ours to Master and to Own*, ed. Immanuel Ness and Dario Azzellini (Chicago: Haymarket Books, 2011).

148. Victor Wallis, "Workers Control and Revolution," in *Ours to Master and to Own: Workers' Control from the Commune to the Present*, eds. Immanuel Ness and Dario Azzellini (Chicago: Haymarket Books, 2011).

149. Donny Gluckstein, "Workers' Councils in Europe: A Century of Experience," in *From Ours to Master and to Own*, ed. Immanuel Ness and Dario Azzellini (Chicago: Haymarket Books, 2011).

150. Colin Barker, eds., *Revolutionary Rehearsals* (Chicago: Haymarket Books, 1987, 2002).

151. Immanuel Ness and Dario Azzellini, *From Ours to Master and to Own* (Chicago: Haymarket Books, 2011).

152. Victor Wallis, "Workers Control and Revolution" in *Ours to Master and to Own: Workers' Control from the Commune to the Present*, eds. Immanuel Ness and Dario Azzellini (Chicago: Haymarket Books, 2011).

153. Colin Barker, ed., *Revolutionary Rehearsals* (Chicago: Haymarket Books, 1987, 2002).

154. Ibid.

155. Ibid.

156. Victor Wallis, "Workers Control and Revolution" in *Ours to Master and to Own: Workers' Control from the Commune to the Present*, eds. Immanuel Ness and Dario Azzellini (Chicago: Haymarket Books, 2011).

157. Donny Gluckstein, "Workers' Councils in Europe: A Century of Experience," in *From Ours to Master and to Own*, ed. Immanuel Ness and Dario Azzellini (Chicago: Haymarket Books, 2011).

158. Dennis Kosuth, "Hungary 1956: Revolution in a Workers' State," *Internationalist Socialist Review* 51 (2007).

159. Sheila Cohen, "The Red Mole: Workers' Councils as a Means of Revolutionary Transformation," in *From Ours to Master and to Own*, ed. Immanuel Ness and Dario Azzellini (Chicago: Haymarket Books, 2011).

160. Ibid.

161. Ibid.

162. Duncan Hallas, "Towards a Revolutionary Socialist Party," in *Party and Class* (London and Chicago: Bookmarks, 1971).

163. Ibid: 52.

164. Ibid.

165. Immanuel Ness and Dario Azzellini, *From Ours to Master and to Own* (Chicago: Haymarket Books, 2011).

166. Ibid.

167. Victor Wallis, "Workers Control and Revolution," in *Ours to Master and to Own: Workers' Control from the Commune to the Present*, eds. Immanuel Ness and Dario Azzellini (Chicago: Haymarket Books, 2011).

168. Chris Harman, "How the Revolution Was Lost," *International Socialism* 1, no. 30 (1967).

169. Ibid.

170. Ibid.

171. Hal Draper, "Why the Working Class?" *Socialistworker.org*, September 14, 2012, http://socialistworker.org/2012/09/14/why-the-working-class.

172. Karl Marx and Friedrich Engels, *The Communist Manifesto* (Chicago: Haymarket Books, 1848, 2005).

173. Hal Draper, "Why the Working Class?" *Socialistworker.org*, September 14, 2012, http://socialistworker.org/2012/09/14/why-the-working-class.

174. Karl Marx and Friedrich Engels, *The Communist Manifesto* (Chicago: Haymarket Books, 1848, 2005): 634.

175. Sheila Cohen, "The Red Mole: Workers' Councils as a Means of Revolutionary Transformation," in *From Ours to Master and to Own*, eds. Immanuel Ness and Dario Azzellini (Chicago: Haymarket Books, 2011).

176. Ibid.

177. Donny Gluckstein, "Workers' Councils in Europe: A Century of Experience," in *From Ours to Master and to Own*, eds. Immanuel Ness and Dario Azzellini (Chicago: Haymarket Books, 2011).

178. Thamy Pogrebinschi, "Participation as Representation: Democratic Policymaking in Brazil," in *New Institutions for Participatory Democracy in Latin America: Voices and Conse-*

quence, eds. Maxwell A. Cameron, Eric Hershberg, and Kenneth E. Sharpe (London: Palgrave MacMillan, 2012).

179. Ibid: 70.

180. Felipe J. Hevia de la Jara, and Ernesto Isunza Vera, "Constrained Participation: The Impact of Consultative Councils on National-Level Policy in Mexico," in *New Institutions for Participatory Democracy in Latin America: Voices and Consequence*, eds. Maxwell A. Cameron, Eric Hershberg, and Kenneth E. Sharpe (New York: Palgrave MacMillan, 2012).

181. Goran Music, "Yugoslavia: Workers' Self-Management as State Paradigm," in *Ours to Master and to Own: Workers' Control from the Commune to the Present*, eds. Immanuel Ness and Dario Azzellini (Chicago: Haymarket Books, 2011).

182. Ibid: 177.

183. Ibid: 189.

184. Douglas Kellner, "Theorizing Globalization," *Sociological Theory* 20, no. 3 (2002): 285–503.

185. Peter Evans, "Counter-Hegemonic Globalization: Transnational Social Movements in the Contemporary Global Political Economy," *The Handbook of Political Sociology: States, Civil Societies, and Globalization*, ed. Thomas Janoski (Cambridge, UK: Cambridge University Press, 2012).

186. Waldon, Bello, *Deglobalization: Ideas for a New World Economy* (London: Zed Books, 2005).

187. Boaventura De Sousa Santos, "Beyond Neoliberal Governance: The World Social Forum as Subaltern Cosmopolitan Politics and Legality," in *Law and Globalization from Below: Towards a Cosmopolitan Legality*, eds. Boaventura De Sousa Santos and Cesar A. Rodriguez-Garavito (Cambridge, UK: Cambridge University Press, 2005): 29–63.

188. John Holloway, *Zapatista! Reinventing Revolution in Mexico* (London: Pluto Press, 1998).

189. John Holloway, *Change the World Without Taking Power* (London: Pluto Press, 2002).

190. John Dale, *Free Burma: Transnational Legal Action and Corporate Accountability* (Minneapolis: University of Minnesota Press, 2011).

191. Dan La Botz, "The New Movement for Global Justice." *Against the Current* 88 (September–October 2000).

192. Willelm Assies, "David Versus Goliath in Cochabamba: Water Rights, Neoliberalism and the Revival of Social Protest in Bolivia," *Latin American Perspectives* 30, no. 3 (2003).

193. Peter Evans, "Is an Alternative Globalization Possible?" *Politics and Society* 36, no. 2 (2008): 272.

194. Ibid: 271–298.

195. Ibid.

196. Ibid.

197. Christopher Chase-Dunn, Alessandro Morosin, and Alexis Alvarez, "Social Movements and Progressive Regimes in Latin America: World Revolutions and Semiperipheral Development," in *Handbook of Social Movements Across Latin America*, eds. Paul Almeida and Allen Cordero Ulate (Dordrecht, Netherlands: Springer, 2015): 13–23.

198. Nicolás M. Somma, "Social Movements in Latin America: Mapping the Literature," in *The Oxford Handbook of the Sociology of Latin America*, eds. Xóchitl Bada and Liliana River-Sánchez (Oxford, UK: Oxford University Press, 2020).

199. Karl Marx and Friedrich Engels, *The Communist Manifesto* (Chicago: Haymarket Books, 1848, 2005): 39.

200. Ibid.

Chapter Three

Popular Power, Participatory Democracy, and the Communes from Punto Fijismo to the Present

Underneath a busy highway in Caracas, Venezuela, thirty to forty community members, sitting on tattered couches and an array of plastic and wooden chairs, collectively decide what type of projects and services they would like to implement in their neighborhoods. Accompanied by live music, pets, children of all ages, and the constant noise of passing traffic, members of the communal council engage in lively debates and vote on public policy and projects that directly affect their daily lives. There is a communal, almost extended-family feel to the gathering. On this particular day in La Cascada, the assembly is discussing possibilities to build a stage with bathrooms and dressing rooms, a sports court, a daycare center, and a soup kitchen to serve community members. Whatever decisions are made by the council are binding. If the council decides to build a daycare center and a sports court, the mayor and local officials are bound to abide by the council's decision.

On the other side of Caracas in the parish of Antimano, the Clavellinas Communal Council, a council that was formed in 2006 with 350 families, is working to receive grants for home, sidewalk, and alleyway repairs. La Cascada and Clavellinas are just two of the thousands of registered Communal Councils in Venezuela. Funding for these communal councils comes mostly from municipal, state, and city governments and goes directly to the community (Fox and Leindecker 2008; Azzellini 2013). La Cascada and Clavellinas give us a glimpse of the self-government mechanisms that are cropping up all over Venezuela where marginalized communities who previously had no say, now participate in decision making that is collective rather than individual, direct rather than representative, and active rather than passive.

Since the 1998 election of Hugo Chávez Frias, Venezuela has undergone significant changes. For one, networks of popular power through popular organizations like the communal councils, land committees, and communes are far more prevalent today than any time before the Chávez era. Often these changes are seen as the sole result of the election of Chávez. This formulation downplays the broader context of the development of social movements in both Venezuela and the region. The extent of Chavismo's successes and the achievements of the Bolivarian Revolution would be unthinkable without the social movements and civil society that support and give viability to the Chavista government.

One important achievement of the Bolivarian Revolution is the inclusion and participation of broader social sectors in the democratic process. This new participation has manifested itself in various forms, including local public planning councils that work to develop public policy, participatory budget-allocation, co-management of state-owned factories, workers' councils, Bolivarian circles, social "missions," community radio, and most importantly communal councils. Although the communal councils undeniably received a huge boost when they were legitimized, promoted, and began to receive funds from the Venezuelan government, communal councils and neighborhood associations were organizing themselves independently and outside of the state prior to their official recognition by the Chavista government. Many of these forms of popular organizations that were formed under Chávez have distinct genealogies that predate the Chávez government and are part of a long history of social movements in Venezuela. Contemporary expressions of popular power and community-based organizations were shaped throughout fifty years of political activity. Communal council and commune activists trace their heritage to the clandestine movements against the military regime in the 1950s, the guerilla struggles of the 1960s, and the urban committees of the 1990s. With this in mind, this chapter will explore these genealogies as we look at social movements, the left and popular organization from the restoration of formal liberal democracy in 1958 to the present.

This chapter will further explore the dynamic between the Venezuelan state (primarily during the Chávez years), which committed itself to a discourse on grassroots political participation, and civil society, which responded to this call in ways that often exceeded and challenged the expectations of the government. The Bolivarian process has raised Venezuelans' expectations of the state, and its very success depends on both the actions of grassroots activists and the Chavista government. While the government has opened up spaces for grassroots organization, what social movement actors in Venezuela see as radical transformation still requires direct confrontation with those in political power. The Bolivarian process is not something that can be decreed from above, but must involve struggle, organization, and ordinary people's ability to act independently of the state.

Part one gives a brief history of popular organization and the left in Venezuela from 1958 to the *Caracazo*. Part two analyzes the economic and social crises leading up to Hugo Chávez's election in an attempt to understand the broader context of resistance and social movements in which he came to power. Part three analyzes the relationship between civil society and the state by looking at the 2002 coup, the creation of the 1999 constitution, the radicalization of Chávez, and the activity of popular movements. Part four focuses on participatory democracy as a form of popular power.

A HISTORY OF POPULAR ORGANIZATION AND THE LEFT IN VENEZUELA FROM 1958 TO THE *CARACAZO*

The Jimenez Dictatorship and the Rise of Punto Fijismo

Representative democracy was established with the overthrow of Dictator Perez Jimenez in 1958. Soon after the ouster of Jimenez, the leaders of the non-communist parties who opposed the dictatorship signed what was called the Pacto De Punto Fijo. The power-sharing agreement was signed by Accion Democratica (AD), the Comite de Organizacion Politica Electoral Independiente (COPEI), and the Union Republicana Democratica (URD), with the URD resigning four years later. The pact was intended to preserve Venezuelan democracy by respecting the outcomes of popular elections, minimizing public interparty rivalries, and avoiding efforts for the military to exploit political divisions and to incorporate losing parties in their cabinets.[1] But the pact also included many anti-democratic measures that served to curtail the role of the left by excluding left-wing parties from the political process. Many of the left-wing parties that were critical to the overthrow of Jimenez were formally excluded. The Venezuelan Communist Party (PCV), for example, who was part of the prodemocracy umbrella group Junta Patriotica (Patriotic Council), had garnered significant support in the barrios for their role in the overthrow of the dictatorship. Their exclusion from the pact and the consolidation of power between the AD and COPEI served to tame and channel the energies of the popular masses that struggled to remove the dictator from power and deny them access to official levers of power.

As George Ciccariello-Maher argues, it was with the establishment of formal democracy that a new struggle for substantive democracy and equality was born.[2] Student movements, movements of the left parties, and later the guerrilla movement were all struggling against this exclusionary form of liberal democracy. These movements were a direct predecessor to movements today. Not only are many ex-guerillas in the Bolivarian government today but also the seeds for a whole layer of social movements against liberal democracy came out of these movements. The new struggle was a struggle for more radical change rather than gradual, for more direct and participatory democracy rather than limited forms of formal, representative democracy.

Guerilla Movement

In the early 1960s, the Venezuelan left turned to armed struggle. Many of those who participated in the struggle against military rule became quickly disillusioned and dissatisfied with the exclusionary form of democracy of *puntofijismo* as well as the repression that came with it. The state targeted repression against parties left of AD (the PCV was eventually made illegal), and the militants of these parties were tortured and executed.[3] Students, workers, campesinos, and the unemployed who took to the streets to radicalize the new liberal government were attacked and gunned down. As a result of this and repression, and few options, the Venezuelan left turned to guerrilla struggle. Leftists and revolutionaries began to form small guerilla units in the mountains and barrios. In April of 1960, a section of militant youth left the ruling AD party to form the Movement of the Revolutionary Left (MIR). Inspired by the Cuban Revolution and the exclusion from the Punto Fijo Pact, various guerilla factions formed the Armed Forces of National Liberation (FALN). The FALN was made up of the PCV and the MIR, along with independent militants, dissident soldiers, and communists.[4]

The guerillas carried out a wide range of actions, including hijacking a cargo ship, burning a Sears Roebuck factory, and kidnapping the deputy head of a U.S. military mission. From the very beginning, the guerilla movement faced severe repression under the AD government. In 1963 alone, the government cracked down on opposition deputies and arrested and jailed some 1,200 suspected communists, including one of its principal leaders Teodoro Petkoff.[5]

In the mid-1960s the PCV shifted its attention away from armed struggle and toward prisoner release. The retreat from armed struggle created tension within the movement resulting in the expulsion of Douglas Bravo, another principal leader of the movement. The FALN continued its armed struggle until the early 1970s, where, failing to win widespread support, the armed struggled collapsed. Though the armed guerilla movement was short-lived, the memory of the struggle remained, and as Sujatha Fernandes argues:

> The partial autonomy of urban social movements was established during these years of armed struggle, especially in the parishes such as 23 de Enero. Guerilla activists forged an alternative pole of historical memory that existed alongside and in contrast with deepening clientelist relationships between barrio residents and the state.[6]

With the 1969 election of Rafael Caldera of COPEI began the pacification process, which effectively disarmed the guerilla movement. The left responded to the failure of the strategy of armed struggle in various ways. Some formed political parties, like the Movimiento al Socialismo (MAS) led by Petkoff; some began to engage in cultural activism, while others created mass fronts.[7] Many on the left began to organize cultural workshops calling for a democratization of culture. Neighborhoods like 23 de Enero began to form cultural and community-based organizations. Community-based organizing that was pushed to the sidelines during the armed struggle began to emerge. Rather than a focus on state power, these organizations focused on more local concerns, including the creation of theater and sports groups, drug awareness campaigns, and demands on local government for improvements in sanitation, health, and infrastructure.[8] Neighborhood associations grew to become more prominent in the 1980s.

ECONOMIC AND SOCIAL CRISES LEADING UP TO THE ELECTION OF HUGO CHÁVEZ

In order to provide the reader with the basic grounding necessary to understand popular power in Venezuela, it is important to first give a brief history of the region from the Great Depression to the social and economic crises of the 1980s and 1990s. From the Great Depression to the late 1960s, import substitution industrialization (ISI) was the prevalent trade and economic policy in Latin America. ISI promoted "inner directed" development involving the replacement of imported goods with goods produced domestically. Government manipulation of the exchange rate, import tariffs, subsidized credit for substitutive investments, and direct or indirect subsidies to hold down costs of inputs for substitutive production were all policy instruments used to achieve inner directed development.[9, 10, 11, 12, 13, 14, 15, 16]

This strategy relied heavily on state intervention to control trade and investment. ISI policies deepened the dependence of developing countries on developed world economies, as the former relied heavily on imported finished products like machinery. Overvalued exchange rates exacerbated the problem as income inequalities between urban and rural areas widened drastically. Debt in Latin America had been a constant characteristic, as local markets were not large enough to sustain any firms. Consequently, the funding of capital goods was through loans and trade deficits. An already weak and indebted Latin America was devastated by the oil crisis in the 1970s, which caused foreign debt and interest rates to skyrocket.[17, 18, 19]

The Bretton Woods institutions, the World Bank, the International Monetary Fund (IMF), and later the World Trade Organization (WTO) began to set terms of financial settlements between nearly bankrupt countries and international lenders. Structural adjustment programs, the packages of policy prescriptions necessary for a developing country to receive loans, became the standard economic policy in Latin America.[20, 21, 22] State interventionist policies were replaced by market oriented, "laissez-fair" economic doctrine, later known as neoliberalism.

By the 1980s, neoliberalism had become the dominant political ideology in the region. Neoliberalism, which meant fiscal austerity, privatization of state assets, liberalization of trade, deregulation, and free trade, did not have the results its adherents had claimed. The aggregate trade deficit of lowincome countries increased from US$6.5 billion to US$34.7 billion between 1980 and 1992. The IMF and World Bank lent out more money to cover growing trade deficits, and as a result, international indebtedness increased from US$134 billion to US$473 billion between 1980 and 1992.[23] Inflation in Latin America increased twenty-six times between 1981 and 1990.

Neoliberal structural adjustment also disproportionately affects the poor, primarily by: 1) the distribution of real income by the market, and 2) the provision of public goods by the state.[24, 25, 26, 27, 28, 29, 30] Inflation due to devaluation mainly affects the poor who do not own any land or real assets. Public workers, such as teachers (in Africa), have faced a 33 percent decrease in salaries.[31] The poor are further disadvantaged by cuts in subsidies for essential commodities, healthcare, and education. Many countries reduced labor costs, downsized the labor force, reduced real wages, and intensified work. The minimum wage in Latin America fell by 25 percent in the 1980s, and average earnings in the informal economy decreased by 42 percent.[32] The cost of living increased dramatically as a result of structural adjustment. From 1980–1999 per capita growth in South America was 11 percent compared to the 80 percent growth during the twenty years prior to the neoliberal period. Between 1960 and 1995, the ratio of average income between the world's poorest and richest countries increased from 18–1 to 37–1. Neoliberalism also contributed to a number of economic crises in Latin America, including Argentina in 2001 and Mexico in 1994. Despite these realities for many Latin Americans, the wealth redistribution toward the rich and the accumulation of financial and political power led many in the world's upper class to see neoliberalism as a resounding success.[33]

In Venezuela the picture was similar. Venezuela's twenty-year economic decline began in 1979 due in large part to heavy indebtedness, increasing oil production costs, and neoliberal policies. Real per capita income suffered a steady decline of 27 percent from 1979–1999, a decline that was greater than any other country in the region. By the early 1980s, poverty and inequality skyrocketed to the highest levels in Latin America. Poverty increased from 17 percent in 1980 to 65 percent in 1996.[34] The lower classes increasingly felt isolated and excluded from public decisions and power.[35]

The 1989 *Caracazo*

The dissatisfaction came to a head in February 1989. In the 1988 presidential campaign, Carlos Andres Perez ran on an anti-neoliberal platform. Just a few weeks after taking office, Perez implemented a harsh neoliberal IMFimposed structural adjustment program. On the morning of the 27th, ten days after Perez announced the SAP, commuters who traveled to the city by bus noticed that, because of the increase in gas prices, the fares had doubled. Venezuelans immediately began protesting. By mid-morning, protests had spread to the country's major cities. Buses were overturned and burnt; shops and supermarkets were looted and destroyed. The protests and destruction turned into an outright rebellion that lasted a few days. The rebellion, later called the *Caracazo*, was followed by brutal military repression. Perez reacted to the rebellions by unleashing the police and military to squash not only the protesters but also the poor population. By the end of the *Caracazo* between 300 and 3,000 people had been killed.[36, 37]

Much like elsewhere in Latin America, the failures of neoliberalism to accomplish its economic promises resulted in a rise of resistance against the economic doctrine across Latin America. The Zapatistas directly challenged the Mexican State, the Landless Peasants Movement (MST) in Brazil organized large land occupations, and indigenous movements in Bolivia and Ecuador mobilized in defense of natural resources and the environment. Venezuela was not different.

Primarily as a consequence of the *Caracazo*, new human rights groups, social movements, civil and community associations, and political parties emerged. Community organizations and networks of Afro-Venezuelans, indigenous, and woman's organizations were established, and a flood of neighborhood assemblies developed.[38] Many of the predecessors to community and neighborhood associations that exist today, including the communal councils, can be traced back to the aftermath of the *Caracazo*. One such organization is the Coordinadora Símon Bolívar, a grouping of fourteen grassroots collectives that cropped up in one of Venezuela's neighborhoods in response to the police repression of the *Caracazo*. Grassroots indigenous movements like the Regional Organization of the Indigenous Peoples of the Amazonian State (ORPIA), Indigenous Federation of the State of Bolívar (FIB), and the National Indigenous Council of Venezuela (CONIVE) also began to organize themselves to insert their political goals well into the 1990s.

The 1992 Coup

Another consequence of the *Caracazo* was increased membership and support for the Revolutionary Bolivarian Movement 200 (MBR 200). Founded by Chávez, the MBR-200 began as a secret cell within the army with the aim to seize power of the state. The movement came out of a general disillusionment with corrupted democratic institutions. One major influence on both Chávez and the MBR-200 was Douglas Bravo. Bravo, who was introduced to Chávez in the early 1980s by Chávez's brother, had the idea to take over the state not through guerilla warfare but rather to infiltrate and take power through the armed forces. Because an overwhelming majority of the armed forces were made up of workers and peasants, Bravo saw the military ripe for infiltration. For Bravo, an alliance between civilians and the military was crucial. The goal was to take power through a coup led by a mix of civilian and military leaders. The MBR-200 was thus formed to spread revolutionary ideology in the ranks of the military.

The Venezuelan military is unique relative to others in Latin America. The military historically recruited out of the working class and peasantry, making its makeup uniquely of the popular classes. But perhaps more importantly, starting with the Andres Bello plan in the 1970s, members of the armed forces were permitted to leave the barracks to attend universities.[39, 40] Many soldiers studied philosophy, political economy, philosophy, engineering, medicine, sociology, and learned professional skills and social sensitivity. The university setting also provided a forum where officers and soldiers could engage with others in the university and have radical debates.[41, 42]

Though the clandestine organization was formed in 1982, it was not until the massive repression of the *Caracazo* that their ranks began to swell. When the Carlos Andres Perez government called on the army to put down the rebellion, many in the armed forces were appalled by the use of excessive force. On February 4th, MBR-200 took over various key strategic locations in Caracas, Maracaibo, and Maracay. It was not long before the plan began to unravel. Communication began to break down, expected support from both other military units and civilians didn't materialize, and rebels failed to capture the presidential palace. Recognizing defeat and wanting to avoid further bloodshed, Chávez called on his comrades to surrender. As a condition of surrender, the Perez administration permitted Chávez to address the nation on television. In addition to calling for his comrades to lay down their weapons, the speech did two things that catapulted Chávez from a little-known soldier into the national spotlight. First, he took full responsibility for the failed coup. This was significant for a country who had grown accustomed to political scandals, corruption, and a climate where political leaders rarely took responsibility for their actions. Second, he called for his comrades to surrender and said that the rebels had failed to achieve their objectives *por ahora* ("for now"), suggesting that this was only a minor setback for the Bolivarian Revolution and that the struggle had only begun. Chávez was subsequently arrested and sentenced to prison.

Military coups are not uncommon in Latin America. Traditionally military coups in Latin America, especially during the 1970s, were orchestrated by elite members of the armed forces and generally were in line with rightwing interests and to protect the privileges of the wealthier classes. What makes the 1992 coup attempt unique is that it was carried out not by elite officers but rank-and-file soldiers and middle-level officers. That MBR-200 was a left-wing movement and that members were radicalized over the course of ten years of clandestine activity also distinguish the 1992 coup from other coups in Latin America.[43, 44]

Between the Coup and the Election of Chávez (1992–1998)

Shortly after a military second coup attempt, Perez was removed from power in what amounted to a congressional coup. After the *Caracazo*, two failed military coup attempts, and multiple charges of corruption, Perez lost the support of elites in AD. Congress charged Perez with corruption, and he later resigned.[45] Rafael Caldera, who left COPEI to form a new political party, Convergence, won the 1993 elections. In 1994, Caldera fulfilled his promise and pardoned Chávez and other members of the MBR-200 who participated in the coup. Like Perez before him, Caldera quickly turned to the IMF for loans conditioned by neoliberal SAPs. Also, like Perez, he did so in direct contradiction to his campaign promises. These reforms further aggravated the problems of poverty in Venezuela due to its cuts in social spending, privatization, and the increasing costs of services.[46] The passage of these reforms further contributed to the loss of credibility for Venezuela's political class. The social and economic crisis, the de-legitimization of the major political parties and the political elites, and the emergence of grassroots social movements opened a space and created the conditions for Chávez's electoral triumph in 1998.

Meanwhile, the MBR-200 maintained their opposition to elections until 1997 when they transitioned into a new party, the 5th Republic Movement (MVR), to represent a shift in strategy from armed struggle to electoral politics. The party was formed to support the electoral goals of the MBR200, most importantly the 1998 presidential campaign of Hugo Chávez.

The years leading up to the 1998 election were marked by neoliberal structural adjustment and austerity. Neoliberal policies in the 1980s and 1990s resulted in drastic increases in poverty and inequality. In 1978, the poverty rate was 10 percent, while 2 percent lived in extreme poverty. By 1998, the poverty rate had reached 81 percent, while 48 percent lived in extreme poverty.[47]

Several factors contributed to Chávez's electoral success in 1998. Among them were general disillusionment with rises in poverty and inequality, disillusionment with traditional political parties, frequent charges of corruption and incompetence, as well as the political establishment's unwavering support for unpopular austerity and neoliberal policies. The MVR joined with various other small leftist parties to form a broad coalition called the *Polo Patriótico* (Patriotic Front). The Patriotic Front included the PCV (*Partido Comunista de Venezuela*), MAS (*Movimiento al Socialismo*), MEP (*Movimiento Electoral del Pueblo*), and the PPT (*Patria Para Todos*). Chávez ran on an anti-neoliberal platform that called for a constitution to replace the existing document drafted during the *puntofijismo* period. Chávez's electoral success in the 1998 elections can be attributed greatly to his opposition to the neoliberal policies and that he came from outside and was independent from the political establishment.

Community organizations and networks of Afro-Venezuelans, indigenous, and women's organizations that had emerged from the *Caracazo* and before were challenging and offering a different narrative of democracy opposed to what many saw as the limitations of representative democracy. These organizations were assuming a greater role in society.

THE RELATIONSHIP BETWEEN CIVIL SOCIETY AND THE STATE

Constitution

One of the first acts of the Chávez administration was rewriting the constitution. He was able to achieve this because of the tremendous dissatisfaction with the current political system. The constitution was approved in a popular referendum in December of 1999. The new constitution added two branches of government, changed the country's name, introduced popular referenda and local planning councils, recognized Venezuela's large indigenous population, recognized housework as an economic activity, and in some ways strengthened presidential power. Many commentators argue that Venezuela has the world's most progressive constitution in the sense that it provides for broad citizen participation and comprehensive human rights protections.[48] Title III includes more than a hundred articles directly addressing a wide range of civil and human rights. Human rights were a central component in the constitution and often went far beyond what most constitutions incorporate and often beyond liberal notions of human rights.[49] Not only are civil and political rights included but also social and economic rights such as the right to employment, education, healthcare, and dignified housing. These rights are seen as fundamental and an obligation of the state. For some the constitution has come under some criticism for guaranteeing more than what the state should provide its citizens.[50, 51] Nevertheless, the constitution and its framing in the language of human rights and participatory democracy served as a launching pad from which social movements could base their struggle. What is important for this chapter is not so much the content of the constitution but the role of civil society and social movements in its construction. Additionally, important are the ways in which civil society and social movements have used the human rights language in the constitution to bring the document to life.

One of the most unique aspects of the constitution is that it was written with the direct participation of the Venezuelan people. They were able to follow the debates on television, as well as participate in public forum sessions. One such movement is the *Centro de Estudios de la Mujer* (CEM— Center for Women's Studies), based at the *Universidad Central de Venezuela* (UCV—Central University of Venezuela). In addition to being a research center, the CEM has played a significant role in pushing for women's rights and pushing the agenda of the women's movement. Article 88 in the constitution (the aforementioned provision that recognizes work in the home as an economic activity and therefore eligible for social security) was the result of proposals from the CEM. Other provisions in the constitution including sexual and reproductive rights, the use of gender-neutral language, the right to decide how many children to have, equality with men, and affirmative action for women were proposals that were taken to the constituent assembly by people from the CEM. Since the approval of the constitution, the CEM has continued to push the government to institute initiatives and programs that live up to the principles of the constitution, including the Women's Development Bank, the Inamujer-National Women's Institute, and the social mission *Madres del Barrio* (Mothers of the Slums Mission).[52]

Another group that was instrumental in the construction of the constitution was indigenous peoples. Indigenous organizations participated in the construction of the constitution with an exceptional level of access. One of the most important indigenous organizations in this process was the National Indigenous Council of Venezuela (CONIVE). CONIVE convoked various forums and consultations to mobilize support for their proposals to the National Assembly. The result was the Venezuelan constitution dedicated an entire chapter to indigenous peoples. The constitution recognizes collective cultural rights of indigenous peoples—their languages, customs, culture, and traditional lands. Indigenous peoples were granted various entitlements, communal land titles, and the right to their own educational institutions.[53]

Not only did existing social movements participate in the construction of the constitution, but new social movements were created in the process. One such movement is the Network of Afro-Venezuelan Organizations, which is made up of over thirty groups and takes on issues that uplift Venezuela's black population.

Popular Movements

In his first two years, Chávez's social and economic policies were strikingly similar to his predecessors. No redistributions of wealth, no limitations on profit, and no expropriations had taken place. In fact, the emergence of the opposition had more to do with the elimination of governing elites from centers of power and a forced vote on the leadership of the Confederation of Workers of Venezuela (CTV). Chávez's first years in office, despite his radical speeches, were quite modest. He was elected primarily by the Venezuelan middle class who desperately wanted a solution to the corrupt and inefficient political system without disrupting the status quo. The poor, who were later to be Chávez's primary base of supporters, voted for Chávez but had much lower rates of participation and registration. Unlike later elections, Chávez would have never been elected by the poor themselves in the 1998 election.[54] By the recall referendum in 2004, the middle class had abandoned Chávez and the poor became his primary base of support. This section examines how the relationship between civil society, neighborhood associations, and the state brought about this change.

One example of this relationship is the development of community media. Catia TVe, born out of the Manicomio Film Club and the repression of the 1980s, was one of Venezuela's first community television stations. During the 2002 coup, as the private media ramped up their anti-Chávez campaign, Catia TVe and other community stations helped the Venezuelan people get accurate information. For example, they reported that Chávez had not resigned and that he was being held against his will. Prior to the coup, community media was not a top priority for the government, but the role of community media in defeating the coup was obvious. Shortly after Chávez returned to power, the government began to support community media by providing equipment, funding, and broadcast licenses.[55]

As demonstrated in the example of Catia TVe, advances in Venezuelan society during the Chávez era have been the result of popular movements pushing for more radical changes. Some of these movements include, but are not limited to, communal councils, workers councils, Bolivarian circles, grassroots community organizations, community media, and the labor movement. Worker takeovers of factories, land reforms, concerns related to housing, corruption, and infrastructure have been among the issues addressed by grassroots organizations. Popular movements supported Chávez in implementing these reforms and even pressured him to deepen these reforms.[56] Carlos Martinez et al. locate the rise of popular power in a dialectic between the self-organization of ordinary Venezuelans and the Chávez government's receptivity to these movements from below:

Venezuelans have created cooperatives; taken over factories; occupied urban and rural lands; launched community radio and television stations; built centers for culture and popular education; participated in creating national legislation and found numerous other means of bringing the government's discourse of popular power into a reality. Many of these actions have been motivated by the words of President Chávez or have been facilitated by government initiatives. Meanwhile many people behind these actions continue to pressure the government to survive or succeed. [7]

While taking of power has been from above in the sense that the government was stimulating and facilitating much of this activity, social movements have played an integral role in building popular power that goes beyond the scope of government and in implementing the process of change. Movements that have been organizing before the election of Chávez simply took advantage of the opportunities the Chávez administration had created.[58]

Neighborhood associations and community groups had been organizing around issues of improving the water supply, healthcare, land distribution, and other government programs prior to Chávez's election. It was not until 2006, eight years after being elected, that the government began to legitimize their self-organization by passing the Communal Council Law.

The labor movement has also been an impetus for radical change. When the conservative CTV sided with the coup-makers in 2002, a new union federation was formed, the National Union of Venezuelan Labor (UNT). The UNT has grown to be larger than the CTV and has supported radical reforms like the taking over of idle factories and transforming them into worker selfmanaged or co-managed factories. The labor movement understood that Chávez, and now Maduro, must be pressured and criticized in order for their movement to advance.

Many of the community groups throughout the country pre-date Chávez. One such organization is the *Coordinadora Símon Bolívar*, a grouping of fourteen grassroots collectives that cropped up in one of Venezuela's neighborhoods in response to the police repression of the *Caracazo*. Grassroots indigenous movements like the Regional Organization of the Indigenous Peoples of the Amazonian State (ORPIA), Indigenous Federation of the State of Bolívar (FIB), and the National Indigenous Council of Venezuela (CONIVE) were organizing themselves to insert their political goals in the 1990s. Another example is the Popular Education Centers (PECs) that were established in the mid-1970s. PECs were responsible for carrying out various projects in the community, including training centers, transportation, and human resource training. These centers worked until 1994 when the boom of neighborhood associations and communal councils began to emerge as the popular mode of community organization.

It was only in 2006 with the Communal Council Law that the government began to promote their self-organization. These groups are the most outspoken about the shortcomings of the government and keep the issues of corruption, the slowness of reform, and participatory democracy on the top of the government's agenda.[59] Through the introduction of comprehensive social programs, promotion of cooperatives, workers councils and communal councils, the nationalization of industries, and the regulation of capital, Venezuela has gone further than any other country in reversing neoliberal policies. Many of the advances in social programs and participatory democracy would not have been achieved without pressure from below by community groups, social movements, and marginalized Venezuelans.

2002 Coup

One example of this relationship is the activity of Venezuelan civil society in the aftermath of the 2002 coup. The 2002 coup also provides further evidence, manifested in the response from Venezuela's oil company (PDVSA), of the threat that Bolivarian process posed for neoliberal policies. Had it not been for the mobilization of the Venezuelan people and social movements, Chávez's presidency would have ended in 2002. As part of Venezuela's re-nationalization of the nation's oil production, Chávez transformed minority state participation into majority participation. In response, the oil company (PDVSA) organized a general strike for April 11, 2002. On the morning of the 11th, opposition protestors started a march from the state-owned oil company. On the other side of town, Chávez supporters gathered around the presidential palace. Breaking with its announced plan, the opposition march changed course and headed toward the presidential palace. Amid the confusion of the merging marches, snipers began shooting into both crowds. The private media, primarily Radio Caracas Television (RCTV), reported that the Chávez supporters instigated the violence against the demonstrators and broadcasted manipulated video images of Chávez supporters on a bridge shooting opposition demonstrators below.[60, 61] This video served as a major justification for the coup. Videos taken from other angles later showed that the images shown by RCTV were manipulated and that the Chávez supporters were shooting at snipers who were openly firing upon their march.[62, 63, 64]

Soon after the opposition kidnapped Chávez, RCTV announced that Chávez had willingly resigned. Shortly after the kidnapping, Pedro Carmona, the president of businessmen's federation, *Fedecámeras*, and one of the principal organizers of the coup, assumed the presidency. He then organized a cabinet of like-minded business colleagues, suspended all democratic rights, dissolved the National Assembly and the Supreme Court, and revoked the 1999 constitution. Although the private media had announced that Chávez had resigned, grassroots word-of-mouth networks spread the word that Chávez in fact had not resigned and that the dead and injured in Miraflores were Chávez supporters. As word spread through the barrios, ordinary Venezuelans sprang to action. Over a million Chávez supporters began to rally around the presidential palace in support of their democratically elected president. When demonstrators surrounded the palace in attempts to reinstate Chávez, the private media orchestrated a complete blackout on the demonstrations, instead showing reruns of *Tom and Jerry* cartoons and the movie *Pretty Woman*. As the protestors and military officers loyal to Chávez surrounded the palace, Carmona had no choice but to step down. In just fortyseven hours, the coup was over and Chávez was reinstated. It was through the organization and mobilization of civil society, social movements, and the poor from the barrios that Chávez was returned to power. Had it not been for the active participation of various sectors of Venezuelan society, the Chávez regime would have ended in 2002.[65, 66, 67]

PARTICIPATORY DEMOCRACY

Democracy is based on the idea that the general public should participate in the decision-making process that impacts their daily lives. In this conception, the shortcomings of representative democracy are becoming more and more apparent in our contemporary society. As economic power becomes more concentrated and powerful, its influence on representative politics increases. Powerful economic interests are becoming increasingly able to make their desires felt in the legislative process. This is accomplished in a variety of ways, including the calculated use of corporate media, the funding of powerful lobbies, and various methods of manipulating the electorate. Representatives depend more on lobbies than their constituents during election cycles, resulting in lobbies having a greater influence on policy than everyday voters. The media often relies on images and personalities rather than the debate on important issues. According to the Center for Responsive Politics, in 93 percent of House of Representative races and 94 percent of Senate races (in the United States), the candidate that spent the most money ended up winning. Most of the money that comes from political financing comes from corporate donations, political action committees, and wealthy individuals. The concept of "one person, one vote" is becoming harder to reconcile with representative democracy. Money, not people, tends to have more influence on the political process. The intention of the "rule of the people" was to guarantee that political decisions were inspired by and dictated by the interests of the people. When representatives make the decisions, there is no guarantee that political decisions will reflect the desires of the people.

The concept of participatory democracy holds that citizens should be active participants in the process of governing the country. In this model citizens must play a significant role in developing government policy and prioritizing budgets and projects in a way that the needs of the entire community are considered. The main principle behind participatory democracy is the constant participation, consultation, and discussion by citizens in the political process. This conception of democracy is quite different than the representative model where the extent of participation among citizens is going to the voting booth once every two to four years. The constant participation of citizens in the political process serves to better ensure self-determination. Participatory democracy strives to create an active political culture, opportunities for the incorporation of broader sectors of the population into the political process, and a healthier civil society in general.

The Bolivarian Constitution provides for broad citizen participation in the democratic process. This new participation has manifested itself in various forms, including local public planning councils that work to develop public policy, participatory budget-allocation, co-management of state-owned factories, workers' councils, Bolivarian circles, social "missions," community radio, and most importantly communal councils.[68]

For the purposes of this chapter, I will discuss two of the aforementioned forms of participatory democracy practiced in Venezuela, the local public planning councils (CLPPS) and communal councils. Largely modeled after participatory local budgeting in Porte Alegre, Brazil, CLPPs aim to provide citizens the necessary tools to influence decisions that affect their well-being. The law of Local Public Planification Councils was established in article 182 of the Constitution. The law required that 335 municipalities implement them by October 12, 2002. Currently many sectors of the civil society are being represented in the CLPPs, including education, health, transportation, culture, sports, ecology, security, women, people with disabilities, land committees, and others. Citizens in CLPPs develop annual budgets and actively supervise its implementation. The idea behind the people directly participating and influencing local planning and the allocation of resources is that they have the most comprehensive understanding of their own communities.

This is not to say that the CLPPS are not without their problems. Not all citizens can attend meetings, the degree of participation across different councils varies, elected officials still often have the final say on the realization of decisions made by the council, and the councils are not supported by all mayors, governors, public officials, and those in the government. Nevertheless, the institution of CLPPS is a positive step toward participatory democracy.[69]

Perhaps the most widespread and most effective instrument of self-organization and self-government so far in the Bolivarian process are the communal councils and the communes. Since the passage of the 2006 Law of Community Councils, over 47,000 communal councils and over 3,000 communes have been established. These councils are grassroots, neighborhood-based bodies that bring together existing community organizations that have emerged in mostly poor neighborhoods around issues of water, electricity, health, education, and media. The communes are a larger body of selfgovernance that make up a collection of communal councils. Decisions made in communal councils and the communes are made in citizen assemblies and are open to the whole community. Communal councils are funded by the state and are encouraged to play a direct economic role, such as creating cooperatives or taking over idle factories.[70, 71, 72]

Like the CLPPS, communal councils are also not without problems. Although communal council decisions are binding and give ordinary Venezuelans more direct control over their own lives, they have no power to influence national and international policies. Despite their shortcomings, the emergence of communal councils, workplace councils, CLPPS, participatory budget allocation, Bolivarian circles, co-management, and cooperatives have resulted in a growing incorporation of broader social sectors into the decision-making process.

Although early experiments in participatory democracy can be found in the West, notably classical Greece and parts of Spain in the Spanish Civil War, in our contemporary age, the global south is taking a lead in its promotion and practice in participatory democracy. While Western notions of representative democracy are losing favor in many parts of the global south, citizens are reconfiguring democracy under their own terms. Since 1989, participatory budgeting in Porte Alegre, Brazil has allowed residents to directly participate in the allocation of city funds. Budgeting decisions are made by dozens of assemblies made up of poor and middle-class men and women across the city. Currently more than 50,000 residents participate in the budgeting process in a city of a 1.5 million people.[73]

Responding to the economic crisis of 2001, workers in Argentina created hundreds of neighborhood assemblies. Argentines also began to take control of factories. The number of occupied and worker-controlled factories subsequently grew into the hundreds.[74] Building off factory occupations that took place during the Dirty War of the 1970s, workers cooperatively run the factories, decisions are made democratically by worker assemblies rather than professional managers, and profits are distributed equitably to all workers.[75]

Experiments with participatory budgeting, worker-controlled workplaces, communal councils, local public planning councils, in short, experiments with participatory democracy, are not without their own shortcomings and limitations, but they do offer an alternative path to economic development and a more democratic polity.

NOTES

1. Miguel Tinker Salas, *Venezuela: What Everyone Needs to Know* (Oxford, UK: Oxford University Press, 2015).

2. George Ciccariello-Maher, *We Created Chávez: A Peoples History of the Venezuelan Revolution* (Durham, NC: Duke University Press, 2013).

3. Ibid: 28.

4. Michael McCaughan, *The Battle for Venezuela* (New York, NY: Seven Stories Press, 2005): 58.

5. Ibid.

6. Sujatha Fernandes, *Who Can Stop the Drums? Urban Social Movements in Chávez's Venezuela* (Durham, NC: Duke University Press, 2010): 49.

7. Ibid.

8. Ibid: 52.

9. Laura Enriquez, "The Varying Impacts of Structural Adjustment on Nicaragua's Small Farmers," *European Review of Latin America and Caribbean Studies* 69 (October 2000).

10. Jon Jonakin, "The Interaction of Market Failure and Structural Adjustment in Producer Credit and Land Markets: The Case of Nicaragua," *Journal of Economic Issues* 31, no. 2 (1997).

11. Jon Jonakin and Laura Enriquez, "The Non-Traditional Financial Sector in Nicaragua: A Response to Rural Credit Market Exclusion," *Development Policy Review* 17 (1999).

12. Flavia Echanove, "Globilisation and Restructuring in Rural Mexico: The Case of Fruit Growers," *Tijdschrift Voor Economische en Sociale Geographe* 96, no. 1 (2005): 15–30.

13. Julie Cupples, "Rural Development in El Hatillo, Nicaragua Gender, Neoliberal and Environmental Risk," *Singapore Journal of Tropical Geography* (2004).

14. Howard Waitzkin, Rebeca Jasso-Aguilar, and Celia Iriat, "Privatization of Health Services in Less Developed Countries: An Empirical Response to the Proposals of the World Bank and Wharton School," *International Journal of Health Services* 37, no. 2 (2007).

15. Thomas Walker, *Nicaragua Without Illusions* (Lanham, MD: Rowman and Littlefield, 1997).

16. Giles Mohan, Ed Brown, Bob Milward, and Alfred B. Zack-Williams, *Structural Adjustment: Theory, Practice and Impacts* (London and New York: Routledge, 2000).

17. David Harvey, A *Brief History of Neoliberalism* (Oxford, UK: Oxford University Press, 2005).

18. David Korten, *When Corporations Rule the World: Second Edition* (San Francisco, CA: Kumarian Press, 2001).

19. Giles Mohan, Ed Brown, Bob Milward, and Alfred B. Zack-Williams, *Structural Adjustment: Theory, Practice and Impacts* (London and New York: Routledge, 2000).

20. Ibid.

21. David Korten, *When Corporations Rule the World: Second Edition* (San Francisco, CA: Kumarian Press, 2001).

22. David Harvey, A *Brief History of Neoliberalism* (Oxford, UK: Oxford University Press, 2005).

23. David Korten, *When Corporations Rule the World: Second Edition* (San Francisco, CA: Kumarian Press, 2001).

24. Jean-Paul Azam, "The Uncertain Distribution Impact of Structural Adjustment in Sub Saharan Africa," in *Structural Adjustment and Beyond in Sub Saharan Africa*, eds. Rolph Van Der Hoeven and Fred Van Der Kraaij (London, UK: Heinemann, 1994).

25. Julie Cupples, "Rural Development in El Hatillo, Nicaragua Gender, Neoliberal and Environmental Risk," *Singapore Journal of Tropical Geography* (2004).

26. Laura Enriquez, "The Varying Impacts of Structural Adjustment on Nicaragua's Small Farmers," *European Review of Latin America and Caribbean Studies* 69 (October 2000).

27. Jon Jonakin, "The Interaction of Market Failure and Structural Adjustment in Producer Credit and Land Markets: The Case of Nicaragua," *Journal of Economic Issues* 31, no. 2 (1997).

28. David Lehmann, *Democracy and Development in Latin America: Economics, Politics and Religion in the Post-War Period* (Philadelphia, PA: Temple University Press, 1992).

29. Giles Mohan, Ed Brown, Bob Milward, and Alfred B. Zack-Williams, *Structural Adjustment: Theory, Practice and Impacts* (London and New York: Routledge, 2000).

30. Howard Waitzkin, Rebeca Jasso-Aguilar, and Celia Iriat, "Privatization of Health Services in Less Developed Countries: An Empirical Response to the Proposals of the World Bank and Wharton School," *International Journal of Health Services* 37, no. 2 (2007).

31. Giles Mohan, Ed Brown, Bob Milward, and Alfred B. Zack-Williams, *Structural Adjustment: Theory, Practice and Impacts* (London and New York: Routledge, 2000).

32. Ibid.

33. Carlos Martinez, Michael Fox, and Jojo Farrell, *Venezuela Speaks! Voices from the Grassroots* (Oakland, CA: PM Press, 2010).

34. Gregory Wilpert, *Changing Venezuela by Taking Power* (London: Verso, 2007).

35. Carlos Martinez, Michael Fox, and Jojo Farrell, *Venezuela Speaks! Voices from the Grassroots* (Oakland, CA: PM Press, 2010).

36. Gregory Wilpert, *Changing Venezuela by Taking Power* (London: Verso, 2007).

37. Richard Gott, *Hugo Chávez and the Bolivarian Revolution* (New York: Verso Books, 2005).

38. George Ciccariello-Maher, *We Created Chávez: A Peoples History of the Venezuelan Revolution* (Durham, NC: Duke University Press, 2013).

39. Michael McCaughan, *The Battle for Venezuela* (New York: Seven Stories Press, 2005).

40. Miguel Tinker Salas, *Venezuela: What Everyone Needs to Know* (Oxford, UK: Oxford University Press, 2015).

41. Michael McCaughan, *The Battle for Venezuela* (New York: Seven Stories Press, 2005).

42. Miguel Tinker Salas, *Venezuela: What Everyone Needs to Know* (Oxford, UK: Oxford University Press, 2015).

43. Steve Ellner, *Rethinking Venezuelan Politics: Class, Conflict, and the Chávez Phenomena* (Boulder, CO: Lynne Rienner, 2008).

44. Miguel Tinker Salas, *Venezuela: What Everyone Needs to Know* (Oxford, UK: Oxford University Press, 2015).

45. Richard Gott, *Hugo Chávez and the Bolivarian Revolution* (New York: Verso Books, 2005).

46. Gregory Wilpert, *Changing Venezuela by Taking Power* (London: Verso, 2007).

47. Sujatha Fernandes, *Who Can Stop the Drums? Urban Social Movements in Chávez's Venezuela* (Durham, NC: Duke University Press, 2010).

48. Gregory Wilpert, *Changing Venezuela by Taking Power* (London: Verso, 2007).

49. Anderson Bean, "Venezuela, Human Rights and Participatory Democracy," *Critical Sociology* 42, no. 6 (September 1, 2016): 827–843.

50. Chesa Boudin, Gabriel Gonzalez, and Wilmer Rumbos, *The Venezuelan Revolution* (New York: Thunder's Mouth Press, 2006).

51. Gregory Wilpert, *Changing Venezuela by Taking Power* (London: Verso, 2007).

52. Carlos Martinez, Michael Fox, and Jojo Farrell, *Venezuela Speaks! Voices from the Grassroots* (Oakland, CA: PM Press, 2010).

53. Ibid.

54. Gregory Wilpert, *Changing Venezuela by Taking Power* (London: Verso, 2007).

55. Carlos Martinez, Michael Fox, and Jojo Farrell, *Venezuela Speaks! Voices from the Grassroots* (Oakland, CA: PM Press, 2010).

56. Gregory Wilpert, *Changing Venezuela by Taking Power* (London: Verso, 2007).

57. Carlos Martinez, Michael Fox, and Jojo Farrell, *Venezuela Speaks! Voices from the Grassroots* (Oakland, CA: PM Press, 2010): 4.

58. Ibid.

59. Gregory Wilpert, *Changing Venezuela by Taking Power* (London: Verso, 2007).

60. Eva Golinger, *The Chávez Code: Cracking the US Intervention in Venezuela* (London, UK: Pluto Press, 2007).

61. Chesa Boudin, Gabriel Gonzalez, and Wilmer Rumbos, *The Venezuelan Revolution* (New York: Thunder's Mouth Press, 2006).

62. Eva Golinger, *The Chávez Code: Cracking the US Intervention in Venezuela* (London: Pluto Press, 2007).

63. Richard Gott, *Hugo Chávez and the Bolivarian Revolution* (New York: Verso Books, 2005).

64. Michael McCaughan, *The Battle for Venezuela* (New York: Seven Stories Press, 2005).

65. Eva Golinger, *The Chávez Code: Cracking the US Intervention in Venezuela* (London: Pluto Press, 2007).

66. Richard Gott, *Hugo Chávez and the Bolivarian Revolution* (New York: Verso Books, 2005).

67. Michael McCaughan, *The Battle for Venezuela* (New York: Seven Stories Press, 2005).

68. Chesa Boudin, Gabriel Gonzalez, and Wilmer Rumbos, *The Venezuelan Revolution* (New York: Thunder's Mouth Press, 2006).

69. Sarah Wagner, "Women and Venezuela's Bolivarian Revolution," in *Venezuela's Bolivarian Process*, ed. Gregory Wilpert (Venezuelaanalysis.com, 2004).

70. Dario Azzellini, "Venezuela's Solidarity Economy: Collective Ownership, Expropriation, and Workers Self-Management," *The Journal of Labor and Society* 12 (2009): 171–191.

71. Dario Azzellini, "The Communal State: Communal Councils, Communes, and Workplace Democracy," *North American Congress on Latin America* 46, no. 2 (2013).

72. Steve Ellner, *Rethinking Venezuelan Politics: Class, Conflict, and the Ch á vez Phenomena* (Boulder, CO: Lynne Rienner, 2008).

73. David Lewit, "Porto Alegre's Budget of, by, and for the People," *Yesmagazine.org*, December 31, 2002, https://www.yesmagazine.org/issues/what-would-democracy-look-like/ 562.

74. Marina Sitrin, ed., *Horizontalism: Voices of Popular Power in Argentina* (Chico, CA: AK Press, 2006).

75. Peter Ranis Peter, "Factories Without Bosses: Argentina's Experience with Worker-run Enterprises," *Labor: Studies in Working-Class History of the Americas* 3, no. 1 (2006).

Chapter Four

Networks of Popular Power

Communes as Globalization from Below

COMMUNES AND GLOBALIZATION FROM BELOW

Globalization can be considered as a series of processes that embody an intensification of worldwide social relations, interconnectedness, interdependence (local happenings shaped by events occurring in other parts of the world and vice versa), and the compression of time and spatial distances. Although people, ideas, and goods have been moving across the globe and becoming more interconnected for centuries, it was not until the rise of neoliberalism in the late 1970s and its consolidation in the early 1980s that globalization took a new and accelerated form. Neoliberalism is an economic doctrine that comes from a variety of sources, including classical liberalism, the Austrian School of Economics and Friedrich Hayek, as well as the Chicago School of Economics and Milton Friedman. Neoliberal philosophy claims that free trade and unfettered free markets are the most efficient way to produce the greatest social, political, and economic good. Policies often associated with neoliberalism include the privatization of public assets, economic liberalization, the reduction or elimination of trade tariffs and barriers, fiscal austerity, deregulation, reductions in government spending, and free trade among others. But as David Harvey argues, neoliberalism should not merely be seen as a litany of economic policies but also as a concerted effort by the capitalist class to reconstitute and restore power.[1] In other words, neoliberalism is a class project to re-establish the conditions for capital accumulation and to reconstitute the power of economic elites.[2, 3]

Further, Wendy Brown argues that neoliberalism is also a mode of the modern form of power that Foucault calls "governmentality" (i.e., knowledge and techniques that are concerned with the regulation of everyday conduct, even non-economic contexts).[4, 5] Aihwa Ong argues that this extension of market rationality (through neoliberal governmentality) can predominate even in contexts where neoliberalism as an economic doctrine is not central.[6] Sujatha Fernandes suggests that this is the case in Venezuela where:

> A post neoliberal formation has adopted anti-neoliberal reforms, while its ongoing subjection to the requirements of a global economy has given impetus to neoliberal rationalities and techniques in a range of state and nonstate arenas.[7]

But globalization is not just a political project promoted and facilitated by economic and political elites from above. In what has been called alternative globalization,[8] globalization from below, counter-hegemonic globalization, or deglobalization, transnational social movements from below have fought to create alternatives to corporate-led globalization. Not simply a reaction to or resistance to top-down globalization, globalization from below is also a movement, or movement of movements,[9, 10] to create a different kind of globalization, one based on democracy and social justice. To use Peter Evans' definition, counter-hegemonic globalization is a "a globally organized effort to replace the neoliberal global regime with one that maximizes democratic political control and makes the equitable development of human capabilities and environment stewardship its priorities."[11] Movements for globalization from below not only take advantage of spaces, instruments, and institutions that have been created by corporate globalization but have also played a role in creating spaces and institutions to struggle for a more socially just and democratic globalization. However, globalization from below can also press for *less* socially just and undemocratic globalization, for example, Daesh (a.k.a. the Islamic State) or Al-Qaeda (which seek to institutionalize a global Umma). Just because it comes "from below," does not make it more socially just.

As discussed in chapter 3, various examples and theories of globalization from below include: transnational social movements,[12] deglobalization,[13] the World Social Forum,[14] the Zapatista movement,[15, 16] the Free Burma Movement,[17] the Global Justice Movement,[18] and the Bolivian Water Wars,[19] among others. These authors are interested in the ways in which counterhegemonic social movements have played a role in shaping our global world and challenging hegemonic neoliberal globalization from above.

The Bolivarian Process, in which the communes are a central component, have played an important role in movements of democratic globalization from below, both as a resistance to corporate-led globalization with the struggle to defeat the Free Trade Agreement of the Americas (FTAA) and as a movement to create alternative forms of globalization with the creation of various institutions that promote regional integration, including The Bolivarian Alliance for the Peoples of Our America (ALBA), The Bank of the South (BancoSur), The New Television Station of the South (TeleSUR), and the Andean Community of Nations (CAN). These institutions together can be called "south-south integration."

In 1994, the United States, Canada, and Mexico signed the North American Free Trade Agreement (NAFTA), a neoliberal policy measure for regional commercial integration. NAFTA set the tone for the expansion of "free trade" in the region. Nearly a decade later, with the hopes of expanding "free trade" across the whole region, U.S. policymakers proposed the Free Trade Area of the Americas (FTAA). De La Barra et al. explains what was at stake:

> The acceptance of the FTAA by Latin American and Caribbean countries would have amounted to an economic order characterized by less accounting, less transparency, less respect to the human rights, less preoccupation for reducing poverty, more damage to the environment, and further increases in the already massive external debt. [20]

De la Barra et al. goes on to say that the FTAA agreement would further impede democratization and weaken national sovereignty.[21]

Knowing very well the impacts that NAFTA had on Mexico, and the repercussions of a continuation and deepening of neoliberal policies throughout the region, a broad movement against FTAA emerged. Protests, demonstrations, popular plebiscites, and forums organized by nascent transnational social movements began to take form. A broad range of organizations, committees, and activist groups mobilized against FTAA. As a result of the growing regional opposition to FTAA, the United States was given a decisive blow; in 2005, FTAA was declared dead. With the defeat of the FTAA, Latin American social movements won their first struggle against neoliberalism. This victory opened the door for the creation of alternative paths of development in the region.[22, 23, 24]

South-south integration is an economic and social development model promoted by social movements and left-leaning governments in Latin America. South-south integration comes as a response to neoliberal, finance-led development and its emphasis on (uneven) competition, individualism, free trade, privatization, competitive advantage, and deregulation. The key components that drive south-south integration are, therefore, cooperation, solidarity, sustainability, cooperative advantage, and participatory democracy. Among the initiatives taken by South American governments to promote regional integration and growth are the Bolivarian Alternative for the Americas (ALBA), the Bank of the South, Fund of the South, Television of the South (Telesur), Andean Community of Nations (CAN), Union of South

American Nations (UNASUR), and the Common Southern Market (Mercosur). These regional integration initiatives have impacted development to varying degrees and have experienced various successes and failures.

ALBA was proposed by Venezuela President Hugo Chávez in the context of and as a response to the failure of FTAA. Breaking from neoliberal tradition, ALBA aims to "promote trade and investment between member governments based on cooperation, and with the aim of improving people's lives, not making profits."[25] Free healthcare, education, alternative media, state ownership of natural resources, environmental sustainability, and a promotion of social movements are the stated objectives of ALBA.

According to Thomas Muhr, ALBA's integration initiatives employ five mechanisms that make it a counter-hegemonic globalization project.[26] Regionalist inter-state, bi-national, multi-national, sub-regional, and transnational agreements allow the project to compete with capitalist globalization across local, national, regional, and global spheres through popular social movements, workers' and communal councils, cooperatives, and state-worker-managed factories. ALBA should be seen as a form of developmental regionalism, meaning that it is interventionist but does not delink from the global economy. Central to this regionalism is the Venezuelan notion of endogenous development. Endogenous development promotes a needs-based economy based on human need before profit and with an emphasis on the community.[27]

The Bank of the South and the Fund of the South, also proposed by Chávez, aims to utilize monetary reserves to provide assistance with no conditionalities to protect against speculative global capital, and as a regional credit mechanism to finance integration infrastructure and regional development. The role of the Bank of the South and the Fund of the South is to serve as an alternative to the World Bank.

UNASUR is a regional organization with the intention to form a continental bloc, modeled on the United Nations. The parliament is located in Cochabamba, Bolivia, and the bank in Caracas, Venezuela. The Telesur initiative has introduced alternative media programming regionally to serve as a counterbalance to the monopolization of media by transnational corporations. MERCOSUR, developed by former Argentine president Nestor Kirchner, is the largest trading bloc in South America and was created with an interest to eliminate obstacles to regional trade. CAN is a smaller regional trading bloc comprising the countries of Colombia, Peru, Ecuador, and Bolivia.

The Bolivarian movement was fundamental in the construction of various institutions of regional integration. But it is important to note that the communes are central to the Bolivarian process as a whole, and the future of the process depends on the future of the communes. Here one communal organizer I spoke with explains the relationship between the communes and Bolivarian process:

> The relationship is basic. It is the root of the Chavista project. The relationship between the state and the communes are basic in the sense that the roots of the revolution are to take power, to transfer power to the people through their territories and the only way to do that is to have an organization, this organization is called communal councils. So the territory, the new power of the territory, the new establishment of power is going to be represented by the commune but actually the main role of the communal council is to take power and to organize themselves. This situation will be a way of self-governing of the people and this self-governing will go against the traditional set or forms of power and institutions, like the governor, the county, or even the president. So the victory of socialism is about the construction of this power to the territories. They have to take power through territories around organizations of communal councils and represent through the parliament of the communes (Alex Interview 7).

The transfer of power from traditional structures of power to structures of popular power and the masses through communal councils and communes that is at the core of the Bolivarian process, which is at its core an alternative to neoliberal models of development.

COMMUNES AS GLOBALIZATION FROM BELOW

The communes in particular should be considered an example of democratic globalization from below for two reasons. First, they are a central part of a global movement against corporate-led globalization and neoliberal forms of economic development. Communes are an experiment of a different kind of grassroots development, opposed to IMF and World Bank prescribed reforms like privatization and free trade. In other words, in addition to being a central component of the Bolivarian process that promotes south-south integration as a means to break from the political, economic, and military control by hegemonic forces from the global north, the communes also offer alternative modes of production and development to the privatization and free trade policies championed by those very hegemonic forces, including international financial institutions like the World Bank and the IMF. Second is the way in which the communes have coordinated and cooperated with other transnational movements in an effort to build new democratic spaces for a more just globalization. The alternative models of development and the ways in which the communal movement works with other movements for similar aims are an important way in which the poor and working people exercise agency in the face of corporate globalization.

ALTERNATIVE MODEL TO NEOLIBERALISM

My argument that the communal movement offers alternatives to corporate globalization and is an important component to south-south integration projects rests on four characteristics that I have identified. The four characteristics will be discussed in turn and include the following: participatory decision making instead of top-down decision making, endogenous development instead of neoliberal development, communal markets instead of the free market, and communal ownership over production instead of private ownership. These four components are central to the ways in which workers, through networks of popular power, exercise agency over their own development.

Participatory Democracy

Participatory democracy is an integral component of the Bolivarian process, and it should be seen as a deeper and more inclusive form of democracy than representative democracy, which is often promoted by Western governments and liberal human rights organizations. In the representative model, political participation is often limited to the electoral sphere. Citizens elect representatives and those representatives are, in theory, held accountable to their voters through decisions. Democracy, therefore, is exercised through the periodic activity in elections, rather than the day-to-day activities of governance. Participation, therefore, is confined to activities within the framework of consent to be governed.

The concept of participatory democracy holds that citizens should be active participants in the process of governance and decision making over the territory in which they live or work. In this model citizens must play a significant role in developing government policy and prioritizing budgets and projects in a way that benefits the entire community. The proportion to which a decision affects a particular individual or community, those affected are to have the same proportion of decision-making power over that decision. The main principle behind participatory democracy is the constant participation, consultation, and discussion by citizens in the political process. This conception of democracy is quite different than the representative model, where the extent of participation among citizens is choosing every two to six years which person they entrust to make decisions for them. The constant participation of citizens in the political process serves to better ensure selfdetermination. Participatory democracy strives to create an active political culture, opportunities for the incorporation of broader sectors of the population into the political process, and a healthier civil society in general.

The Bolivarian Constitution provides for broad citizen participation in the democratic process. This new participation has manifested itself in various forms, including local public planning councils that work to develop public policy, participatory budget-allocation, co-management of state-owned factories, workers' councils, Bolivarian circles, social "missions," community radio, and most importantly communal councils and communes.

The 2006 Communal Council Law (which was later updated in 2009) and the 2010 Organic Law of Communes established two important levels of participatory democracy, the communal councils and the communes, respectively. The Law of the Communes consists of sixty-five articles relating to the organization and establishment of communes across the country. According to Assembly member Ulises Daal, the Law was the result of open debates in which over 61,850 communal council *voceros* (spokespeople) participated.[28] Communal councils and communes are grassroots neighborhood bodies of popular power that bring together community organizations to make decisions that directly affect their lives. Rather than local, state, or federal elected officials making decisions that affect the community, the community themselves through the communes and communal councils, are making these decisions. The communes and councils are permanent governing structures that enable previously excluded social sectors into the political decisionmaking process. Through these structures of popular power, everyday Venezuelans are encouraged to directly manage public policy and projects that affect their daily lives. The levels of participatory democracy begin with the communal council at the most neighborhood level, then are the communes which are collections of communal councils, followed by communal cities, and then eventually the communal state. Each of these are to be structures of participatory self-administration. At this point in the Bolivarian process, the highest state that has been achieved is the commune, though we have seen the collaboration of large groups of communes giving us a glimpse of what the communal cities can look like.

All decisions made in the communal councils and the communes are made in popular assemblies. The assemblies are open to the whole community, and every citizen over the age of fifteen can vote. According to the Law of Communes, decisions are made by a simple majority, and 30 percent of the members of the commune must be present to vote. Each communal council elects a spokesperson to represent their council in the commune, and typically a spokesperson from each communal council must be present for a vote in the commune. The needs and goals of the commune and the projects aimed to achieve these goals are decided by the communes themselves. The commune conducts participatory diagnostics of the community and decides in the assemblies what the community needs most and what projects they want to carry out.

Here, one communal organizer explains how the communes through these diagnostics determine what are the most pressing needs of the community:

We have made plans, short, middle and long term in every single centimeter of the territory. So we, because of our communal discussions, made decisions to do certain things, and those certain things are related to our problems so that we can make decisions about food, construction of houses, education, health, sports. For example, through participatory diagnosis we decided to build houses because it was the main problem of the comuna, through this diagnosis we saw the main need was to build houses, so we started to build houses first (Jose, Interview 7).

Decisions about what is to be built, what projects are a priority, and how the budget is spent, whether that be houses, education, health, or sports, are participatory. Commune activists are very conscious of how the levels of participation that exist today are very different from how projects were carried out and decisions were made prior to the creation of the communes. Rosa, a *comunera* from a communal council in Guarenas, speaks about this difference:

The CCs and the communes are songs of the revolution, they are the expression of popular power and the participation of people in the decisions that they are making. Before, popular power wasn't making the decisions or participating in the political sphere. So, the participation of people, the mentality that we are the ones to provide for our own community is something completely and totally different than the ways we have done things in the past (Rosa, Interview 9).

Diarobis, a *comunera* from a commune in Caracas, compares how community problems were solved before the creation of her commune to how they are solved now:

The communes took place when the revolution delivered power to the people, it delivered the participation of the people. So the communal councils are constituted by the same necessities and the same problems like water or other issues. And they shared the same problems. So before these associations, the people told the state their problems and the state went and tried to solve the problems. With the communes it is different because we make our projects and we ourselves develop these projects. So we ourselves solve the problems. There are not private enterprises who do the projects. But our people are the ones that work in the projects. So it is not like before where the associations put forward a proposal to the state and the state would contract a private enterprise. Now we ourselves develop the project. So before these neighbors associations did not have a legal background. Now the CCs and the Communes have a legal background. There are laws of the CCs and the law of communes and the law of popular power. They are now legally protected (Diarobis, Interview 2).

So rather than the state or private enterprises, or the state contracting out private enterprises, it is through the participation of those in the community that not only defines and prioritizes the problems of the community but that also develops projects and actively works in these projects to solve the problems they may have in their territory.

Not only are everyday Venezuelans actively participating in decisions that directly affect them, but the decisions that are made in the communes and communal councils are binding. Local and state officials must abide by the decisions made in the communes. If the commune decides they want to construct a basketball court in their community, the Law of the Communes states that those officials must abide by that decision. That this power that is granted to the communes is significant in terms of the actual decisionmaking power that is vested in the direct participation of citizens through the communal citizen assemblies. This distinction makes the Venezuelan communes distinct from similar neighborhood councils around the world, like, for example, the consultative councils in Mexico discussed in chapter 3. The consultative councils in Mexico play only an ancillary role to established institutions; they consult in the formulation of policies, evaluate policies, and make recommendations for specific issues to government agencies. But ultimately the decision remains in the established institutions. In practice, these councils and the decisions are often used by local officials as simply a formal window dressing, so they can tell their constituents that they met and consulted with the community, even if decisions made by the community were not ultimately implemented. With the communes in Venezuela, this is not the case; decisions made by the communes are binding. As Jose, a *vocero* from the Pio Tamayo Commune told me:

> If someone wants to make decisions for us, on our behalf, from the ministry or any governmental institutions, they can't. Decisions are first discussed here [in the commune] and decisions are made here [in the commune]. Nobody can come here from the outside with a decision that has been made in another place. We the members [of our commune] make decisions about our community and these decisions are binding (Jose, Interview 6).

Endogenous Development

The dominant approach to economic development is neoliberalism. This development model rests on the idea that the most effective way to foster development in the developing world is to remove any barriers to the free market. Growth, according to the neoliberal model, is best achieved by full integration into the world market. Some common policies associated with neoliberalism include the removal of the state from control, regulation or ownership from the economic system; decreases in government spending; the reduction of labor, trade, or environmental regulations; and reduction in tariffs and barriers to attract foreign investment and production that is guided by export-led development based on the needs of the world market.

Endogenous development is a socioeconomic model of development that is driven from within or from the inside (of the state or local community), rather than development from without or from the outside. This model focuses on development based on the country's developmental needs rather than by the demand of goods on the international market. In other words, as neoliberal development rests on the privatization of government industries by selling them to foreign owners, endogenous development is development that is inwardly creating (Howard 2008). In the case of Venezuela, that means focusing on Venezuela's own unique assets, preserving Venezuela's traditional farming methods and native seeds, as well as native seeds rather than using genetically modified seeds imported from abroad. [29] The Bolivarian Constitution promotes the concept of what is called "integral rural development," which both encourages new collective forms of property as well as increased food production to fight against food insecurity. The goal is not only to make the Venezuelan economy more self-sufficient, one that would favor products made in Venezuela, rather than simply producing for the export, but also development that is organized from below, one that motivates community participation and planning in the economy through new forms of organization and is based on the values of cooperation and solidarity.[30]

One of the central new forms of organization that promotes endogenous development is the communes. A lot of the production that takes place in the communes is still bought and sold by the private companies and the state, but a growing percentage is produced for local and domestic needs rather than for the international market. Decisions about what is produced are often made in citizen's assemblies taking into account the direct needs of the local community. The once-abandoned Brahma beer factory is one example. When the commune decided to take over the factory, the community, through citizen's assemblies and participatory diagnostics of the community and its needs, decided that what the community needed the most was a clean, reliable source of potable water. So based on the needs of the community rather than the needs of the international market, the decision was made to turn the factory in to a water-production plant. The decision was made with community participation, was based in the existing capacities and necessities of the community, was organized from below, and was based on the values of cooperation and solidarity.

The factory takeover in *Comuna El Sur Existe,* and the subsequent projects that developed from the takeover, is another example of endogenous development. The commune decided, once again in a citizen's assembly, to use the factory to produce textiles. Ricardo, a *vocero* in *Comuna el Sur Existe*, put it bluntly when he responded to my question about why they decided to produce school uniforms:

Why do we produce school uniforms? Well, because that is what our community needs, too many of our children don't have the necessary attire to go to school five days a week so that's what we decided to prioritize (Ricardo, Interview 8).

The community saw a need for school uniforms for local school-age students and decided to produce uniforms for the children. The decision was not made because school uniforms would be able to be sold for a high profit margin on the international market but rather the community assessed the needs unique to their community and decided to produce school uniforms to meet those needs.

The communal markets discussed below are another mechanism by which the communes produce directly for the country's developmental needs based on the values of cooperation, participation, and solidarity. The communal market is an attempt to break the dependence on the private sector for the production of basic goods, as well as a way to circumvent the vagaries of the world market. Food that is produced in the communal markets are distributed directly to local communities and are sold at regulated prices. Endogenous development is therefore a counterstrategy to the neoliberal model, whereby the neoliberal principles of private production, production for the global market, and development that is driven by international capital is replaced by collective production, production for domestic needs, and the socioeconomic development driven from within.

Communal Control of Production

The private production of goods and services, and by extension the privatization of public assets, is central to neoliberal globalization from above. This section will show how communal control of the means of production offers an alternative to private, top-down production processes. But before I discuss the Venezuelan experiments of communal control of production, I will first discuss the centrality of private production to the neoliberal project of globalization.

The privatization of the means of production has long been promoted by hegemonic forces in the global north. These measures have been imposed through financial institutions like the World Bank and the IMF as conditionalities for indebted countries to receive loans. The nationalization of previously privately-owned firms has also been a key factor in various coups in Latin America. Two prominent examples are the U.S.-backed coups of Guatemalan president Jacobo Arbenz in 1954, and Chilean president Salvador Allende in 1973. Prior to the coup in Guatemala, Arbenz passed an agrarian reform that nationalized land owned by U.S.-based United Fruit Company. In the case of Allende, one of the key reasons for his ouster was the nationalization of large-scale industries, most notably copper, banking, and the healthcare and education systems.

Privatization is also central to the neoliberal project in the form of what David Harvey calls accumulation by dispossession.[31] Accumulation of dispossession is the act of centralizing wealth and property into the hands of the few by dispossessing the public of their wealth or land most commonly by transferring property from public ownership to private property. This serves the interests of the capitalist class as it transfers common property to privatized property. The privatization of water is but one example. The Bolivian water wars of 2000 and the sale of the public water system to a consortium of private multinational corporations is one clear example of this phenomena.

Facing an economic meltdown marked by high rates of inflation, the Bolivian government looked to the IMF to bail them out. In return for loans from the IMF, the Bolivian government signed a number of structural adjustment programs that required, as conditions for loans, that the government privatize its airlines, railways, telephone systems, hydrocarbons, and water. Bolivia put its state-owned water company SEMAPA up for sale. Only one party bid on the project, Aguas del Tunari, a consortium of companies led by the U.S.-backed Bechtel company. In order to legally sell the company, the Bolivian government had to first pass law 2029, which verified the contract. Law 2029 gave Aguas Tunari monopoly control over all water resources, created broader restrictions on water used for irrigation and other community-based uses, and also required Bolivians to apply for a permit to collect rainwater from their roofs. Before the law was passed, it was common for Bolivians to collect rainwater for various purposes on the roofs of their houses, but the privatization of water prohibited Bolivians from utilizing what was previously common property for anyone to use. The process of accumulation by dispossession in Bolivia transferred property from public ownership to private property, Bolivians have been effectively dispossessed from what used to be a commonly owned resource.

The instances where communes control the means of production stand in stark contrast to the relations of production that are promoted and facilitated by powerful states and international financial institutions like the IMF and the World Bank. The first level of popular power, the communal council, was originally formed to manage budgets and work on infrastructural projects like water, electricity, health, education, media, parks, and community centers. This was also the original function of the communes. Like the communal councils, the communes initially focused primarily on infrastructural projects like water, electricity, roads, and parks, among others. Though most of communal production is done in rural communes, production is also taking place in urban areas. As I discussed in chapter 2, by 2015, many communes had shifted their focus to production. In 2015 alone, communes produced over 60,000 hectares of agricultural production, including corn, rice, beans, coffee, cereals, and so on. Sixty thousand hectares amounted to about onetwelfth of agricultural products that Venezuelans consume per year, and this number is expected to increase. The ministry of communes estimated that communal agricultural production would exceed 100,000 hectares in 2016. Unfortunately, the ministry stopped releasing this data in 2016.

Communes have taken over production through various different channels. Some have taken over abandoned buildings like the small textile factory in the case of *Comuna El Sur Existe*, and Brahma, the abandoned beer factory in *Comuna Pío Tamayo*. Communes also use communal funds to start production from scratch.

When I spoke with members of the *Pío Tamayo* commune, for example, they explained to me how funds that are earned from the beer factory are used for the buying or selling of pigs. The pig farm is used mostly for meat production for members of the community. In *El Sur Existe*, communal funds were used to start both a grocery store and a paper store. In some cases, the production in a commune is completely self-sufficient. In still other cases, production is heavily reliant on funds that come directly from the government or different government ministries. Other times, production is financed through a mixed system in which some of the money used in production comes from the government while the rest comes from earnings generated from that production. One example of this is in *Comuna Socialista Agroecoturistica el Aranero Latinamericano* (CSAAL), a mixed commune (composed of both urban and rural communal councils) located in the state of Portuguesa. CSAAL controls both a series of coffee plantations and plant that processes bananas in order to produce baby food. The finances for this project come from funds that communal councils receive from the government and from profits earned from selling the coffee and baby food produced in the commune.

Comuna El Maizal, a rural commune in the state of Lara, controls 2,000 hectares of land, 800 of which are used for production while the remaining 1,200 are a national reserve protected by the commune. The land controlled by the commune was expropriated from the wealthy Alvarado family in 2009. But this was not simply a gift from the government; the expropriation was a result of years of struggle from community members in that area to retain collective control of the community on grounds that the land originally belonged to the people in the area until a group of wealthy families took the land from them.

Lara state has a rich history of struggle, and that this particular community was well organized prior to the passage of the Law of Communes benefited them in their struggle for expropriation. That not all communities have the same rich history of popular organization and struggle explains part of the reason why the development of communes has been an uneven process, a topic to which we will return.

The Communal Market

Neoliberalism, and by extension neoliberal globalization, is rooted in the notion that unfettered free markets are the most efficient way to produce the greatest social, political, and economic good. The free market is to determine prices of products, wages of employees, what is produced, how it is produced, and how it is exchanged. Any obstruction to this formula is seen as government overreach and a hindrance to the market's ability to function properly. International financial institutions like the IMF, World Bank, and powerful states push national and local governments to deregulate the market (this may include labor, trade, or environmental regulations) liberalize trade; and reduce tariffs, barriers, and import controls in order to liberate the market from any government interference. Structural adjustment programs promoted by the IMF and World bank require nations to push through many of these reforms as conditions to receive loans.

In the midst of the economic crisis in Venezuela, communes decided to break from the free market model of production, prices, and exchange. Communes created *mercados comunales*, or communal markets, in the second half of 2015 as an alternative to the traditional distribution and exchange of goods dictated by the market. As goods and services struggled to make it to the supermarkets—whether that be because of hoarding, contraband, corruption related to the abuse of preferential exchange rates for imports, or simply the vicissitudes of the market—communal markets were created as a strategy to break with the dependence of the market for the distribution of goods. The government and the communes established an alliance for the creation of communal markets, which integrates communal production with state national distribution.

The call for communal markets came out of a February 2014 national communal economy conference in the state of Barinas. The conference was attended by 567 delegates representing 225 different communes. By early 2016, there were already over 1,000 communal markets throughout the country and according to various representatives from the Ministry of the Communes the number was expected to expand (again, it is difficult to determine the current number of communal markets as the ministry stopped releasing this data in late 2016). Communal markets are spaces for direct distribution, from producer to consumer, without intermediation. This is a space where the communes are bypassing the free market and private or state intermediaries to distribute products produced by the communes directly to the consumers. Circumventing the private sector middlemen has another advantage in that it avoids the expensive speculative rates and fees associated with private distribution services, which tend to drive up food prices and cut into producers' incomes.

Each weekend in several localities in the country, communal products are transported directly to communal markets. This is a space where different communal producers can bring their products to distribute, and the transportation of the goods to the market is also owned and controlled by the communes. The majority of products distributed in the communal markets are agricultural, but textiles can also be found in these markets. The dates and times of where the food will be distributed is announced beforehand, and anyone is welcome to come buy the products that are sold at regulated prices. As mentioned in chapter 2, production for the free market can create a number of problems. First, when global commodity prices oscillate according to the needs of the market, as we have seen with the fluctuation of oil prices, it can create crises that often lead to limited access to basic goods. Also, producing for the free market, even if produced in a commune, can reproduce the same patterns of accumulation and exploitation as production in the state or private sphere. Producing for the communal market, as a system of direct distribution of goods based on need, in theory is supposed to avoid some of the limitations of the free market. Since the creation of the communal market, much of the production from the communes is still bought and sold by private companies and the state, but the percent that is being distributed through the communal markets has increased significantly.

Communal markets are, in a sense, markets that are created to resist the market. But these are not the only forms of exchange and distribution that were formed to resist capitalist markets. Bolivian sociologist Silvia Rivera Cusicanqui's work focuses on similar forms of anti-market markets. One of these is the *qhatu*, an ancient traditional market where indigenous communities in colonial times would barter or negotiate prices at the local level. Some continue to exist today in Aymara and Quechua communities in Bolivia. Cusicanqui describes *qhatus* as conscious markets in the sense that what is exchanged, bartered, or sold is a product of cooperation and negotiation, not one mediated by the logic of market competition. She distinguishes these markets from depersonalized capitalist markets where the relationship of producers and consumers is simply an economic transaction shaped by prices of commodities.[32] Both the *qhatu* and the communal markets allow us to rethink markets as not just exploitative modes of exchange and distribution, and more importantly forces us to think more carefully about what we mean by the market in different political economies.

Much like *qhatus*, Venezuela's communal markets are organized not by the logic of market competition but rather through cooperative planning and negotiation. The communes that are producing the goods, and the community who will be consuming the goods (two groups that are not necessarily mutually exclusive), cooperate and negotiate what they think is fair and equitable, both in terms of what is produced and the prices at which they are sold. This is very different than capitalist markets where it is the vagaries of market supply and demand that determine both prices and how transactions between producer and consumer take place. Communal markets are thus part of a larger project of counterhegemonic globalization that resists the global capitalist market, and all that it entails, with the goal of replacing it with more cooperative participatory planning methods of production and distribution of goods.

Cooperation with Other Transnational Movements

In addition to the ways in which the communal movement offers an alternative to the top-down neoliberal model of globalization and development, the communes also cooperate and coordinate with other transnational movements in an effort to construct new democratic spaces for a more just globalization.

One council I observed, *Communal Council El Socuy*, collaborated and shared ideas and strategies with the Zapatistas in Chiapas, Mexico. Located in the northern Venezuelan state Zulia, Socuy is one of the many indigenous communal councils in the country. The council is in the community *Wayuu Mana*, which means the place of the Wayuu people. The Wayuu are an indigenous group mostly located in the Guajira Peninsula in northern Colombia and northwest Venezuela.

The Zapatista Army of National Liberation (EZLN) took up arms on January 1, 1994, symbolically on the day when the North American Free Trade Agreement came into effect and declared war on the Mexican state. The mostly indigenous EZLN began to seize towns and cities in the southern Mexican state of Chiapas. After years of negotiations, refusals from the Mexican government to abide by San Andres Accords (which were to grant autonomy, recognition, and rights to the indigenous population of Mexico), and an increased military presence, the Zapatistas decided to unilaterally enact in their own communities the principles of the San Andres Accords, which the government refused to acknowledge. The Zapatistas created "liberated areas" where the population would gain "the right to freely and democratically elect their own administrative authorities." These liberated areas, or what were later called Rebel Zapatista Autonomous Municipalities (MAREZ), were created all throughout Chiapas.

Currently, there are thirty-two autonomous municipalities in southern Mexico. These municipalities are self-governed, and all decisions made in autonomous municipalities are made through various participatory mechanisms, one of which was through general assemblies. These meet regularly and are open to everyone in the community. Each autonomous municipality has elected delegates that can be revoked at any time, and that serve on a rotation basis. The idea is that at some point every member of the community will be able to serve as a delegate. These delegates form an assembly called

Juntas de Buen Gobierno or Councils of Good Government (JBG), which oversees programs on health, education, food, and taxation. The autonomous municipalities are also organized in small groups called *caracoles*. *Caracoles* are where collections of autonomous municipalities convene, and they also house different social programs education programs, language schools, and clinics, among others.

On various occasions many of the Wayuu people, from the El Socuy communal council traveled to Chiapas to meet with and share ideas about the way they have organized their communities and how they have struggled for indigenous rights and representation. Perhaps because of the collaboration between the two movements, both the autonomous municipalities in Chiapas and the El Socuy communal council in Venezuela have various similarities. For example, they make decisions in assemblies open to the whole community, have their own systems of education, and grow their own food. On the cooperation between the two groups, a Wayuu activist and organizer in the El Socuy communal council told me:

> [We] got invited by Subcomandante Marcos to pass along the word of what is going on in Venezuela, what is the relationship with the government, what is going on with the coal mining struggle, what the Wayuu people are doing, what's going on in Venezuela and Colombia, and do we support Chávez. All these things were topics that they thought was interesting to share with the restof the communities. And also, to bring the lessons and discipline of the Zapatista people to have it as a reference there in the community. Solidarity between those really respected and admired. They are really present in terms of reference for our community (David, Interview 15).

Thus, collaboration between the two movements is not just a mechanism to share how to organize their own respective communities but also a way to discuss each of their own particular struggles as well as their own political perspectives about different political questions that each group face. It is also important to highlight the two-way knowledge sharing; both movements learn from and gain perspectives from the other.

I was in a *caracol* named Oventic, home to one of the five Juntas of Good Government, where they house a language school for both internationals and indigenous people who are interested in learning Spanish or Tzotzil (an indigenous language native to southern Mexico), a school that trains teachers and a clinic that is open to the various autonomous municipalities in the area. The notion of solidarity and the idea that workers, peasants, and indigenous people in all countries have similar interests and similar enemies, and how this idea drives the collaboration between Zapatistas and other movements from below, like the communes in Venezuela, was highlighted in a discussion I had with a Zapatista in Oventic during my field work in Chiapas.

Anderson: Does the Mexican Government still attack Zapatista Autonomous municipalities or the Caracoles?

Manuel: Yes, there was an attack on a Tzeltal [A Mayan ethnic group and the largest indigenous group in Chiapas] community just the other day.

Anderson: How frequent are the attacks?

Manuel: There is an attack on the Zapatistas and our communities almost every day.

Anderson: When was the last attack on Oventic? Manuel: There hasn't been one in a long time.

Anderson: Is that because the government knows that the language school is here and there are likely to be foreigners here? Perhaps the government knows that attacking poor indigenous peasants may not garner the same domestic or international scandal and outcry as if the government were to attack or kill a U.S. citizen or a European. Do the foreigners here in the language school then provide some kind of safety or security from attacks from the government? Manuel: Anderson, you all are not foreigners, you are internationals; the Mexican government, they are the ones who are the foreigners. (Manuel, Interview 25)

So before answering my question about whether the presence of "foreigners" provide some kind of safety from attacks from the state, Manuel wanted to make it clear that to the Zapatistas, other members of the working class and peasants who come to Zapatista municipalities and *caracoles* on the basis of solidarity and cooperation, are not foreigners, are not alien to the land which belongs to the people. The Mexican government, who is not welcome and does not have legitimacy to the land and resources that belong to the people, are the ones who are viewed as foreign. This notion of solidarity, that workers and peasants of all countries are part of the same struggle that was extended to me and the other "internationals" that were at Oventic is the same principal that drives much of the cooperation and collaboration that the Zapatistas and the communes in Venezuela share with one another and with other international struggles. In other words, it is not us, workers from outside of Zapatista-controlled lands or even from outside of the political boundaries of Mexico that are seen as "foreigners," but rather it is the Mexican government themselves, who represent different material interests than workers and peasants internationally, that are seen as foreigners.

CHALLENGES AND LIMITATIONS

Communes in a Capitalist State?

On January 30, 2005, in a speech to the World Social Forum in Porto Alegre, Brazil, Hugo Chávez announced that he supported the creation of socialism in Venezuela under the banner of "twenty-first century socialism." Though the details of twenty-first-century socialism were vague, it was clear that the goal of the Bolivarian Process was to follow down a socialist path, no matter how unclear this "socialism" may look. In the subsequent years, various changes were made in the country, many of which have been explored above, but despite the far reach of the communal movement in Venezuela, the shift in the communes to communal production and the creation of the communal market as an alternative to the free market, Venezuela remains a capitalist country, which comes with various limitations to the communal movement and could ultimately bring about its downfall. This section explores the relationship between the communal movement and the capitalist state, and the limitations communes face existing in a capitalist economy.

As I showed in chapter 4, the Bolivarian Process (particularly during the Chávez era) has committed itself to a discourse on political participation, opened up spaces for grassroots organization, nationalized various private industries, created social missions that focus on health and education among others, and increased expenditures on social programs. But despite many of these important gains for working people (again mostly during the Chávez era), the overwhelming majority of the means of production have remained in the hands of the private sphere and the capitalist class. And despite its progressive language on participatory democracy and human rights, the 1999 Chavista constitution gives significant protection to private property (article 15).

In a discussion on whether Venezuela has achieved a social or political revolution, sociologist Jeffery R. Webber says that rather than achieving a revolution, much less socialism:

> Venezuela has witnessed a series of rebellions from below with wide-scale popular participation, and other actions from above with lesser popular participation, which have forced significant concessions from factions of the ruling class, produced significant changes in the personnel of state management, led to the transformation of some old political organizations as well as the creation of new ones, and allowed for major social improvements through the distribution of a greater share of the oil-rent to the popular classes in a context of high oil prices on the world market.[33]

So again, despite some major changes within the country since the beginning of the Bolivarian Process, the control of the economy still remains in the hands of private capital. In fact, between 1999 and 2011, the private sector's share of economic activity actually increased from 65 to 71 percent. [34] Production for private profit still dominates the economy, the production and distribution of goods and services, including key industries like the major food import and processing operations, pharmaceuticals, and auto-parts, are still controlled by the private sector, and the bourgeoisie state apparatus (though perhaps weakened) still endures. Even in instances where the state does own the means of production, for example in the state-owned oil and natural gas company PDVSA and the concrete and asphalt industries, it is the state bureaucracy that controls and makes all decision in these industries, rather than the workers. And in the instances of state control of industry, in particular PDVSA, production and distribution are shaped by the logic of capital, capital accumulation and are produced for the market. The oil industry represents 95 percent of the country's total exports, which is to say sold on the world market. In other words, despite various examples of workers' control throughout the country, whether control by workers' councils or by the communes, in neither the large extant private sector nor in the majority of state-owned industries do workers have control of the means of production.

According to Chávez, the transition to twenty-first-century socialism rests on the expansion of the communes, and then later the expansion of communal cities, and then eventually to the creation of the communal state, which is to replace the bourgeois state. Chávez commented that "the ownership of the means of production should be in the hands of the commune."[35] But even Chávez himself openly spoke about how the transition to socialism has yet to come to fruition and that Venezuela remains a capitalist country and socialism is not in the near future. Here is Chávez on his weekly radio and television show *Alo Presidente*:

> Who would think to say that Venezuela is a socialist country? No, that would be to deceive ourselves. We are in a country that still lives in capitalism, we have only initiated a path; we are taking steps against the world current, including towards a socialist project; but this is for the medium or long term.[36]

So what challenges and limitations does the communal movement face as they operate in what continues to be a capitalist economy? The next section will look at three issues and how they present challenges to the communal movement: hoarding, speculation, and production driven by the needs of the free market.

Production for the Market

Production for the market produces a number of problems. When production is driven by the needs of the market, fluctuations in global prices of commodities can have strong negative consequences. In the case of Venezuela, the drop in global prices of oil had disastrous impacts on a country where 95 percent of total exports and about half of the government's revenue comes from the oil industry. In the summer of 2014, oil prices began to drop, and by the beginning of 2016, the price of a barrel of oil had dropped by more than 70 percent, the lowest rate in over thirteen years. [37, 38] The drop in oil prices resulted in high inflation rates and consequently high rates of capital flight. The problem of dropping oil prices is exacerbated by the government's failure to diversify its economy and its dependence on oil revenues. The drop of global oil prices, and consequently the drastic cutback in revenues, puts the government in a difficult situation to fund both its social programs and the communes.

Not only does the production for the market by state and private sectors create problems for the communes, but communes who themselves control production face challenges due to the logic of producing according to the needs of the market. Not all communes strictly produce for the market (as some produce for the communal market as I described above), but for those that do, production for the market can undermine the democratic elements of the commune itself, decisions that in theory are made by the council are often influenced by the capitalist marketplace in which it operates. For example, the market dictates what is to be produced and the prices for commodities, influencing decisions in the council.

Hoarding

Venezuela subsidizes basic goods like flour, black beans, chicken, milk, gas, diapers, and eggs in order to ensure that products that were unaffordable under previous administrations are accessible to the majority of Venezuelans. This opened the door for capital speculation and hoarding by the capitalist class. Hoarding by the business class has manifested itself in two ways. First is the problem of contraband where much of the food and regulated goods are hoarded and then sold on the black market at exorbitant prices or across the border, particularly in Colombia, at often a 100 percent markup. A second strategy of the business class is hoarding not to resell on the black market or across the border but simply to manufacture shortages as an attempt to destabilize the economy and undermine the Maduro government. Government officials have on various occasions found warehouses full of basic goods, rotting because the private companies wanted to create the sensation that there are no products in the country and make the argument that it is the result of mismanagement of an incompetent government.

In one case, in the municipality of San Francisco in the state of Zulia, the government found a warehouse by the company Herrera C. A. that had over 1.5 million diapers; 360,000 kilos of detergent; 277,000 units of soap; and 14,000 units of baby formula, in addition to corn flour, black beans, rice, shampoo, and other items.[39] In another case, the government found a warehouse in the state of Aragua where they found fourteen million syringes, and two million surgical gloves among a whole slew of other medical equipment.[40] And this is while the supermarkets are severely lacking these products and Venezuelans are waiting for hours to purchase scarce products.

Hoarding, corruption, and capital speculation impact the communes in a variety of ways. First, the activity of the private sector, and the government's inaction to confront these issues, undermines the whole Bolivarian process on which the communal movement relies. Secondly, hoarding and capital speculation impact all sectors of Venezuelan society, including the communes. Shortages in basic goods, for example, limit communes' access to key materials needed for the normal functioning of the commune, and waiting in queues at supermarkets for hours upon hours limits individuals' ability to participate in communal organizing. Also, lost state revenue due to corruption and speculation can dry up much needed state funding that goes to the communes. Lastly, the more the opposition and private capitalist are able to make gains against the Bolivarian process, the more it can embolden the right wing and encourage violent attacks on the communes, like the attacks on *Comuna El Maizal* in the summer of 2015.[41]

Capital Speculation

In the early years of the Bolivarian process, a number of economic measures were taken to defend the process against sabotage orchestrated by the capitalist class. The two most important of these measures were to implement foreign exchange controls and price controls on basic food products. The former was to prevent capital flight and the latter to defend the purchasing power of the poor. Eventually, the capitalists found a way to circumvent these measures.

First, let's take a look at the ways that private capitalists have circumvented price controls. The Venezuelan government put in place various price controls to regulate the prices of basic goods, including milk, black beans, chicken, pre-cooked flour, medicines, soaps, and toilet paper, among others. The idea behind these controls was to keep the prices low for key necessities so people can meet their most basic needs. But a large majority of private producers refused to produce products that are covered by the price controls. To circumvent regulated prices for rice, for example, businesses have produced flavored varieties, which are not covered by price controls. [42] It is also important to note that the private sector has a near monopoly of food production and distribution on many basic products in the country. Jorge Martin points out another way the private sector bypasses the price controls:

> To this we have to add a thousand and one different ways in which the private sector breaks the price regulation regime. Maize flour is permanently scarce, but *arepas* are always well stocked [Maize is the key ingredient to *arepas*]. Chickens are almost impossible to purchase at regulated prices, but roast chicken joints never lack them. Wheat flour can't be bought at the official price, and the bakeries use lack of flour as an argument not to produce the normal loaf of bread (the price of which is regulated), but then they are mysteriously able to produce any other variety of bread, cakes and biscuits, which we have to assume are made with flour. What's behind this mystery?

The fact that private wholesale producers do supply these establishments, but of course not at regulated prices.[43]

In addition to circumventing price controls, private capitalists have also found a way around currency controls. But first it is important to take a quick look at Venezuela's complex currency system, which included three different exchange rates. The first, called DiPro, is the official exchange rate used for the import of food, medicine, and raw materials used for domestic production of goods and services.[44] DiPro is also used for Venezuelan students studying abroad. The DiPro rate is now currently around thirteen bolivares to the dollar. The second official exchange rate, DiCom, is a floating exchange rate, which is currently somewhere between 300 and 700 bolivares to the U.S. dollar and is used to cover all transactions not covered in DiPro. The third exchange rate is the black-market rate that has reached 4,000 bolivares to the dollar.[45]

The chasm between the black-market rate and the DiPro exchange rates has opened the door for corruption and currency speculation. The government provides businesses dollars at the DiPro exchange rate in order to import goods and services. Many of these businesses end up selling these preferential dollars on the black market to make huge profits. If playing with exchange rates, if making money off speculation and corruption is more profitable than providing important services to the public like importing, selling, or manufacturing goods and services, then more and more businesses are going to focus on speculation than those more useful activities. Because so many of the dollars that businesses are getting at the DiPro rate that are supposed to be used for importing goods are instead being sold on the illegal black market, there has been serious scarcities in a number of key goods. In other words, rather than importing goods those dollars are siphoned into the black market, creating scarcity of a variety of goods. One estimate of the total lost due to the manipulation of currency controls is $300 billion.[46]

So while the currency system put in place in 2003 to prevent capital flight just after the 2002–2003 oil lockout may have made sense at the time, why has the Maduro government not changed the these controls which would eliminate many of the incentives for corruption and speculation by the capitalist class? Part of this answer lies in the alliances that the government has made with certain sectors of the private sector who are benefitting handsomely from the status quo, a topic I will develop further in the following section.

The Bolivarian State and the Future of the Communes

In addition to challenges that the communes face existing in a capitalist economy, the success of the communes is also contingent on the success of the Bolivarian process more generally. The future of the communes is very much connected to the future of the Bolivarian process. If the Bolivarian process fails, the communal movement will likely also fail. Opponents of the Bolivarian process are not only those who openly identify as part of the opposition but also opportunists who are nominally a part of the process but whose interests do not align with the interests of genuine popular power and a transition to socialism, and the latter group often includes many in the government and the PSUV itself. Challenges to the success of the Bolivarian process, and by extension the communes, therefore, do not just come from without, or from the right-wing opposition but also from contradictions within the process itself. This a particularly important discussion, as the Bolivarian process is currently going through one of its toughest periods to date, with an unprecedented inflation rate reaching over a million percent by 2018 coupled with shortages of basic consumer goods and long queues outside of supermarkets where Venezuelans can be found waiting for hours to buy basic goods. The following section will explore these contradictions.

One such contradiction originates from the founding of the United Socialist Party of Venezuela (PSUV). The party was formed in 2007 to bring together all the existing organizations that supported Chávez and the Bolivarian process's goal for "socialism of the twenty-first century." It was to be an open mass democratic party of the left. After the first six weeks, the party claimed six million members. One of the key components of the whole Bolivarian process is its emphasis on popular power and participatory democracy. This language is in the 1999 Chavista constitution, and these concepts have driven the creation of various participatory and popular power institutions, including the social missions, participatory budget allocation, co-management of state-owned factories, community radio, communal councils, and of course the communes. But despite the importance of participatory democracy and popular power to the process, the PSUV leaves little room for popular participation in the party itself.

Though in the first years of the PSUV, hundreds of militants in the party participated in community assemblies and various currents within the party had representatives and could make proposals, the party was still a highly centralized party with Chávez at the top of the pyramid. The party always relied on the hyper-leadership of Chávez, and it never developed a collective leadership outside of Chávez. This worked for some time because of his charisma and his ability to connect with people in the popular sectors, but after his death and with the election of Nicolas Maduro, the limits of this model started to become more pronounced.

Under Maduro, the extent to which popular participation was permitted in the party decreased further, as a new ruling bureaucracy within the party began to become more powerful. This new bureaucracy controls the large public sector budget and has made alliances with various parts of the private sector. This is not to say that Chávez had no alliances with any parts of the private sector, but these alliances grew after the eruption of violent rightwing protests called the *guarimbas*, which began in February of 2014 and lasted until April of the same year. The anti-government protests were calling for "*la salida*," "the exit" of the elected government of Maduro. The protestors blocked roads and communities, burned trash in the streets, attacked state-run health clinics, destroyed billboards, and burned buses. There were some reports of anti-government protestors stringing wire across the road to decapitate motorcyclists.[47] Maduro's method to resolve the *guarimba* violence was to negotiate with the business class.

In a strategy for reconciliation with sectors of the capitalist class and the political opposition, Maduro called for what were called "peace" negotiations. Maduro met with business leaders and powerful private capitalists including the Venezuelan Federation of Chambers of Commerce (Fedecámaras), an organization that was instrumental in the failed 2002 coup d'etat which temporarily overthrew Chávez, and Lorenzo Mendoza, owner of the Polar Company, Venezuela's largest domestic food producer and perhaps the most powerful private capitalist in Venezuela. But perhaps more important than those who *were* invited to these negotiations was those who were *not* invited. Gonzalo Gomez, a member of *Marea Socialista*, a Trotskyist current that was in the PSUV from its inception until they left the party in February of 2014, wrote at the time:

> Only representatives of the right wing, not those of the working class and popular sectors have been invited [to the peace negotiations]. So far, the negotiations have functioned as a way to push Maduro into making further concessions to the interests of the capitalists as a "pragmatic" way forward— though the base of Chavismo favors a very different response.[48]

While it may be true that the biggest challenges to the Bolivarian process and the communal movement more specifically may come from the right-wing political opposition (speculation, hoarding) and that the communes are operating in a capitalist economy (drops in oil prices, production for the market), the government has done very little to combat these issues. The reason why the government has done so little to solve these problems may very well be related to the internal contradictions in the Bolivarian process itself and maybe even more so with the alliances that the Maduro government made with the same sectors of private capital that are resisting a radical advancement of the Bolivarian process. And again, it is important to point out that these alliances were made without the involvement or participation of workers, the left and popular sectors of the Venezuelan society, or in other words without the radical base, the real motor force of the Bolivarian process.

In the age of neoliberal globalization, as corporations and the concentration of capital increase and rules of the market pervade more and more of our lives, workers, through networks of popular power created from struggles from below can exercise agency over their own development. The Venezuelan communes and communal councils are a glimpse of how workers both formal and informal can push for greater control of their lives and can create alternative models of development to the neoliberal model promoted by international financial institutions and powerful nation states.

With the construction of networks of communes and communal councils, more sectors of Venezuelan society have been incorporated into the political decision-making process than at any other point in Venezuelan history. By restructuring how power is distributed and decisions are made, councils and communes have significantly increased popular participation. The constant participation of citizens in the political process has augmented citizens' self-determination in their own communities. The inclusion and participation of community members in decisions about how to allocate communal budgets, what to produce, how to produce, and how to distribute goods demonstrate one important way that workers, through these networks of popular power can exercise agency over their own development.

The four primary characteristics of the communal movement all function to deepen direct democratic community control over the resources and development of local communities. Furthermore, the networks between communes and communal councils deepens the direct democratic control of even larger geographic and political spaces. Participatory democracy in the communes enables citizens to be active participants in the process and decision making over the area in which they live or work. Member of the communes play a significant role in developing projects that benefit the entire community. Moreover, participatory democracy in the communes remedies some of the exclusionary aspects of representative democracy. This is apparent in the citizens' assemblies where historically excluded sectors of society—the poor, indigenous, and other marginalized groups—are prominent. Endogenous development in the communes enables communes to make decisions internally based on the needs of the community, enhancing community control over the resources and development of local communities.

Communal control over production not only allows for community members themselves to decide what is produced, how it is produced, and how it is distributed but it also gives workers in these production sites the power to make decisions about their own working conditions, compensation, work hours, and vacation time. The communal market gives workers further control over their own development in that it enables communes to produce directly based on the needs of the community rather than the market dictating what should be produced, how it is distributed, and more or less the prices of those goods and services produced. Through these four components of the communes, workers have more self-determination and control over their own development.

The successes that the communes have achieved so far are impressive and would be difficult to dispute, but they do confront a series of various serious obstacles. The obstacles are varied and come from both within and without the process. First is the limitations that come with communal production and distribution in the midst of a capitalist economy, both domestically and the global market economy. Second are the explicit challenges from the rightwing opposition, whether that being hoarding, speculation, or outright violence. And finally, the verticalist structure of the PSUV and the hostility to some of the more radical currents of Chavismo that have at various key moments impeded the transfer of power to workers and the popular sectors of society. The survival and spread of the communes require a confrontation with these three obstacles and the further building of popular power from below, and a deepening of the Bolivarian process as a whole. When asked what concretely can be done to confront the very apparent obstacles to the success of the communal movement, Alex Alayo, a communal organizer at the *El Maizal Commune* responded:

We have to control the means of production. We need the resources, the land, everything that you need to produce, the means of production. We need a communization of power, and the communalization of the territories. There is not another way out to liberate humans from capitalism, only with the construction of the power of the people and the changing of the relationships from the way they are now, the change the relationships of power. It has to be from below and horizontal. Right now there is a coexistence of power and a strong conflict between revolution and reform and revolution against counterrevolution. We have to push further against classic distributions of power. We have to build it from below. We don't want this to end in reformism against revolution, no we have to win. The revolution has to defeat the counterrevolution in the end. And this can't be done by reformism. The power has to change. So all the relationships in power have to change. The only way to win is to deepen the fight. If we don't deepen the fight, the commune will die or will simply become an appendix of the bureaucratic state (Alex, Interview 7).

As I have illustrated in previous chapters, the Bolivarian masses have, on various occasions, both defeated the counter-revolutionary attempts by the opposition to end the process and also pushed those in the Bolivarian government, Chávez included, in a more radical direction. This was the case with the 2002 coup and the oil lockout of the same year and more generally with the widespread reforms that improved the living standards of the majority of Venezuelans and the various initiatives that transferred power to popular sectors of society through participatory democracy, communal councils, communes, and participatory budgeting. It is as George Ciccarriello-Maher argued in his book *We Created Chávez*,[49] that it was (and is) the masses, workers, peasants, the organized left, and social movement actors who created Chávez, Chavismo, the Bolivarian process, and the communes, and it is now more than ever that these popular sectors must once again organize and deepen the process to press against those impeding or in opposition to the movement, which includes both the official right-wing opposition, but also those who may be nominally "Chavista," including the PSUV, Maduro, and more conservative sectors of Chavismo.

NOTES

1. David Harvey, A *Brief History of Neoliberalism* (Oxford, UK: Oxford University Press, 2005).

2. Ibid.

3. Philip McMichael, *Development and Social Change: A Global Perspective, Sixth Edition* (Thousand Oaks, CA: Sage Publications, 2016).

4. Wendy Brown, "Neoliberalism and the End of Liberal Democracy," *Theory and Event* 7, no. 1 (2003): 1–21.

5. Wendy Brown, *Undoing the Demos: Neoliberalism's Stealth Revolution* (New York: Zone Books, 2005).

6. Aihwa Ong, *Neoliberalism as Exception: Mutations in Citizenship and Sovereignty* (Durham, NC: Duke University Press, 2006).

7. Sujatha Fernandes, "Cultural and Neoliberal Rationalities in Postneoliberal Venezuela," in *Neoliberalism, Interrupted: Social Change and Contested Governance in Contemporary Latin America*, eds. Mark Goodale and Nancy Postero (Stanford, CA: Stanford University Press, 2013): 22.

8. Peter Evans, "Is an Alternative Globalization Possible?" *Politics and Society* 36, no. 2 (2008).

9. Jackie Smith, *Social Movements for Global Democracy* (Baltimore: Johns Hopkins University Press, 2008).

10. Manuel Castells, *Networks of Outrage and Hope: Social Movements in the Internet Age* (Cambridge, UK: Polity Press, 2015).

11. Peter Evans, "Is an Alternative Globalization Possible?" *Politics and Society* 36, no. 2 (2008): 272.

12. Ibid.

13. Bello Waldon, *Deglobalization: Ideas for a New World Economy* (London: Zed Books, 2005).

14. Boaventura De Sousa Santos, "Beyond Neoliberal Governance: The World Social Forum as Subaltern Cosmopolitan Politics and Legality," in *Law and Globalization from Below: Towards a Cosmopolitan Legality*, eds. Boaventura De Sousa Santos and Cesar A. RodriguezGaravito (Cambridge, UK: Cambridge University Press, 2005): 29–63.

15. John Holloway, *Zapatista! Reinventing Revolution in Mexico* (London: Pluto Press, 1998).

16. John Holloway, *Change the World Without Taking Power* (London: Pluto Press, 2002).

17. John Dale, *Free Burma: Transnational Legal Action and Corporate Accountability* (Minneapolis: University of Minnesota Press, 2011).

18. Dan La Botz, "The New Movement for Global Justice," *Against the Current* 88 (September–October 2000).

19. Willelm Assies, "David Versus Goliath in Cochabamba: Water Rights, Neoliberalism and the Revival of Social Protest in Bolivia," *Latin American Perspectives* 30, no. 3 (2003).

20. Ximena De la Barra X and Richard Dello Buono, *Latin America After the Neoliberal Debacle: Another Region is Possible* (Lanham, MD: Rowman & Littlefield, 2009): 71.

21. Ibid.

22. Mark Goodale and Nancy Postero, *Neoliberalism, Interrupted: Social Change and Contested Governance in Contemporary Latin America* (Stanford, CA: Stanford University Press, 2013).

23. Eric Hershberg and Fred Rosen, *Latin America After Neoliberalism: Turning the Tide in the 21st Century?* (New York: The New Press, 2007).

24. Rovira Kaltwasser, "Toward Post-Neoliberalism in Latin America," *Latin America Research Review* 46, no. 2 (2001): 225–234.

25. Ximena De la Barra X and Richard Dello Buono, *Latin America After the Neoliberal Debacle: Another Region is Possible* (Lanham, MD: Rowman & Littlefield, 2009).

26. Thomas Muhr, "TINA Go Home! ALBA and Re-theorizing Resistance to Global Capitalism," *Cosmos and History: The Journal of Natural and Social Philosophy* 6, no. 2 (2010).

27. Ibid.

28. Juan Reardon, "Venezuelan National Assembly Passes People's Power 'Law of Communes," *Venezuelanalysis.com*, December 4, 2010, http://venezuelanalysis.com/news/5858.

29. Christina Schiavoni and William Camacaro," The Venezuelan Effort to Build a New Food and Agricultural System," *The Monthly Review*, July 1, 2009, http://monthlyreview.org/2009/07/01/the-venezuelan-effort-to-build-a-new-food-and-agriculture-system/.

30. Gregory Wilpert, *Changing Venezuela by Taking Power* (London: Verso, 2007).

31. David Harvey, *The New Imperialism*, (Oxford, UK: Oxford University Press, 2003).

32. Silvia Rivera Cusicanqui, "Indigenous Anarchist Critique of Bolivia's 'Indigenous State': Interview with Silvia Rivera Cusicanqui," *Upside Down World*, September 3, 2014, https://upsidedownworld.org/archives/bolivia/indigenous-anarchist-critique-of-bolivias-indigenous-state-interview-with-silvia-rivera-cusicanqui/.

33. Jeffery Webber, "Dual Powers, Class Compositions, and the Venezuelan People," *Historical Materialism* 23, no. 2 (2015): 200.

34. Gabriel Hetland, "Why is Venezuela in Crisis," *The Nation*, August 17, 2016b, https://www.thenation.com/article/why-is-venezuela-in-crisis/.

35. Frederick B. Mills, "Chavista Transition to the Communal State," *Open Democracy*, July 22, 2015, towards-communal-state.

36. Ibid.

37. Clifford Krauss, "Oil Prices: What's Behind the Drop? Simple Economics," *New York Times*, March 30, 2016, https://www.nytimes.com/2015/01/13/business/energy-environment/oil-prices.html.

38. Virginia Lopez, "Venezuela's Economic Crisis Worsens as Oil Prices Fall," *Al Jazeera*, January 8, 2016, oil-prices-fall-160108105010345.html.

39. Corey Fischer-Hoffman, "Venezuela Officials Seize Warehouse with Enormous Cache of Hoarded Items as Opposition Calls for Strike," *Venezuela Analysis*, January 14, 2015, https://venezuelanalysis.com/news/11158.

40. Andrew Cawthorne, "Venezuela Seizes Warehouses Packed with Medical Goods, Food." *Reuters*, October 23, 2014.

41. Z. C. Dutka, "Attacks on Venezuelan Commune and Farmland Reported, Crops Destroyed," *Venezuela Analysis*, August 19, 2015, https://venezuelanalysis.com/news/11478.

42. Jorge Martin, "Venezuela—A Last Warning," *In Defense of Marxism*, May 19, 2016, http://www.marxist.com/venezuela-last-warning.htm.

43. Ibid.

44. Gabriel Hetland, "Why is Venezuela in Crisis," *The Nation*, August 17, 2016b, https://www.thenation.com/article/why-is-venezuela-in-crisis/.

45. Gabriel Hetland, "How Severe is Venezuela's Crisis," *The Nation*, June 23, 2016a, https://www.thenation.com/article/how-severe-is-venezuelas-crisis/.

46. Gabriel Hetland, "Why is Venezuela in Crisis," *The Nation*, August 17, 2016b, https://www.thenation.com/article/why-is-venezuela-in-crisis/.

47. Tamara Pearson, "Venezuela Guarimbas: 11 Things the Media Didn't Tell You," *Telesur*, February 11, 2015, Things-the-Media-Didnt-Tell-You-20150211-0025.html.

48. Gonzalo Gomez, "Ten Proposals for Venezuela''s Maduro," *Socialistworker.org*, June 24, 2014, https://socialistworker.org/2014/06/24/ten-proposals-for-maduro.

49. George Ciccariello-Maher, *We Created Chávez: A Peoples History of the Venezuelan Revolution* (Durham, NC: Duke University Press, 2013).

Chapter Five

Crisis, the Decline of the Pink Tide, and the Future of the Communes

DESCRIBING THE CRISIS

Venezuela is currently in its deepest economic crisis of the country's history. Millions of Venezuelans are experiencing ever-increasing vulnerability marked by diminishing access to healthcare, food, and other basic consumer goods. Hospitals go without access to basic public services like water and electricity. Garbage trucks circulate less frequently, leaving trash to accumulate for days. Malnutrition is widespread, and the availability of electricity, clean water, and life-saving medicines are limited and sporadic. Unprecedented rates of inflation, declining wages, and increases in the prices of basic goods have made life more difficult. High levels of insecurity, trauma, and stress have resulted in an exodus of Venezuelans fleeing the country seeking better lives. This section will discuss three major components of the crisis: inflation, purchasing power of wages, and migration.

Venezuela has a long history of inflation and since the early 1980s has experienced constant double-digit inflation. During the Chávez era (1999–2013), inflation was kept relatively low, reaching a low of 12.5 percent in 2001. The country also experienced decreasing inflation rates from 2006 until his death in early of 2013. Inflation rates began to increase again under Maduro. In 2014, the annual inflation rate reached 69 percent, the highest in the world (Patton 2014). The inflation rate continued to rise to 181 percent in 2015, 800 percent in 2016, over 4,000 percent in 2017, and by 2018, the rate was over a million percent, at about 1,700,000 percent.[1, 2]

The government has responded to high inflation rates by regularly decreeing salary increases, but despite its attempts, these increases do not keep up with inflation and the purchasing power of salaries, especially for public employees, has been dramatically reduced. In 2018, after the Economic Recovery Plan, the monthly minimum income was the equivalent to US $30.[3] Today, the monthly minimum wage, according to the Central Bank's May 12, 2020 exchange rate, is the equivalent of US $2.23. After adding the government food bonus, the monthly minimum salary is roughly US $4.47, or about US 15 cents a day.[4] This figure is eight times less than the UN's limit for Absolute Poverty of $1.25 a day. It is important to mention that the monthly minimum wage under Chávez was US $300, over sixty times higher than what it is today.[5] To put today's minimum wage in context, four dollars is about what two pounds of meat cost. In other words, the monthly minimum wage is just enough to buy one kilo of meat. And even this number changes daily, as prices go up every day, sometimes several times a day. Minimum wage is insufficient to cover basic needs, and one can simply not survive on minimum wage alone.

Maduro has also tried to supplement the minimum wage with the creation of organizations called Local Committees for Supply and Production (CLAP), which distribute priority foods through a house-to-house delivery method. However, according to the UN High Commissioner for Human rights, the CLAP program does not meet certain standards related to the right to adequate food, as only three to seven million Venezuelans are receiving this aid, and the program is often used for political propaganda (UNCHR 2018).[6]

A 2020 study conducted by Caritas Venezuela found that severe malnutrition in children under the age of five grew by 5.78 percent rising from 11.5 percent in November of 2019 to 17.3 percent in April of 2020. During that same period, the number of households with access to food subsidized by the state through the CLAP system decreased by a third, from 73 percent to 41 percent, while food insecurity increased from 32 percent to 40 percent, of which 21 percent suffer from severe food insecurity.[7]

Because wages are insufficient to survive, many Venezuelans resort to looking for second jobs or migrating to other countries to enable them to send home money through remittances. Since 2016, millions of Venezuelans have fled their country looking for a better life, most of whom are seeking work abroad in order to send money back home. Between 3,000 and 5,000 Venezuelans are leaving their country every day.[8, 9] According to the United Nations Agency for Refugees, between 2016 and June of 2020, over five million Venezuelans fled the country. If Venezuela maintains this pace, the number of displaced people could reach 6.5 million by the end of 2020.[10] Venezuela currently has the highest number of displaced people in Latin America and the second highest in the world, second only to Syria.[11] Since 2014, the number of Venezuelans who have applied for asylum in other countries has increased by 4,000 percent.[12] The crisis seems to have no end in sight.

EXPLAINING THE CRISIS

This chapter argues that there are four major, interrelated causes of the economic collapse in Venezuela, two domestic and two international. First is the economic war waged by Venezuela's domestic right-wing opposition. Second is the economic and political mismanagement of the Maduro administration. Third is the U.S. sanctions imposed on Venezuela. Lastly is the larger international context, that is, the end of the commodities boom, the drop in oil prices, and the fall of the Pink Tide.

Economic War and the Right-Wing Opposition

The right-wing opposition to the Bolivarian process has attempted a variety of strategies and tactics to undermine and destabilize the project since its inception. In 2002, the right-wing opposition, led by the Venezuelan Federation of Chambers of Commerce (*Fedecámaras*) temporarily overthrew Hugo Chávez. Subsequently, the coup makers suspended all democratic rights, dissolved the National Assembly and the Supreme Court, and revoked the 1999 constitution. As detailed in chapter 4, had it not been for millions of Chávez supporters surrounding the presidential palace to demand the reinstatement of their elected president, the Bolivarian project would have ended in 2002.

Later in 2002, the opposition adopted another strategy, an oil lockout in which the opposition-controlled Venezuelan Workers Federation (CTV), *Fedecámaras*, and the right-wing Democratic Coordination collaborated to bring oil production to a halt, with the stated objective to force Chávez to resign. Next in 2004 came the attempt to use a mechanism made law with the 1999 constitution to recall President Chávez through a referendum. They received enough signatures, as required by the constitution, to have the referendum but ultimately failed, as 58 percent of Venezuelans voted against the recall. In 2005, the opposition boycotted the parliamentary elections. Then with the death of Chávez, they tried the electoral route, but when they lost the elections to the PSUV's Nicolas Maduro they refused to accept the outcome and once again adopted a more violent approach, including violence targeting government-run health clinics, busses, and other public institutions, resulting in the death of seven civilians.[13] In 2014, violence erupted again as opposition activists attacked state security forces and even strung wire across intersections, leading to a decapitation of a motorcyclist.

As detailed in chapter 5, hoarding and capital speculation are two more recent strategies the domestic right-wing opposition has employed to undermine the Maduro administration and wreak havoc on the economy. The existing exchange rates, currency controls, and preferential dollars provided to import companies, discussed in the previous chapter, are exploited by the capitalist class. By selling these preferential dollars to the black market rather than importing goods such as medicine and food, import companies make huge profits. When currency speculation and playing with exchange rates is more profitable than providing critical services for the public, such as importing basic necessities or even producing manufactured goods, then more and more businesses will engage in those activities rather than meeting human needs. It is not just the right-wing capitalist class that has engaged in the profitable market of currency speculation; Maduro loyalists in the military have also cashed in on the enterprise. This is part of the reason why Maduro has yet to make any meaningful alterations to the currency system that would eliminate the incentives for this type of speculation.

Hoarding, as detailed in the previous chapter, is another major component of the economic war that the business class has engaged in. There have been numerous cases of hoarding by the business class of basic goods, including milk,[14] toilet paper,[15] gasoline,[16] food, diapers, medicine, and laundry detergent.[17] By hoarding basic goods and allowing them to rot in warehouses, the opposition was able to create the sensation that there were no products in the country, enabling them to make the argument that the crisis was the result of government mismanagement. Of course, government mismanagement contributed, which will be discussed below, but any discussion of the economic crisis that omits the full-on economic war waged by the right-wing opposition is incomplete. The hoarding of regulated food and medicine by private businesses has had devastating consequences.

It is important to mention here that all of the attempts by the right-wing business class to manufacture crisis and wreck the economy were made possible by the Chávez and Maduro administrations' hesitation to make important class decisions, by delaying significant confrontations with capital, or by leaving, with a few exceptions, capitalist modes of production and the private ownership of the means of production intact. So long as the private capitalist class controls large sections of the economy, which they have throughout the entire period of the Bolivarian process, they are able to disrupt the economy by whatever means they see fit. By recognizing private property as a right in the 1999 constitution and by allowing private capitalists to operate and control large sectors of the economy rather than expropriating their property and transferring the ownership of the means of production to the collective and democratic control of workers, the Venezuelan oligarchy has been able to engage in a variety of practices like hoarding, capital flight, and capital speculation that have greatly contributed to the crisis we see in Venezuela today.

Finally, the most recent attempt by the opposition to undermine the Maduro government was the coup attempt of 2019. On January 23, 2019, Juan Guiadó, the president of the National Assembly, declared himself acting president of Venezuela. Guiadó seemingly came out of nowhere. Before he declared himself president of the Republic, 81 percent of Venezuelans did not even know who he was, and he was only elected to the national assembly with 26 percent of the vote.[18] Nevertheless, the United States, Canada, and several right-wing Latin American countries, namely Brazil, Argentina, and Colombia, recognized Guiadó the same day. Guiadó, the right-wing opposition, and the United States claimed that this maneuver was constitutional by evoking article 233. However, article 233 clearly states that the president of the National Assembly takes over as the interim president if the sitting president abandons his post, dies, retires, becomes too ill to carry out his responsibilities, is recalled in a recall referendum, or is impeached by the supreme court.[19] Since none of these had happened, it was an unconstitutional attempt to seize power. Article 233 of the constitution also states that the interim president only takes charge of the presidency of the republic for thirty days, whereby a new election by universal suffrage and direct ballot should be held.[20] So even if Guiadó's maneuver was constitutional, which it was not, after the thirty days a new election would have needed to be held and Guiadó's interim presidency would have been over. But over a year later Guiadó still claims to be acting president, despite the fact that no election occurred. Ironically, Guiadó's justification for not having a new election is because Maduro never abandoned his post, which was precisely the justification for his coup in the first place, that Maduro had "abandoned his post."

The January coup was long in the making. For over a year, the Donald Trump administration had been secretly meeting with defiant military officers to discuss their plans to overthrow Maduro. [21] Guiadó himself, a member of the far-right party Voluntud Popular, made a trip to the White House in December (before he was the president of the National Assembly), just one month before the coup, presumably making plans for his power play. [22] He then spoke with Vice President Mike Pence the night before the coup, getting the green light from Washington to move forward with the plan. [23] The plan, a U.S.-backed coup against Maduro, would be in contravention of international law, which prohibits any country from infringing upon another nation's national sovereignty.[24]

After the January coup failed to convincingly overthrow Maduro, Guiadó tried again a few months later. On April 30, alongside dozens of defectors from Venezuela's armed forces, Guiadó called on the rest of the armed forces to join them in the "final step of usurping power from Maduro." During the coup attempt, Guiadó's supporters carried out various acts of violence, including ransacking, looting, and setting fire to the headquarters of the Indio Caricuao Commune in Caracas.[25] The operation, "Operation Liberty," failed to attract sizable numbers of deserters and was a complete failure.

After two failed attempts at taking power, and as Guiadó's attempts to convince the world that he was in fact the president were unavailing, he faced another major setback: a corruption scandal. One of Guiadó's most consistent critiques of Maduro was corruption, but within the first six months of his declared "assumption of power," he was embroiled in his own corruption scandal. In June of 2019, it was reported that several of his representatives in Colombia had allegedly misappropriated funds and squandered thousands of dollars on hotels, parties, nightclubs, clothes, and other luxuries. This was humanitarian aid that was supposed to be allocated to accommodations for soldiers who had defected from Maduro and were living across the border in Colombia.[26] The result was that an already divided right-wing opposition became more divided and an already unpopular Guiadó became even less popular. By December of 2019, according to a survey by Meganalisis, just 10 percent of Venezuelans "believe, trust and support" Guiadó.[27]

Mismanagement by the Maduro Administration

The second major cause of the Venezuelan crisis is the mismanagement of the Maduro administration. As discussed in the previous chapter, one major factor leading to the crisis in Venezuela was the drastic drop in oil prices, which began in the summer of 2014. By the beginning of 2016, the price of a barrel of oil had dropped by more than 70 percent, the lowest rate in over thirteen years.[28, 29] The fall of oil revenue resulted in a decline in the ability of the government to import raw materials and foodstuffs, to maintain the social programs and to maintain subsidies on regulated goods that could previously be sold at a loss. One response by the government to the sudden decline in revenue was to print more money. The injection of enormous amounts of money into the economy, the prioritization of the payment of foreign debt over importing goods, and an increase of corruption all led to massive inflation.[30] High inflation rates led to high rates of capital flight, with one estimate that capital flight took $250 billion out of the country between 2013 and 2015 alone.[31] The problem of dropping oil prices was exacerbated by the government's failure to diversify its economy and its dependence on oil revenues. The drop of global oil prices, and consequently the drastic cutback in revenues, put the government in a difficult situation as to how to fund both its social programs and the communes.

The Maduro government also took a series of measures prioritizing the interests of capital over the everyday needs of Venezuelans. For example, in January of 2019, in one of his first policy announcements upon being sworn in, Maduro introduced a $1 billion plan to "beautify" major cities. This announcement, as Alejandro Valesco pointed out, "constituted a major affront to the poorest in Venezuela facing medicine, food and currency shortages."[32] In December of the same year, Maduro announced presidential decree number 4,080, giving tax breaks to companies that import processed goods. The decree is a huge stimulus to big business as it exempts, for six months, the payment of value added tax, tax of importation, and the rate for determination of the customs regime. Most of these imports come from major U.S. retailers like Walmart and Costco. [33] Neoliberal measures such as these continue to benefit fractions of the ruling class bourgeoisie to the detriment of working people. This tax exemption for certain sectors of capital will result in the loss of billions of dollars from taxes, which could be used for wage increases to keep up with inflation or for other social programs to alleviate or at least mitigate the suffering of regular working people.

In 2017, the National Constituent Assembly (ANC) approved the Foreign Investment Law, which improved conditions for foreign capital. Critics of the law have pointed out that it contradicts both Chávez's 2001 Hydrocarbons Law, which ensured Venezuelan control over joint ventures, and a 2007 Chávez decree that capped foreign oil deals at 40 percent.[34] One critic called the law "one of the most servile laws [to capital] in the world."[35] Maduro gave even more incentives to capital when he opened up special economic zones (SEZs), which offer incentives of all types to private investors. The 2021 Law of Special Economic Zones requires the privatization of various state-owned companies and the designation of certain geographic areas to be governed by special laws, distinct from the laws of the rest of the country, that orient toward free market economics in order to attract foreign investment by foreign investors. Under the law, lower tax rates and tariff benefits are offered to foreign investors while national laws that protect workers' rights can be suspended. Across the world, SEZs have a long history of blatant labor rights violations due to the weaker and more relaxed worker protections in these designated areas than in the rest of the country.[36] Oscar Figuera, secretary-general of the Venezuelan Communist Party, rightly described the law as favoring capital over Venezuelan workers' interests.[37]

In August of 2018, the Maduro government unveiled a comprehensive package of economic reforms under the name Economic Recovery, Growth, and Prosperity Plan. While the plan did include a few reforms that temporarily benefited workers, the majority of the measures benefited the business class at the expense of workers. One reform that benefited workers was the monetary reconversion, which knocked off five zeros from the currency while raising the minimum monthly salary, effectively raising the purchasing power of monthly salaries. But this benefit disappeared shortly after its implementation, due to soaring inflation rates. Many of the other measures were concessions to the business class, and in the interests of the opposition to the Maduro regime. Some of these reforms included measures that curtailed workers' rights, gave huge subsidies and tax exemptions to employers, created a de facto elimination of price controls, and eliminated many collective worker contracts that were results of decades of struggle.[38]

Memorandum 2792 is another component of the Economic Recovery Plan that protects the interests of capital. The memorandum severely weakens collective bargaining rights, eliminates the right to strike, and imposes new wage scales, which put further downward pressure on the purchasing power of working-class wages. The memorandum states that when a company faces financial crisis, a special commission would be formed to authorize employer non-compliance with collectively bargained agreements.[39] One example of how this affects workers is the case of the Union of Graphic Arts Workers and the Association of Graphic Arts Industrialists. In the process of collective bargaining, the workers had won some small victories. But when the two sides brought the agreement to the Labor Inspection Office, it was determined that the agreement was "too burdensome for the employer" and the institutional representatives kept the contract from being signed.[40] As Leander Perez points out, the capitalists were, as a result, emboldened and demanded more concessions from the workers.[41]

Perhaps the most egregious concession to capital is the Arco Minero project. In 2016, the Maduro administration opened the Orinoco Mining Belt for mineral exploitation. This territory, which makes up over 12 percent of the country's area, is a repository of minerals like gold, oil, gas, bauxite, and coltan and is the country's principle source of fresh water. The project is certain to be an environmental and social disaster, as it will displace populations, poison rivers and land, destroy mountain ecologies, and disrupt the fragile ecosystem of the rainforests.

The project was promoted as a solution to the country's declining GDP and depleted reserves. Maduro was correct that something had to be done, but this solution was an abandonment of national sovereignty and a return to the same neoliberal, neo-colonial arrangements that social movements, workers' movements, Chávez, and the Bolivarian process had been fighting against for decades. Venezuela was on the cutting edge of anti-neoliberalism in the region at the end of the century, and the Arco Minero was a major reversal and setback to that project. In fact, a similar plan was rejected by Chávez years before due to environmental concerns and in recognition of indigenous communities' human and territorial rights.[42] Maduro's plan of privatization of the nation's extractive industries was also an abandonment and reversal of Chávez's strategy of state control of resources and the socialization of its profits.

For the project, Maduro invited 150 multinational corporations from around the world, including the United States, China, Canada, and Russia, to bid for concessions.[43] Extremely favorable conditions were offered to multinationals to exploit Venezuela's mineral resources. Many of the multinational corporations that Maduro offered favorable contracts to were corporations that Chávez had excluded from the country years before. In fact, the first offer was made to Barrick Gold Corporation, a giant Canadian gold-mining corporation that Chávez had kicked out of the country a decade prior.[44] In 2011, when Chávez nationalized the mines, Barrick demanded hundreds of millions of dollars in compensation. To lure Barrick back into the country,

Maduro not only agreed to pay this "debt" but also offered the corporation both a ten-year tax holiday and pledged to develop the regional infrastructure at the state's expense.[45] Scholar Mike Gonzalez accurately describes the project as "colonialism by invitation."[46]

The Arco Minero project is not just a threat to ecosystems, biodiversity, and indigenous communities, it has also contributed to a rise in violence in the region, intensifying the insecurity and distress that the crisis has wrought. Every year since Maduro's 2016 decree to establish the Arco Minero project, violence has increased in all the municipalities of Bolivar state and all the territory located south of the Orinoco River.[47] Massacres carried out by criminal gangs, armed guerillas and by the Venezuelan state have increased since 2016. In 2018, the number of massacres doubled those in 2017. Most of the violence and massacres have taken place in the southern part of Bolivar state, directly affecting indigenous communities.

Venezuelans living in the mining state of Bolivar face constant harassment, persecution, and murder. Perhaps the most prominent case was the murder of Charlie Peñaloza Rivas in December of 2018. Peñaloza was a member of the Pemón nation, one of the twenty-six indigenous groups in Venezuela. Members of Pemón have long fought against both illegal miners operating in their lands and the Venezuelan state's extractivist plans to open the Orinoco to multi-national corporations for mining. Peñaloza was shot along with two others in a confrontation with military counterintelligence troops in an outpost in Canaima National Park, in the Guayana region of Bolivar state.[48] The military claims that the reason for their operation was to clear the region of illegal mining, despite the fact that members of Pemón were protesting both illegal mining and the Arco Minero mining plan. After the confrontation, the Venezuelan Political Ecology Observatory, which is led by indigenous and environmental leaders, issued a statement declaring that the increased violence in the region was a direct result of the Maduro government's extractivist agenda in the Orinoco Mining Arc. The statement cites the indigenous autonomy provisions in the 1999 constitution, which states that the "principle guardians of the national territory are indigenous, and in the case of Guayana, the Pemón people" and that the Arco Minero developmental plan undermines this indigenous autonomy.[49]

State violence against indigenous communities led to one of the most serious acts of aggression in the Orinoco: the Santa Elena Massacre, which occurred on February 22 and 23 of 2019. The massacre, carried out by state security forces, resulted in eight deaths, five of which were indigenous.[50] Prior to the opening of the Arco Minero, the territorial divisions where the mining is taking place had lower homicide rates compared to the main urban centers. By 2018, municipalities in the Orinoco, like El Callao (620 deaths per 100,000 inhabitants) and Roscio (458 deaths per 100,000 inhabitants), became two of the cities with the highest violent death rates in the country.[51]

The economic mismanagement, extractivist, and anti-worker politics of the Maduro administration are not simply mistakes or poor technocratic decisions. Decisions are not made in the abstract but made in the context of real historical circumstances. It is always important to consider the balance of forces to understand why certain measures are taken and why certain policies are implemented. Part of the reason why the Chávez and the Bolivarian process was able to implement radical, anti-neoliberal, pro-worker measures was because it came at a time of high levels of struggle with massive movements in the streets demanding radical change. Chávez did not make the revolution; it was the revolution that made Chávez. It was massive social movements and the organized activity of revolutionaries that pushed Chávez to the left and radicalized both Chávez and the Bolivarian process. George Ciccariello-Maher's book *We Created Chávez* does an excellent job at exploring this relationship.[52]

The state of movements and the state of the left are not the same as they were in the early years of the Bolivarian process. There are many reasons for this, including the incorporation of social movement activists into the state apparatus, the structure of the PSUV (especially after Maduro took over) limiting popular participation, violence carried out by the right-wing, the development of a new ruling bureaucracy within the party, and concessions and alliances the state made with powerful private capitalists and the repression of movements and more critical sections of the left. As many of the former reasons were discussed in chapter 4, this section will briefly discuss government repression of movements in the popular sectors and the left.

The campaign that the Maduro government has waged against ordinary Venezuelans from the country's popular sectors, independent labor unions, and the government's left-wing critics has become increasingly brutal in recent years. The murder of Charlie Peñaloza and the repression of indigenous resistance to the Arco Minero plan mentioned above is just one example of this campaign.

In June of 2018, healthcare workers began to protest the government's flattening of wages and elimination of worker bonuses, both in contravention to their collective contracts. Other demands included raising wages to equal the cost of the basic family food basket and to respect collective agreements. Other sectors of workers joined the protests: oil, electricity, education, as well as workers in other state agencies. By September, the protests had spread across the country. Ruben Gonzalez, the general secretary of Ferrominera Del Orinoco Union was arrested along with seven other trade unionists after participating in a demonstration in Caracas. A few weeks later, four other unionists were arrested. One worker, Rodney Alvarez, was sentenced to seven years in prison. Thirty other workers and union leaders in Guayana were threatened with prison for promoting and participating in labor protests.[53]

Others on the left have also faced government repression. An investigation conducted by the Venezuelan Program of Education-Action in Human Rights (PROVEA) found that forty-five people, all associated with the left and all identified as Chavistas, were attacked in various ways. Several of them ran candidacies outside of the PSUV and were subsequently arrested. Eleven of them faced retaliation upon reporting corruption in public institutions. Thirteen were dismissed from their public institutions due to critiquing specific government actions.[54]

The attacks and suppression of Marea Socialista is yet another example of the Maduro Government's repression of its left critics. Marea is a Trotskyist socialist organization within the broader Chavista movement in Venezuela. They joined the PSUV in 2008 when Chávez called for a unification of all Chavista political forces. Marea left the PSUV in 2015 due to critiques of the direction that Maduro was taking the country, a direction that they believed was contrary to the legacy of Chávez. Soon after they left the party, they began to face repression from the Maduro government. When Marea requested to be recognized as an official party, the National Electoral Council (CNE) rejected their petition. To be able to nominate candidates for parliamentary or presidential elections political parties must be first recognized, then approved for a party card by the CNE. Marea complied with all the requirements of the law but was denied both recognition as a party and the official card to run candidates. The justification was that Marea Socialista was a "slogan" and could not be used as a name for a political party. [55] Marea was just one of nine organizations in 2015 whom the CNE denied recognition.[56] The following year, a commission of heavily armed police broke into Marea's headquarters "in order to locate objects of criminal interest."[57] Nothing was found in the raid, and the police left without seizing anything. Marea released a public statement denouncing the raid as an attack on their political liberties, an act of intimidation, and an illegal interference of their privacy.[58]

The communes have also faced their share of repression from the government. One example is the case of the commune *Dios Es Fuente de Agua Viva*, located in the state of Portuguesa. Ten members of the commune were arrested in 2010 after they occupied a rice-processing factory to stop the public company from being privatized. The communards' seventy-one-day detention came to an end only after a mobilization organized by dozens of popular movements demanded their release.[59]

Some level of repression to defend the state against coup plotters and imperialists may be necessary, but that is very different from the systematic criminalization of dissent, especially against those who played a significant role in the early years of the Bolivarian process, such as those in the popular sectors, labor unions, communes, the left, and critical and dissident Chavistas.

In short, the Maduro government made alliances with different sectors of Venezuelan society, eventually changing the class character and therefore the politics of the ruling party—the PSUV. Concessions to the business class were easier to push through when there were lower levels of class struggle, which, as argued above, government repression has contributed to. These factors resulted in the Maduro government carrying out class collaborationist neoliberal reforms, albeit under the name of "socialism," which deepened the crisis in Venezuela.

U.S. Sanctions

Although the crisis in Venezuela precedes U.S. sanctions, the sanctions have no doubt exacerbated the crisis and caused untold pain and misery for hundreds of thousands of Venezuelans. The United States under Barack Obama issued its first round of sanctions in December of 2014. The Venezuela Defense of Human Rights and Civil Society Act imposed targeted sanctions on Venezuela, including visa restrictions on various Venezuelan officials and their family members. Just a few months later, on March 9, 2015, Obama signed an executive order declaring Venezuela an "unusual and extraordinary threat to the national security of the United States" and expanded the sanctions further. This executive order, which was the ostensible justification for Obama's second round of sanctions, set the stage for the sanctions that were to come under Donald Trump. All subsequent sanctions implemented by Trump were implemented within the remit of Obama's executive order. Finally, as one of Obama's last acts as president, in January of 2017, he extended the sanctions on Venezuela yet again.

Picking up where Obama left off, in the first month of taking office, Trump renewed and expanded the sanctions and met with opposition leader Leopoldo Lopez's wife a few days afterward. Over the course of Trump's presidency, his administration continued to expand and deepen the sanctions on the Venezuelan government. Most notably was executive order 13884, which froze all Venezuelan government assets in the United States and banned Americans from doing business with the Venezuelan government.[60]

The combination of legal and economic sanctions have imposed a litany of debilitating penalties on the Venezuelan government, driving the Venezuelan economy into even deeper problems than it was already in. The following are but a few of the penalties imposed on the country: prohibited U.S. institutions and citizens from trading in Venezuelan debt; froze all government assets; prevented the country from restructuring its foreign debt or payment schedules; blocked payments sent by countries participating in its program for preferential payment of oil; and banned the sale of billions of dollars in trade credits.[61] The sanctions also closed off Venezuela to its most important oil market, the United States, and confiscated properties abroad, like the U.S.-based Citgo, which the state depended on for sources of income.

The August 2017 sanctions critically impacted Venezuela's oil production, causing a loss of $6 billion in revenue in just 2018 alone.[62] This figure is important because virtually every necessity (food, medicine, clean water, electricity, transportation, etc.), is funded through oil export revenue.[63] Sanctions have frozen $17 billion worth of the country's assets and were expected to cost the country around $11 billion in export losses in 2019.[64] In other words, the sanctions are costing Venezuelans $30 million a day.

The Washington, DC–based Center for Economic Policy Research (CEPR) published a 2019 report detailing the effects of U.S. sanctions on Venezuela. The authors, economists Mark Weisbrot and Jeffrey Sachs, reported that "in the week of March 15, U.S. imports of Venezuelan oil fell to zero for the first time, and they remained at zero for two weeks." Oil export revenues in 2019 were projected to fall by an unprecedented 67.2 percent from 2018 because of the tightening sanctions. They also found that between 2017 and 2018 alone, the sanctions killed an estimated 40,000 Venezuelans and plunged many more into precarity. Over 300,000 people were put at risk due to the lack of medicine and healthcare, including 80,000 HIV-positive Venezuelans who have gone without antiretroviral drugs for years now. Additionally, obtaining needed cardiovascular medicine or insulin is a challenge for the 16,000 Venezuelans who need dialysis, the four million with diabetes and hypertension, and the 16,000 people who have cancer.[65]

The UN Human Rights Council adopted a resolution denouncing the U.S. sanctions, and one of its human rights experts, Idriss Jazairy, said "the use of sanctions by outside powers to overthrow an elected government is in violation of all norms of international law."[66, 67] One UN rapporteur called the sanctions "economic warfare."[68] The strategy of the United States and the domestic right-wing opposition seems to be, to use the words of Richard Nixon, "to make the economy scream."

The End of the Pink Tide

In order to understand the rise and the fall of the Pink Tide and its impacts on the communes, it is important to first understand the era that preceded it. From the late 1930s until the late 1970s, an economic model called import substitution industrialization (ISI) was predominant across Latin America. ISI was a state-led industrialization project in which foreign imports were replaced with domestic production. The idea being that the state would reduce its foreign dependency through the domestic production of industrialized products. Self-sufficiency was to be achieved through the creation of internal markets and local production was to be developed by state intervention in the economy, through methods such as nationalization, subsidization of vital industries, protectionist trade policies, or increased tax regimes.

Economic crises in the late 1970s ended the ISI era, and neoliberalism became the predominant economic ideology in the region. After the world economy went into a recession in the late 1970s and early 1980s, Latin America faced hyperinflation and a severe debt crisis. As a response, rightwing regimes, military dictatorships, and avowedly neoliberal administrations in Latin America resorted to a series of neoliberal measures. During the subsequent decades, the 1980s and 1990s, countries across Latin America went through a period of neoliberal restructuring. Liberalization of international trade and investment, privatization of public enterprises, deregulation of labor and environmental statutes and the gutting of social services were carried out across the region.

During this era, the left was annihilated by right-wing authoritarian regimes across the region. In Argentina, between 1976–1983, the authoritarian regime disappeared 30,000 people, targeting urban labor unions, left political parties, human rights organizations, peasant associations, and women's organizations. The left was similarly decimated under Pinochet in Chile, under Brazil's dictatorship, as well as in Uruguay, Paraguay, and Bolivia. The defeat of the left was a necessary step to the rollout of neoliberal restructuring in the region. By 1990, the Latin American left was at its lowest point in modern history.

The result of decades of neoliberal restructuring was increased levels of poverty, inequality, and informalization of work and the decline of wages.[69, 70] The poverty rate in Latin America increased in the 1980s and 1990s, reaching 44 percent in 2002.[71, 72] The average Gini index for the region increased drastically throughout these decades, increasing by 2.2 points from the early 1980s to 1990, 1.7 points over the 1990s, and a further 1.2 points during the recession of 2001–2002, to a total of 5.1 points over the neoliberal period.[73, 74] By 2002, Latin America continued to be the most unequal region of the world.[75, 76]

In 1998, the region experienced its first crisis in the neoliberal period. Brazil and Argentina experienced the worst financial crises in their history between 1998 and 2002. South America's aggregate GDP was negative for four years in a row.[77] What this meant was that poverty levels, unemployment levels, health indicators, education indicators, and nutritional intake massively deteriorated during those four years. This deterioration occurred from a very low base point to begin with, as this crisis came after decades of neoliberal restructuring. Politically, it is important to point out that all the governments in the region were right or center right and openly and avowedly neoliberal. Their solution to the crisis was more neoliberalism, because their diagnosis of the problem was that neoliberalism was not implemented enough.[78, 79] This may have had some ideological appeal in the early 1980s, but by the turn of the century this was no longer the case.

As a response to the crisis, a proliferation of extra-parliamentary struggles emerged, opening up a completely new period and political terrain in Latin America. Unemployed workers' movements, informal sector workers' movements, indigenous movements, peasant occupations of land, new women's movements, new youth revolts, and revolts of students all emerged in the region, making Latin America the leading edge of anti-neoliberal resistance in the world.

Many of these movements shifted toward electoral politics for a variety of reasons. Left-wing movements across South America moderated their radicalism in a myriad of ways, and their mass bases were subordinated to left parties' electoralism.[80, 81] Social movements were demobilized, and their leaders were absorbed by the institutional left and the capitalist state.[82] The demobilization of radical movements undermined more far-reaching transformations that could address the root causes of poverty and inequality.[83] But what it did lead to was electoral victories.

Between 2003 and 2011, Latin America was characterized principally by left-wing and center-left parties coming to office. This "tide" of left and center left electoral victories came to be known as the Pink Tide. This upset the previous domination of right and center-right governments of the 1990s. These left and left-of-center governments associated with the Pink Tide were able to challenge and even reverse the most egregious components of the neoliberal project.[84] The trend began with the election of Hugo Chávez in Venezuela in 1998 and spread to many other Latin American countries with Bolivia, Ecuador, Brazil, Argentina, Uruguay, Paraguay, Nicaragua, and Honduras all electing left or center-left governments. Essentially every Latin American country in South America except Colombia elected a left or leftof-center government. The shift represented a move toward more progressive economic policies and coincided with a parallel trend of democratization of Latin America following decades of inequality.

Left-leaning movements in the mid to late 2000s improved the standard of living for millions of people by winning social programs funded by a commodity boom that began in 2003.[85, 86, 87] This boom was driven by demand from emerging markets like China and India as the price of primary commodities such as soy, iron ore, copper, and most importantly oil reached new highs.

In addition to increased social spending, the boom also provided these new left-leaning governments leverage against U.S. imperial control over the region, especially as the Bush and Obama administrations were focused on their wars in the Middle East. Additionally, because the Pink Tide coincided with a period of capitalist dynamism, driven by accumulation on the world market, principally but not exclusively by China's industrialization, Pink

Tide governments were able to delay a series of crucial class questions or class decisions. As Jeffery Webber has argued, the commodity boom allowed Pink Tide governments to do two things at once.[88, 89] First, they were able to introduce modest reforms through royalties and tax regimes. With the price of natural gas and oil so high, even a modest increase in royalties and taxes created a huge influx in state revenue. This allowed for the creation of many distribution programs such as cash transfer programs, new infrastructure programs which functioned to meet the most pressing demands of ordinary people, and new jobs programs. During this period, under Pink Tide governments, living standards improved and poverty, income inequality, and unemployment were all reduced.[90, 91, 92]

But while they were able, through modest royalty and tax increases, to fund successful antipoverty programs for ordinary people, there was no real meaningful transformation of social property relations, no transformation of these countries in the international division of labor, and no challenge to the prerogatives of transnational capital.[93, 94] Even in the most radical governments in the Pink Tide, Venezuela, Bolivia, and Ecuador, there was no break with extractivism. All three of these countries deepened their dependence on the export of minerals and hydrocarbons.[95] In fact, Venezuela's dependence on oil exports increased during the Chávez and Maduro era, leaving the country dependent on and beholden to global financial and oil markets.[96, 97]

In other words, because of the commodities boom, left-leaning governments were able to reduce poverty and inequality, and expand a variety of different social programs without confronting capital or the global capitalist order in any serious way.[98, 99, 100] For example, in Venezuela, the most radical of the Pink Tide governments, 70 percent of the economy remained in private capitalist hands throughout the Chavista era.[101] Pink Tide governments became what Eduardo Gudynas called "compensatory states," in which wealth was redistributed but they did not change society's underlying class structure or seriously confront private property or profitability.[102] This model and the mutually beneficial relationship between capital and labor rested on a fragile base and was only temporary because of it being contingent on high commodity prices.

This delicate balance sustained itself until 2011–2012 when China's economy began to slow down. China's rates of growth dropped to the lowest since the 1990s. Once the Chinese economy began to slow, the high commodity prices that sustained the Pink Tide governments began to fall and the crisis came to Latin America. The ability to appease both labor and capital came to an end with the end of the commodities boom. By 2015, commodity prices hit a twelve-year low.[103] The slowdown in the global economy and the drastic drop in the price of basic commodities, especially oil, weakened leftleaning governments in Latin America, leading to the decline of the Pink Tide. The slowdown had perhaps the deepest impact in Venezuela, where oil exports account for 95 percent of its export earnings and oil revenues make up more than 90 percent of the government's budget.

The end of the commodity boom forced Pink Tide governments to make a decision, a class decision that they had managed to delay while commodity prices were high. Now in a situation of austere state revenues, who was going to pay for the crisis? Was it going to be labor and regular working people, the social bases that supported and voted for the Pink Tide governments in power, or was it going to be capital? Almost without exception Pink Tide governments chose the former and instituted austerity packages that disproportionately affected their own bases.[104] [105] Consequently, these governments lost both of their bases of support, labor, who had to pay for the crisis through massive cuts in social spending, and capital, who had learned to live with the left during periods of high net profits but decided to jump ship with the drop of their rates of profit and return to their more natural home, the right. Workers began to revolt against austerity measures, and capital engaged in a variety of different parliamentary and extra-parliamentary strategies, including coups of different types to oust left governments from power.[106, 107]

As a result, the momentum shifted toward the right. The right defeated many of the left-leaning Pink Tide governments electorally with Mauricio Macri in Argentina in 2015, Sebastian Pinera in Chile in 2017, Jair Bolsonaro in Brazil in 2018, and in 2015 the right wing in Venezuela won an important congressional election. When they could not win electorally, they seized power by other means. The coups in Brazil in 2016, Honduras in 2009, and Paraguay in 2008 are a few examples. The problem for the right is that once in office, they had no real solution to the crisis of capitalism.

The Future of the Communes

The economic war, the Maduro economic mismanagement, U.S. sanctions, the end of the commodities boom, and the decline of the Pink Tide have put the communes in the most trying and difficult situation since the 2010 Organic Law of the Communes legitimated the communes as a legitimate form of popular power organization. The crisis has made it not only more difficult for *voceros* and commune and communal council members to organize but also, since a majority of communes rely on some amount of government funding, drastic declines in government revenue have had a deleterious impact. As the crisis deepened, the government largely cutback on funding to local communities, and the communes and communal councils suffered significantly.

The most recent numbers produced by the Ministry of Communes puts the official number of communal councils and communes at 47,000 and 3,000, respectively.[108] It is difficult to attain accurate data on Venezuela because the government has become increasingly unreliable in releasing data. But based on my research and conversations I have had with those in the communes, it is fair to say that while the official number of communes has stayed about the same, the number of communes and communal councils that are active has decreased. The crisis has taken a toll.

Despite all the obstacles of the crisis, there were opportunities for the communes to expand both qualitatively and quantitatively, but these opportunities were stymied. The first was a proposal by the National Network of Comuneros to respond to the crisis of rampant food shortages, malnutrition, and hunger. To combat this problem, the National Network of Comuneros proposed the creation of a national communal enterprise for the production and distribution of food.[109] The idea behind the proposal was for the government to invest in the communes to produce and distribute food to ensure affordable food reached those who needed it most. This proposal would have reduced the dependence on foreign imports, diversified the economy making it less vulnerable to crisis produced by the vicissitudes of the market, and expanded the communes, the most democratic institutions in the country. Maduro rejected the proposal and instead instituted Local Committees for Food Distribution and Production (CLAPs). Despite having the word "production" in the title, all food that is distributed through the CLAPs is imported.[110] The CLAPs are organs of the government and thus are under the control of the local PSUV officials and easier to control. With CLAPS, PSUV officials simply tell people what to do while decisions in the communes are made democratically in citizens' assemblies. When given the choice to either continue to give preferential dollars and subsidies to the business class (the class responsible for the economic war) to import food or to invest in the communes (the bedrock of the Bolivarian process), Maduro chose the former.

Another opportunity for the expansion of the communes occurred when the majority of Venezuelan opposition parties decided to boycott the 2017 elections. This opened spaces in some municipalities for commune *voceros* and other grassroots movements to run alternative candidates to those advanced by the PSUV. Many took advantage of this opening but faced significant resistance from the National Electoral Council (CNE) and the PSUV.[111] The case of Angel Prado is instructive. Angel Prado is a *vocero* in one of the most successful communes in the country, *El Maizal*, located in Lara state. He was elected to the National Constituent Assembly (ANC) in July of 2017. Later that year, Prado decided to run for mayor of his municipality against the PSUV's handpicked candidate. His candidacy had the support of four left-wing parties. He had secured more than 9,000 signatures from local residents in support of his candidacy and nearly a thousand *El Maizal* members marched to the ANC in Caracas to demand that his candidacy was authorized.[112] The CNE blocked his candidacy, stating that he must have permission from the ANC before launching his candidacy. The ANC never made public the reason for denying Prado's candidacy.[113] Reinaldo Iturriza, the former Minister of Communes said that the decision to block a prominent commune *vocero* from participating in the municipal election was a "defeat for all of Chavismo."[114]

Despite facing major setbacks during the crisis, and despite the obstacles of operating within a market economy, the communes and communal councils remain one of the few spaces in Venezuela that dispute power. They remain the most democratic and genuine spaces for building participatory democracy. They remain an alternative to the limitations of liberal representative democracy. And they remain a viable alternative to the policies that drove the economy into the crisis as well as an alternative mode of development to neoliberal development. However, for the communes to achieve their goal of creating a communal state, it will have to be the result of their own self-activity; it will not come from above, not from the Maduro regime, and certainly not come from the hostile right wing, but rather from below, from the initiative of Venezuelans themselves and the communes specifically.

For most of the lifespan of the communes there was a relationship between the Bolivarian state and the grassroots that, while not without its conflicts and contradictions, could be described as cooperative in that the two worked together in a dynamic between bottom-up and bottom-down organization. The organs of communal councils themselves were created and organized by the grassroots, then later formalized and institutionalized by Chávez. There were already thousands of communal councils in existence, although not necessarily by that name, when Chávez drafted the communal council law in 2006, and there were already hundreds of communes operating by the time the law of communes was written into law and formally legitimated. These popular organizations were initiated by the grassroots and then made into government policies, and for a time supported and promoted by the government, though not without some friction and conflict. Legislation tended to follow bottom up initiatives, but that they were initiated at all, and with such enthusiasm, is a testament to the commitment the Chavista government had toward participatory democracy and the inclusion of wider, traditionally excluded sectors of society into the decision-making process. The Chávez government did not just legitimate already existing participatory initiatives from below, he promoted them and broadened them in ways that facilitated the expansion of these organs across the country. Chávez was clear on his support of the communal project. He saw the commune as the fundamental component of the Bolivarian process, the organ of popular power that would serve as the building block for a new kind of society. This was summed up in Chávez's now famous declaration that it was either "*La comuna o nada*" (the commune or nothing), in his last major speech, Golpe De Timon, before he died. The communal state was not meant to be a permanent parallel structure, something to stand beside the bourgeoisie state, or just some other sector among many in society, but rather to overcome, to take over and replace the bourgeoisie state. Despite this being the vision of Chávez and thousands of grassroots *comuneros*, this was not a position that the entire PSUV held or one that even all Chavista officials held. Many local officials and even self-described Chavistas are hostile to communes because they see them as a direct threat to their power, and in a sense they are.

In recent years, the cooperative relationship between the communes and the state has waned. Maduro has proven to be more of an obstacle to the expansion and development of the communes than a proponent. But make no mistake, the right-wing opposition continues to be outright hostile to the communal movement, and a coup-led government would make matters even worse. Nevertheless, the communes can no longer depend on the government for support. Financially, state support for the communes has disappeared due to the crisis, and politically, state support has dried up due to the alliances the Maduro government has made to the business class and the consequent changes in the class character of the PSUV.

Despite the changing relationship between the state and the communes, the latter continues to struggle to transform society and build toward a communal state. Partly because of this waning relationship, the communes that were able to take over production, create their own source of revenue, and gain more autonomy from the state are the ones that have proven to be the most durable and the most likely to maintain high levels of activity. Another major factor in determining the health of communal councils and communes is their connection to other communes and organs of popular power. The unification of communes is integral to building the kind of power necessary to overcome the challenges that the communal movement is facing. There have been a number of examples of communes unifying and collaborating to strengthen their forces. The aforementioned National Network of Comuneros is a network made up of 150 different communes across the country. The *Gran Asamblea Comuna* is made up of twelve communes and 159 communal councils in the states of Lara and Portuguesa. The *Bloque Gran Comunal* in the state of Carabobo is another formal structure in which thirty-six communes coordinate projects in their respective territories. It is these types of unifications of communal and grassroots movements for popular power, coupled with efforts to prioritize taking over the means of production, that are necessary to build the requisite power to overcome the challenges that lay ahead.

NOTES

1. Corina Pons, "Venezuela 2016 hits 800 percent, GDP shrinks 19 percent: document," *Reuters*, January 20, 2017, https://www.reuters.com/article/us-venezuela-economy-idUSK BN154244.

2. Alessandro Di Stasio, "Inflación de 2018 cerró en 1.698.488%, según la Asamblea Nacional," *Efecto Cocuyo*, January 9, 2019, https://www.eluniversal.com/economia/30142/.

3. Cira Pascual Marquina, "Working-Class Struggle in Venezuela: A Conversation with Leander Perez," *Venezuelanalysis*, February 21, 2020, https://venezuelanalysis.com/analysis/14792.

4. Wladimir Abreu, "Economía Informal y Cuarentena, Una Pareja Dispareja," *Aporrea*, May 12, 2020, https://www.aporrea.org/economia/a290423.html.

5. Cira Pascual Marquina, "Working-Class Struggle in Venezuela: A Conversation with Leander Perez," *Venezuelanalysis*, February 21, 2020, https://venezuelanalysis.com/analysis/14792.

6. United Nations Human Rights Office of the High Commissioner, "Violaciones de los Derechos Humanos en la Republica Bolivariana de Venezuela: Una Espiral Descendente que no Parece Tener Fin," *Naciones Unidas Derechos Humanos Oficina Del Alto Comisionado*, June 2018.

7. Caritas Venezuela, "S.A.M.A.N Nutrition Infantil y Seguridad Alimentaria Abril 2020," *Caritas Venezuela*, April 2020, tas-Informe-de-Desnutricion-Abril-2020.pdf.

8. Deutch Welle, "ACNUR: 'Nos preocupa que se invisibilice la crisis de refugiados y migrantes de Venezuela," *Aporrea*, November 29, 2019, https://www.aporrea.org/ddhh/n349504.html.

9. United Nations Human Rights Office of the High Commissioner, "Venezuela: Crisis de Refugiados y Migrantes: El Éxodo Mas Grande de la Historia Reciente de América Latina," May 2020.

10. Ibid.

11. Aporrea-Agencias, "Venezuela es el Segundo País del Mundo con Mayor Número de Desplazados, Según Acnur," *Aporrea*, June 20, 2020, https://www.aporrea.org/ddhh/n356323.html.

12. United Nations Human Rights Office of the High Commissioner, "Venezuela: Crisis de Refugiados y Migrantes: El Éxodo Mas Grade de la Historia Reciente de América Latina," May 2020.

13. Gabriel Hetland, "A History of Violence," *Jacobin Magazine*, September 13, 2016c, https://www.jacobinmag.com/2016/09/venezuela-opposition-maduro-chavez-coup-protests/.

14. Tamara Pearson, "Venezuelan Government Confronts Milk Hoarding," *Venezuelanalysis*, December 7, 2011, https://venezuelanalysis.com/news/6673#:~:text=Venezuelan%20Government%20Confronts%20Milk%20Hoarding%20Since%20confronting%20Italian,offensive%20to%20get%20hoarded%20milk%20to%20the%20people.

15. La Iguana, "3800 More Toilet Paper Packs Found Hoarded," *Venezuelanalysis*, October 22, 2013, https://venezuelanalysis.com/news/10109.

16. Lucas Koerner, "Venezuela Ramps up Anti-Crime Offensive, Targets Hoarding and Contraband," *Venezuelanalysis*, August 10, 2015, https://venezuelanalysis.com/news/11468.

17. Corey Fischer-Hoffman, "Venezuela Officials Seize Warehouse with Enormous Cache of Hoarded Items as Opposition Calls for Strike," *Venezuela Analysis*, January 14, 2015, https://venezuelanalysis.com/news/11158.

18. George Ciccariello-Maher, "Venezuela: Call it What it IsA Coup," *The Nation*, January 25, 2019, https://www.thenation.com/article/archive/venezuela-coup-guaido-maduro/.

19. Bolivarian Republic of Venezuela Constitution of 1999 Article 233.

20. Ibid.

21. Ernesto Londoño and Nicholas Casey, "El Gobierno de Trump discutió un posible golpe de Estado con Militares Rebeldes en Venezuela," *New York Times*, September 8, 2018, https://www.nytimes.com/es/2018/09/08/espanol/trump-golpe-de-estado-maduro.html.

22. Jorge Martin, "Chavistas March Against Imperialism: What Is the Next Step in Trump's Coup?" *Venezuelanalysis*, February 19, 2019, https://venezuelanalysis.com/analysis/14311.

23. Jessica Donati and Vivian Salama, "Pence Pledged U.S. Backing Before Venezuela Opposition Leader's Move," *The Wall Street Journal*, January 25, 2019, https://www.wsj.com/articles/a-call-from-pence-helped-set-an-uncertain-new-course-in-venezuela-11548430259.

24. Gabriel Hetland, "Stop Talking About Coups," *Jacobin Magazine*, September 17, 2019, https://jacobinmag.com/2018/09/venezuela-maduro-coup-trump-united-states-intervention.

25. Frederico Fuentes, "Venezuela's Crisis: A View from the Communes," *Green Left Weekly*, May 10, 2019, https://www.greenleft.org.au/content/venezuela-crisis-view-communes.

26. Orlando Avendaño, "Enviados de Guaidó se Apropian de Fondos Para Ayudar Humanitaria en Colombia," *Panam Post*, June 18, 2019, https://es.panampost.com/orlando-avendano/2019/06/14/enviados-de-guaido-se-apropian-de-fondos-para-ayuda-humanitaria-en-colombia/.

27. Jim Wyss, "Poll Shows Venezuela's Guaidó Is Losing Popularity and Has Shrunk to Maduro Level," *Miami Herald*, December 4, 2019, tion-world/world/americas/article238040219.html.

28. Clifford Krauss, "Oil Prices: What's Behind the Drop? Simple Economics," *New York Times*, March 30, 2016, https://www.nytimes.com/2015/01/13/business/energy-environment/oil-prices.html.

29. Virginia Lopez, "Venezuela's Economic Crisis Worsens as Oil Prices Fall," *Al Jazeera*, January 8, 2016, oil-prices-fall-160108105010345.html.

30. Juan Manuare and Carlos E. Juarena,"Venezuela: A Balance Sheet of 2016 and Perspectives for 2017," *In Defence of Marxism*, February 27, 2017, la-a-balance-sheet-of-2016-and-perspectives-for-2017.htm.

31. Heirbert Barreto, "Fuga de Capitales y Desfalco en Venezuela (1999–2013) Datos Para una Auditoria, Ponencia de Heibet Barreto," *Aporrea*, June 9, 2015, http://www.aporrea.org/contraloria/n271878.html.

32. Alejandro Valesco, "A Call for Cooler Heads on Venezuela: How to Criticize Maduro While Opposing U.S. Regime Change," *In These Times*, March 11, 2019, times.com/article/21789/venezuela-maduro-trump-barrios-intervention-sanctions-chavismoguaido.

33. LaClase.info, "Maduro Entrega Seis Meses de Privilegios Fiscales a Los Empresarios Importadores," *LaClase.info*, January, 2020, meses-de-privilegios-fiscales-a-los-empresarios-importadores/.

34. Paul Dobson, "Venezuela Assumes OPEC Presidency, Unveils Foreign Oil Investment Deals," *Venezuelanalysis*, January 9, 2019, https://venezuelanalysis.com/news/14213.

35. Cira Pascual Marquina, "How to Get Venezuela's Economy Going Again: A Conversation with Luis Enrique Gavazut," *Venezuelanalysis*, January 3, 2019, https://venezuelanalysis.com/analysis/14203.

36. J. John, "Special Economic Zones: Their Impact on Labour," *Labour File* 6, no. 5 (2008).

37. Luis Britto Garcia, "Upcoming Legislation in Venezuela: Special Economic Zones," *Venezuelanalysis*, May 24, 2021, https://venezuelanalysis.com/analysis/15212.

38. Cira Pascual Marquina, "Working-Class Struggle in Venezuela: A Conversation with Leander Perez," *Venezuelanalysis*, February 21, 2020, https://venezuelanalysis.com/analysis/14792.

39. Ibid.

40. Ibid.

41. Ibid.

42. Mike Gonzalez, *The Ebb of the Pink Tide: The Decline of the Left in Latin America* (London: Pluto Press, 2019).

43. Ibid.

44. Ibid.

45. Ibid.

46. Ibid: 130.

47. Cesar Romero, "Evolucion de la violencia en el entorno minero del estado Bolivar (marzo de 2016-febrero de 20190," *Observatorio de Ecología Política de Venezuela*, May 26, 2020.

48. Bill Weinberg, "Forgotten Voices in Venezuelan Crisis," *Countervortex*, January 24, 2019, https://countervortex.org/blog/forgotten-voices-in-venezuela-crisis/#:~:text=Things%20are%20approaching%20a%20crisis%20point%20in%20the,thousands%20of%20supporters%20in%20Caracas%20on%20Jan.%2023.

49. Vladimir Aguilar Castro, "Los Episodios de Kanaimo (Canaima) en Tiempos de Jurisdicciones Indígenas en Venezuela," *Observatorio de Ecología Política de Venezuela*, December 13, 2018.

50. Cesar Romero, "Evolucion de la violencia en el entorno minero del estado Bolivar (marzo de 2016-febrero de 20190," *Observatorio de Ecología Política de Venezuela*, May 26, 2020.

51. Ibid.

52. George Ciccariello-Maher, *We Created Chávez: A Peoples History of the Venezuelan Revolution* (Durham, NC: Duke University Press, 2013).

53. Nacional Web, "Sindicalistas: En 2019 Recrudecerá Persecución para Impedir las Protestas," *El Nacional Web*, January 4, 2019, tas-2019-recrudecera-persecucion-para-impedir-las -protestas_265128/.

54. Vanessa Moreno Losada, "Provea: 45 Representantes del Chavismo Disidente Han Sido Agregados Por el Gobierno de Maduro," *Efecto Cocuyo*, November 6, 2018, https:// efectococuyo.com/politica/provea-45-representantes-del-chavismo-disidente-han-sido-agredidos -porel-gobierno-de-maduro/.

55. Carlos Crespo, "CNE: Marea Socialista no es una Denominación Partidista Sino Una Frase," *Crónica Uno*, May 19, 2015, https://cronica.uno/cne-marea-socialista-no-es-una -denominacion-partidista-sino-una-frase/.

56. Politika UCAB, "CNE Niega a Vente Venezuela y Marea Socialista Inscribirse como Partidos," *Politika UCAB*, May 18, 2015, https://politikaucab.net/2015/05/18/cne-niega-avente -venezuela-y-marea-socialista-inscribirse-como-partidos/.

57. Bernardo Luzardo, "Allanaron Sede del Movimiento Marea Socialista," *Globovision*, October 6, 2016, socialista.

58. Equipo Operativo Nacional de Marea Socialista, "Allanan Sede Nacional de Marea Socialista," *Rebelión*, November 6, 2016.

59. Ricardo Vaz, "Venezuela: Popular Movements Secure Release of Detained Communards," *Venezuelanalysis*, April 24, 2019, https://venezuelanalysis.com/news/14441.

60. Executive Order No. 13884, Federal Register, Vol. 84, No. 152, August 7, 2019, https:// www.treasury.gov/resource-center/sanctions/Programs/Documents/13884.pdf.

61. Branko Marcetic, "Sanctions Are Murder," *Jacobin Magazine*, May 6, 2019, https:// jacobinmag.com/2019/05/venezuela-sanctions-trump-intervention/.

62. Joe Emersberger, "Trump's Economic Sanctions Have Cost Venezuela about $6bn Since August 2017," *Venezuelanalysis*, September 27, 2018, https://venezuelanalysis.com/ analysis/14073.

63. Branko Marcetic, "Sanctions are Murder," *Jacobin Magazine*, May 6, 2019, https:// jacobinmag.com/2019/05/venezuela-sanctions-trump-intervention/.

64. Edward Wong and Nicholas Casey, "U.S. Targets Venezuela With Tough Oil Sanctions During Crisis of Power," *The New York Times*, January 28, 2019, https://www.nytimes.com/ 2019/01/28/us/politics/venezuela-sanctions-trump-oil.html.

65. Mark Weisbrot and Jeffrey Sachs, "Economic Sanctions as Collective Punishment: The Case of Venezuela," *Center for Economic and Policy Research*, April 2019.

66. General Assembly Resolution 37/L.34, Human Rights and Unilateral Coercive Measures, 37/ A/HRC/37/L.34 (March 19, 2018) available from https://undocs.org/A/HRC/37/L.34.

67. United Nations Human Rights Office of the High Commissioner, "Venezuela Sanctions Harm Human Rights of Innocent People, UN Expert Warns," January 31, 2019, https://www .ohchr.org/en/NewsEvents/Pages/DisplayNews.aspx?NewsID=24131&LangID=E%20.

68. Branko Marcetic, "Sanctions are Murder," *Jacobin Magazine*, May 6, 2019, https:// jacobinmag.com/2019/05/venezuela-sanctions-trump-intervention/.

69. William I. Robinson, "Latin America's Pink Tide: The Straightjacket of Global Capitalism," in *Latin America's Pink Tide: Breakthroughs and Shortcomings*, ed. Steve Ellner (Lanham, MD: Rowman and Littlefield, 2020.)

70. Jeffery R. Webber, *The Last Day of Oppression and the First Day of the Same: The Politics and Economics of the New Latin American Left* (Chicago: Haymarket Books, 2017).

71. Luis Reygadas, "Latin America: Persistent Inequality and Recent Transformations" in *Latin America After Neoliberalism: Turning the Tide in the 21st Century*, eds. Eric Hershberg and Fred Rosen (New York City: The New Press, 2007): 122.

72. Jeffery R. Webber, *The Last Day of Oppression and the First Day of the Same: The Politics and Economics of the New Latin American Left* (Chicago: Haymarket Books, 2017).

73. Ibid.

74. Giovanni Andrea Cornia, "Inequality Trends and Their Determinants: Latin America Over the Period 1990–2010," in *Falling Inequality in Latin America: Policy Changes and Lessons*, ed. Giovanni Andrea Cornia (Oxford Scholarship Online, 2014): 25.

75. Luis Reygadas, "Latin America: Persistent Inequality and Recent Transformations," in *Latin America After Neoliberalism: Turning the Tide in the 21st Century*, eds. Eric Hershberg and Fred Rosen (New York City: The New Press, 2007): 122.

76. Jeffery R. Webber, *The Last Day of Oppression and the First Day of the Same*: *The Politics and Economics of the New Latin American Left* (Chicago: Haymarket Books, 2017).

77. Ibid.

78. Ibid.

79. Jeffery R. Webber, "The Retreat of the Pink Tide in Latin America," *International Socialist Review* 110 (April 5, 2018).

80. Jeffery R. Webber, *The Last Day of Oppression and the First Day of the Same*: *The Politics and Economics of the New Latin American Left* (Chicago: Haymarket Books, 2017).

81. William I. Robinson, "Latin America's Pink Tide: The Straightjacket of Global Capitalism," in *Latin America's Pink Tide: Breakthroughs and Shortcomings*, ed. Steve Ellner (New York: Rowman and Littlefield, 2020).

82. Ibid.

83. Ibid.

84. Ibid.

85. Jeffery R. Webber, *The Last Day of Oppression and the First Day of the Same*: *The Politics and Economics of the New Latin American Left* (Chicago: Haymarket Books, 2017).

86. Jeffery R. Webber, "The Retreat of the Pink Tide in Latin America," *International Socialist Review* 110 (April 5, 2018).

87. Giovanni Andrea Cornia, "Inequality Trends and Their Determinants: Latin America Over the Period 1990–2010," in *Falling Inequality in Latin America: Policy Changes and Lessons*, ed. Giovanni Andrea Cornia (Oxford Scholarship Online, 2014): 25.

88. Jeffery R. Webber, *The Last Day of Oppression and the First Day of the Same*: *The Politics and Economics of the New Latin American Left* (Chicago: Haymarket Books, 2017).

89. Jeffery R. Webber, "The Retreat of the Pink Tide in Latin America," *International Socialist Review* 110 (April 5, 2018).

90. Giovanni Andrea Cornia, "Inequality Trends and Their Determinants: Latin America Over the Period 1990–2010," in *Falling Inequality in Latin America: Policy Changes and Lessons*, ed. Giovanni Andrea Cornia (Oxford Scholarship Online, 2014): 25.

91. Jeffery R. Webber, *The Last Day of Oppression and the First Day of the Same*: *The Politics and Economics of the New Latin American Left* (Chicago: Haymarket Books, 2017).

92. Jeffery R. Webber, "The Retreat of the Pink Tide in Latin America," *International Socialist Review* 110 (April 5, 2018).

93. William I. Robinson, "Latin America's Pink Tide: The Straightjacket of Global Capitalism," in *Latin America's Pink Tide: Breakthroughs and Shortcomings*, ed. Steve Ellner (New York: Rowman and Littlefield, 2020).

94. Jeffery R. Webber, *The Last Day of Oppression and the First Day of the Same*: *The Politics and Economics of the New Latin American Left* (Chicago: Haymarket Books, 2017).

95. William I. Robinson, "Latin America's Pink Tide: The Straightjacket of Global Capitalism," in *Latin America's Pink Tide: Breakthroughs and Shortcomings*, ed. Steve Ellner (Lanham, MD: Rowman and Littlefield, 2020).

96. Rene Rojas, "The Latin American Left's Shifting Tides," *Catalyst* 2, no. 2 (2018): 7–71.

97. William I. Robinson, "Latin America's Pink Tide: The Straightjacket of Global Capitalism," in *Latin America's Pink Tide: Breakthroughs and Shortcomings*, ed. Steve Ellner (Lanham, MD: Rowman and Littlefield, 2020).

98. Giovanni Andrea Cornia, "Inequality Trends and Their Determinants: Latin America Over the Period 1990–2010," in *Falling Inequality in Latin America: Policy Changes and Lessons*, ed. Giovanni Andrea Cornia (Oxford Scholarship Online, 2014): 25.

99. Jeffery R. Webber, *The Last Day of Oppression and the First Day of the Same*: *The Politics and Economics of the New Latin American Left* (Chicago: Haymarket Books, 2017).

100. Jeffery R. Webber, "The Retreat of the Pink Tide in Latin America," *International Socialist Review* 110 (April 5, 2018).

101. William I. Robinson, "Latin America's Pink Tide: The Straightjacket of Global Capitalism," in *Latin America's Pink Tide: Breakthroughs and Shortcomings*, ed. Steve Ellner (Lanham, MD: Rowman and Littlefield, 2020).

102. Eduardo Gudynas, "Estado comprensador y nuevos extractivismos: Las ambivalencias del progresismo sudamericano," *Nueva Sociedad* 237 (January–February 2012): 128–146.

103. John Ficenec, "Commodity Prices Collapse to Lowest in 12 Years," *The Telegraph*, January 29, 2015, prices-collapse-to-lowest-in-12-years.html.

104. Jeffery R. Webber, *The Last Day of Oppression and the First Day of the Same: The Politics and Economics of the New Latin American Left* (Chicago: Haymarket Books, 2017).

105. Jeffery R. Webber, "The Retreat of the Pink Tide in Latin America," *International Socialist Review* 110 (April 5, 2018).

106. Jeffery R. Webber, *The Last Day of Oppression and the First Day of the Same: The Politics and Economics of the New Latin American Left* (Chicago: Haymarket Books, 2017).

107. Jeffery R. Webber, "The Retreat of the Pink Tide in Latin America," *International Socialist Review* 110 (April 5, 2018).

108. Ministerio de las Comunas, Bolivarian Republico of Venezuela, https://www.mp comunas.gob.ve/.

109. Frederico Fuentes, "Venezuela's Crisis: A View from the Communes," *Green Left Weekly*, May 10, 2019, https://www.greenleft.org.au/content/venezuela-crisis-view-communes.

110. Ibid.

111. Lucas Koerner and Rachael Boothroyd Rojas, "Venezuela: Commune Leader Blocked from Running for Mayor," *Green Left*, December 1, 2017, tent/venezuela-commune-leader-blocked-running-mayor.

112. Ibid.

113. Ibid.

114. Ibid.

Bibliography

Abreu, Wladimir. "Economía Informal y Cuarentena, Una Pareja Dispareja." *Aporrea*, May 12, 2020. https://www.aporrea.org/economia/a290423.html.

Ackerman, John. "Co-governance for Accountability: Beyond Exit and Voice." *World Development* 32, no. 3 (2003): 447–463.

Ansley, Fran. "Local Contact Points at Global Divides: Labor Rights and Immigrant Rights as Sites for Cosmopolitan Legality." In *Law and Globalization from Below: Towards a Cosmopolitan Legality*. Eds. Boaventura de Sousa Santos and Cesar A. Rodriquez-Gravito. Cambridge, UK: Cambridge University Press, 2005. 158–181.

Aporrea-Agencias. "Venezuela es el Segundo País del Mundo con Mayor Número de Desplazados, Según Acnur." *Aporrea*, June 20, 2020. https://www.aporrea.org/ddhh/n356323.html.

Arblaster, Anthony. *Democracy*. 3rd edition. Buckingham, UK: Open University Press, 2002.

Arnstein, S. R. "A Ladder of Citizen Participation." *Journal of the American Institute of Planners* 35, no. 4 (1969).

Assies, Willelm. "David Versus Goliath in Cochabamba: Water Rights, Neoliberalism and the Revival of Social Protest in Bolivia." *Latin American Perspectives* 30, no. 3 (2003).

Avendaño, Orlando. "Enviados de Guiadó se Apropian de Fondos Para Ayudar Humanitaria en Colombia." *Panam Post*, June 18, 2019. https://es.panampost.com/orlando-avendano/2019/06/14/enviados-de-guaido-se-apropian-de-fondos-para-ayuda-humanitaria-en-colombia/.

Avritzer, Leonardo. "New Public Spheres in Brazil: Local Democracy and Deliberative Politics." *International Journal of Urban and Regional Research* 30, no. 3 (2017): 623–37.

Azam, Jean-Paul. "The Uncertain Distribution Impact of Structural Adjustment in Sub Saharan Africa" In *Structural Adjustment and Beyond in Sub Saharan Africa*. Eds. Rolph Van Der Hoeven and Fred Van Der Kraaij. London and Portsmouth: Heinemann, 1994.

Azzellini, Dario. "Venezuela's Solidarity Economy: Collective Ownership, Expropriation, and Workers Self-Management." *The Journal of Labor and Society* 12 (2009): 171–191.

———. "The Communal State: Communal Councils, Communes, and Workplace Democracy." *North American Congress on Latin America* 46, no. 2 (2013).

———. *Communes and Worker's Control in Venezuela: Building 21st Centruy Socialism from Below*. Leiden, Netherlands: Brill, 2016.

Bada, Xóchitl, and Liliana Rivera-Sánchez. *The Oxford Handbook of the Sociology of Latin America*. Oxford, UK: Oxford University Press, 2020.

Baiocchi, Gianpaulo, and Ernesto Ganuza. *Popular Democracy: The Paradox of Participation*. Stanford, CA: Stanford University Press, 2017.

Barber, Benjamin. *Strong Democracy*. Berkeley: University of California Press, 2003.

Barker, Colin, ed. *Revolutionary Rehearsals*. Chicago: Haymarket Books, 1987, 2002.

Barreto, Heibert. "Fuga de Capitales y Desfalco en Venezuela (1999–2013) Datos Para una Auditoria, Ponencia de Heibet Barreto." *Aporrea*, June 9, 2015. http://www.aporrea.org/contraloria/n271878.html.

Bean, Anderson. "Venezuela, Human Rights and Participatory Democracy." *Critical Sociology* 42, no. 6 (2016): 827–843.

Bello, Waldon. *Deglobalization: Ideas for a New World Economy*. London: Zed Books, 2005.

Bolivarian Republic of Venezuela Constitution of 1999 Article 233.

Boudin, Chesa, Gabriel Gonzalez, and Wilmer Rumbos. *The Venezuelan Revolution*. New York: Thunder's Mouth Press, 2006.

Brewer-Carias, Allan R. *Dismantling Democracy in Venezuela: The Chávez Authoritarian Experiment*. Cambridge, UK: Cambridge University Press, 2010.

Brown, Wendy. "Neoliberalism and the End of Liberal Democracy." *Theory and Event* 7, no. 1 (2003): 1–21.

———. *Undoing the Demos: Neoliberalism's Stealth Revolution*. New York: Zone Books, 2005.

Bruce, Ian. *The Real Venezuela: Making Socialism in the 21st Century*. London: Pluto Press, 2008.

Buxton, Julia. "Venezuela After Chávez." *New Left Review* 99 (May–June 2016).

Cairns, James, and Alan Sears. *The Democratic Imagination: Envisioning Popular Power in the Twenty-First Century*. Toronto: University of Toronto Press, 2012.

Cameron, Maxwell, Eric Hershberg, and Kenneth E. Sharpe, eds. *New Institutions for Participatory Democracy in Latin America: Voices and Consequence*. New York: Palgrave MacMillan, 2012.

Canovan, Margaret. *Populism*. Toronto: Junction Books, 1981.

Caritas Venezuela. "S.A.M.A.N Nutrition Infantil y Seguridad Alimentaria Abril 2020." *Caritas Venezuela*. April 2020. http://caritasvenezuela.org/wp-content/uploads/2020/06/Caritas-Informe-de-Desnutricion-Abril-2020.pdf.

Castells, Manuel. *Networks of Outrage and Hope: Social Movements in the Internet Age*. Cambridge, UK: Polity Press, 2015.

Castoriadis, Cornelius. *The Imaginary Institution of Society*. Cambridge, MA: MIT Press, 1975.

Castro, Vladimir Aguilar. "Los Episodios de Kanaimo (Canaima) en Tiempos de Jurisdicciones Indígenas en Venezuela." *Observatorio de Ecología Política de Venezuela*. December 13, 2018.

Catt, Helena. *Democracy in Practice*. London: Routledge, 1999.

Cawthorne, Andrew. "Venezuela Seizes Warehouses Packed with Medical Goods, Food." *Reuters*, October 23, 2014.

Chase-Dunn, Alessandro Moosin, and Alexis Alvarez. "Social Movements and Progressive Regimes in Latin America: World Revolutions and Semiperipheral Development." In *Handbook of Social Movements Across Latin America*. Eds. Paul Almeida and Allen Cordero Ulate. Dordrecht, Netherlands: Springer, 2015.

Chávez, Hugo. 2012. "Propuesta del Candidato de la Patria Comandante Hugo Chávez para la gestión Bolivariana Socialista 2013–2019." Sistema de Información de Tendencias Educattivas en America Latina, 2012. Available at http://www.chavez.org.ve/Programa-Patria-2013-2019.pdf.

Chávez, Hugo. "Strike at the Helm." *The Monthly Review* (April 2015).

Ciccariello-Maher, George. *We Created Chávez: A Peoples History of the Venezuelan Revolution*. Durham, NC: Duke University Press, 2013.

———. *Building the Commune: Radical Democracy in Venezuela*. London: Verso 2016.

———. "Venezuela: Call it What it Is—A Coup." *The Nation*, January 25, 2019. https://www.thenation.com/article/archive/venezuela-coup-guaido-maduro/.

Cohen, Sheila. "The Red Mole: Workers' Councils as a Means of Revolutionary Transformation." In *Ours to Master and to Own: Workers' Control from the Commune to the Present*. Eds. Immanuel Ness and Dario Azzellini. Chicago: Haymarket Books, 2011.

Constitución de la República Bolivariana de Venezuela 1999. Retrieved on July 10, 2020. https://www.cijc.org/es/NuestrasConstituciones/VENEZUELA-Constitucion.pdf.

Cornia, Giovanni Andrea. "Inequality Trends and Their Determinants: Latin America Over the Period 1990-2010." In *Falling Inequality in Latin America: Policy Changes and Lessons.* Ed. Giovanni Andrea Cornia. Oxford Scholarship Online (2014): 25.

Crespo, Carlos. "CNE: Marea Socialista no es una Denominación Partidista Sino Una Frase." *Crónica Uno,* May 19, 2015. https://cronica.uno/cne-marea-socialista-no-es-una-denominacion-partidista-sino-una-frase/.

Cupples, Julie. "Rural Development in El Hatillo, Nicaragua Gender, Neoliberal and Environmental Risk." *Singapore Journal of Tropical Geography* (2004).

Cusicanqui, Silvia Rivera. "Indigenous Anarchist Critique of Bolivia's 'Indigenous State': Interview with Silvia Rivera Cusicanqui." *Upside Down World,* September 3, 2014. https://upsidedownworld.org/archives/bolivia/indigenous-anarchist-critique-of-bolivias-indigenous-state-interview-with-silvia-rivera-cusicanqui/.

Dahl, Robert. *Democracy and its Critics.* New Haven, CT: Yale University Press, 1989.

Dale, John. *Free Burma: Transnational Legal Action and Corporate Accountability.* Minneapolis: University of Minnesota Press, 2011.

De la Barra, Ximena, and Richard Dello Buono. *Latin America After the Neoliberal Debacle: Another Region Is Possible.* Lanham, MD: Rowman & Littlefield, 2009.

Dello Buono, Richard, and Jose Bell Lara. *Imperialism, Neoliberalism, and Social Struggles in Latin America.* Chicago, IL: Haymarket Books, 2006.

de la Jara, Felipe J. Hevia, and Ernesto Isunza Vera. "Constrained Participation: The Impact of Consultative Councils on National-Level Policy in Mexico." In *New Institutions for Participatory Democracy in Latin America: Voices and Consequence.* Eds. Maxwell A. Cameron, Eric Hershberg, and Kenneth E. Sharpe. New York: Palgrave MacMillan, 2012.

De Sousa Santos, Boaventura. "Beyond Neoliberal Governance: The World Social Forum as Subaltern Cosmopolitan Politics and Legality." In *Law and Globalization from Below: Towards a Cosmopolitan Legality.* Eds. Boaventura De Sousa Santos and Cesar A. Rodriguez-Garavito. Cambridge, UK: Cambridge University Press, (2005): 29–63.

———. "Human Rights as an Emancipatory Script? Cultural and Political Conditions." In *Another Knowledge Is Possible: Beyond Northern Epistemologies.* Eds. Boaventura De Sousa Santos and Cesar A. Rodriguez-Garavito. London: Verso, (2008): 3–40.

della Porta, Donatella. *Can Democracy Be Saved?* Malden, ME: Polity Press, 2013.

della Porta, Donatella, and Dieter Rucht. *Meeting Democracy: Power and Deliberation in Global Justice Movements.* Cambridge, UK: Cambridge University Press, 2013.

Di Stasio, Alessandro. "Inflación de 2018 cerró en 1.698.488%, según la Asamblea Nacional." *Efecto Cocuyo,* January 9, 2019. https://www.eluniversal.com/economia/30142/.

Dobson, Paul. "Venezuela Assumes OPEC Presidency, Unveils Foreign Oil Investment Deals." *Venezuelanalysis,* January 9, 2019. https://venezuelanalysis.com/news/14213.

Donati, Jessica, and Vivian Salama. "Pence Pledged U.S. Backing Before Venezuela Opposition Leader's Move." *The Wall Street Journal,* January 25, 2019. https://www.wsj.com/articles/a-call-from-pence-helped-set-an-uncertain-new-course-in-venezuela-11548430259.

Draper, Hal. "Why the Working Class?" *Socialistworker.org,* September 14, 2012. http://socialistworker.org/2012/09/14/why-the-working-class.

Draper, Hal. "Marx on Democratic Forms of Government." *Socialist Register,* 1974.

Dryzek, John S. "Discursive Democracy vs. Liberal Constitutionalism." In *Democratic Innovation: Deliberation, Representation and Association.* Ed. Michael Saward. London and New York: Routledge, 2000.

Dutka, Z. C. "Attacks on Venezuelan Commune and Farmland Reported, Crops Destroyed." *Venezuela Analysis,* August 19, 2015. https://venezuelanalysis.com/news/11478.

Echanove, Flavia. "Globilisation and Restructuring in Rural Mexico: The Case of Fruit Growers." *Tijdschrift Voor Economische en Sociale Geographe* 96, no. 1 (2005: 15–30).

Ellner, Steve. *Rethinking Venezuelan Politics: Class, Conflict, and the Chávez Phenomena.* Boulder, CO: Lynne Rienner, 2008.

———. "A New Model with Rough Edges: Venezuela's Community Councils." *NACLA Report on the Americas* 42, no 3 (2009): 11–14.

———. "Venezuela's Social-based Democratic Model: Innovations and Limitations." *Journal of Latin American Studies* 43, no. 3 (2011): 421–449.

————. "It is Necessary to Contextualize the Pragmatic and Populist Policies of the Chavista Government: An Interview with Steve Ellner." *Venezuelanalysis*, September 15, 2015. https://venezuelanalysis.com/analysis/11505.

————. "Beyond the Boliburguesia Thesis." *North American Congress on Latin America*. (June 9, 2016).

————. *Latin America's Pink Tide: Breakthroughs and Shortcomings*. Lanham, MD: Rowman & Littlefield, 2020.

Emersberger, Joe. "Trump's Economic Sanctions Have Cost Venezuela about $6bn Since August 2017." *Venezuelanalysis*, September 27, 2018. https://venezuelanalysis.com/analysis/14073.

Enriquez, Laura J. "The Varying Impacts of Structural Adjustment on Nicaragua's Small Farmers." *European Review of Latin America and Caribbean Studies* 69 (October 2000).

Epstein, Barbara. *Political Protest and Cultural Revolution: Nonviolent Direct Action in the 1970s and 1980s*. Berkeley: University of California Press, 1991.

Evans, Peter. "Is an Alternative Globalization Possible?" *Politics and Society* 36, no. 2 (2008): 271–305.

————. "Counter-Hegemonic Globalization: Transnational Social Movements in the Contemporary Global Political Economy." *The Handbook of Political Sociology: States, Civil Societies, and Globalization*. Ed. Thomas Janoski. Cambridge, UK: Cambridge University Press, 2012.

Equipo Operativo Nacional de Marea Socialista. "Allanan Sede Nacional de Marea Socialista." *Rebelión*. November 6, 2016.

Executive Order No. 13884, Federal Register, Vol. 84, No. 152. August 7, 2019. https://www.treasury.gov/resource-center/sanctions/Programs/Documents/13884.pdf.

Fernandes, Sujatha. "Growing Movement of Community Radio in Venezuela." *Z Magazine*. December 24, 2005.

_____. *Who Can Stop The Drums? Urban Social Movements in Chávez's Venezuela*. Durham, NC: Duke University Press, 2010.

————. "Radio Bemba in an Age of Electronic Media: The Dynamics of Popular Communication in Chávez's Venezuela." In *Venezuela's Bolivarian Democracy: Participation, Politics and Culture*. Eds. David Smilde and Daniel Hellinger. Durham, NC: Duke University Press, 2011. 131–156.

————. "Cultural and Neoliberal Rationalities in Postneoliberal Venezuela. In *Neoliberalism, Interrupted: Social Change and Contested Governance in Contemporary Latin America*. Eds. Mark Goodale and Nancy Postero. Stanford, CA: Stanford University Press, 2013.

Ficenec, John. "Commodity Prices Collapse to Lowest in 12 Years." *The Telegraph*, January 29, 2015. https://www.telegraph.co.uk/finance/commodities/11376321/Commodity-prices-collapse-to-lowest-in-12-years.html.

Fitzpatrick, Tony. "The Two Paradoxes of Welfare Democracy." *International Journal of Social Welfare* 11 (2002).

Fischer-Hoffman, Corey. "Venezuela Officials Seize Warehouse with Enormous Cache of Hoarded Items as Opposition Calls for Strike." *Venezuelanalysis.com*, January 14, 2015. https://venezuelanalysis.com/news/11158.

Foot, Paul. *The Vote: How it Was Won and How it was Undermined*. London: Viking, 2005.

Foster, John Bellamy. "Chávez and the Communal State: On the Transition to Socialism in Venezuela." *Monthly Review* 66, no. 11 (2015).

Fox, Michael, and Silvia Leindecker. *Beyond Elections: Redefining Democracy in the Americas*. Oakland. CA: PM Press, 2008.

Fuentes, Frederico. "Venezuela: New Moves to Build People's Power." *Green Left Weekly* 831 (2010).

_____. "Venezuela's Crisis: A View From the Communes." *Green Left Weekly*, May 10, 2019, https://www.greenleft.org.au/content/venezuela-crisis-view-communes.

Ganuza, Ernesto, Heloise Nez, and Ernesto Morales. "The Struggle for a Voice: Tensions between Associations and Citizens in Participatory Budgeting." *International Journal of Urban and Regional Research* 38, no. 6 (2014): 2274–2291.

Garcia, Luis Britto. "Upcoming Legislation in Venezuela: Special Economic Zones." *Venezuelanalysis.com*, May 24, 2021. https://venezuelanalysis.com/analysis/15212.

Geier, Joel. "Year of Revolutionary Hope." *International Socialist Review* 59 (2008): May–June.

General Assembly Resolution 37/L.34, Human rights and unilateral coercive measures, 37/ A/ HRC/37/L.34 (March 19, 2018). Available from https://undocs.org/A/HRC/37/L.34.

Ginsborg, Paul. *Democracy: Crisis and Renewal.* London: Profile Books, 2008.

Gluckstein, Donny. "Workers' Councils in Europe: A Century of Experience." In *Ours to Master and to Own: Workers' Control from the Commune to the Present.* Eds. Immanuel Ness and Dario Azzellini. Chicago: Haymarket Books, 2001.

Goldfrank, Benjamin. *Deepening Democracy in Latin America: Participation, Decentralization, and the Left.* University Park: Pennsylvania State University Press, 2012.

Golinger, Eva. *The Chávez Code: Cracking the US Intervention in Venezuela.* London: Pluto Press, 2007.

Gomez, Gonzalo. "Ten Proposals for Venezuela's Maduro." *Socialistworker.org,* June 24, 2014. https://socialistworker.org/2014/06/24/ten-proposals-for-maduro.

Gonzalez, Mike. *Hugo Chávez: Socialist for the Twenty-First Century.* London: Pluto Press, 2014.

Gonzalez, Mike. *The Ebb of the Pink Tide: The Decline of the Left in Latin America.* London: Pluto Press, 2019.

Goodale, Mark, and Nancy Postero. *Neoliberalism, Interrupted: Social Change and Contested Governance in Contemporary Latin America.* Stanford, CA: Stanford University Press, 2013.

Gott, Richard. *Hugo Chávez and the Bolivarian Revolution.* New York: Verso Books, 2005.

Grattan, Laura. *Populism's Power: Radical Grassroots Democracy in America.* Oxford, UK: Oxford University Press, 2016.

Guernos-Meza, Valeria, and Mike Geddes. "Local Governance and Participation under Neoliberalism: Comparative Perspectives." *International Journal of Urban and Regional Research* 34, no. 1 (2010): 115–129.

Gudynas, Eduardo. "Estado compensador y nuevos extractivismos: Las ambivalencias del progresismo sudamericano," *Nueva Sociedad* 237 (January–February 2012): 128–146.

Habermas, Jürgen. *The Structural Transformation of the Public Sphere: An Inquiry into a Category of Bourgeoise Society.* Cambridge, MA: MIT Press, 1991.

Hallas, Duncan. "Towards a Revolutionary Socialist Party." In *Party and Class.* London: Bookmarks, 1971.

Hammond, John. *Building Popular Power: Workers' and Neighborhood Movements in the Portuguese Revolution.* New York: Monthly Review Press, 1988.

Hanson, Rebecca. "Deepening Distrust: Why Participatory Experiments Are Not Always Good for Democracy." *The Sociological Quarterly* 59, no. 1 (2018): 145–167.

Harman, Chris. "How the Revolution was Lost." *International Socialism* 1, no. 30 (1967).

———. "Latin America: The Return of Popular Power." *International Socialism* 114 (2007).

Harvey, David. *The New Imperialism.* Oxford, UK: Oxford University Press, 2003.

———. A *Brief History of Neoliberalism.* Oxford, UK: Oxford University Press, 2005.

Hawkins, Kirk A., and David Hanson. "Dependent Civil Society: The Circulos Bolivarianos in Venezuela." *Latin American Research Review* 41 (2006): 102–132.

Hershberg, Eric, and Fred Rosen. *Latin America After Neoliberalism: Turning the Tide in the 21st Century?* New York: The New Press, 2007.

Hetland, Gabriel. "The Crooked Line: From Populist Mobilization to Participatory Democracy in Chávez-Era Venezuela." *Qualitative Sociology* 37 (2014): 373–401.

———. "How Severe Is Venezuela's Crisis?" *The Nation,* June 23, 2016a. https://www.the nation.com/article/how-severe-is-venezuelas-crisis/.

———. "Why Is Venezuela in Crisis?" *The Nation,* August 17, 2016b. https://www.thenation .com/article/why-is-venezuela-in-crisis/.

———. "A History of Violence." *Jacobin Magazine,* September 13, 2016. https://www .jacobinmag.com/2016/09/venezuela-opposition-maduro-chavez-coup-protests/.

———. "From System Collapse to Chavista Hegemony: The Party Question in Bolivarian Venezuela." *Latin American Perspectives* 44, no. 212 (2017): 17–36.

———. "The Promise and Perils of Radical Left Populism: The Case of Venezuela." *Journal of World-Systems Research* 24, no. 2 (2018): 277–290.

———. "Stop Talking About Coups." *Jacobin Magazine*, September 17, 2019. https://jacobin mag.com/2018/09/venezuela-maduro-coup-trump-united-states-intervention.

Holloway, John. *Zapatista! Reinvinting Revolution in Mexico*. London: Pluto Press, 1998.

———. *Change the World Without Taking Power*. London: Pluto Press, 2002.

Howard, April. "Venezuela: Creating an Endogenous Cooperative Culture." *Upside Down World*, September 4, 2008. http://upsidedownworld.org/main/venezuela-archives-35/1457 -venezuela-creating-an-endogenous-cooperative-culture.

Huntington, Samuel P. *Political Order in Changing Societies*. New Haven, CT: Yale University Press, 1965.

James, C. L. R. "Every Cook Can Govern." *Correspondence*, 2 no. 12 (1956).

John, J. "Special Economic Zones: Their Impact on Labour." *Labour File* 6, no. 5 (2008).

Jonakin, Jon. "The Interaction of Market Failure and Structural Adjustment in Producer Credit and Land Markets: The Case of Nicaragua." *Journal of Economic Issues* 31, no. 2 (1997).

Jonakin, Jon, and Laura Enriquez. "The Non-Traditional Financial Sector in Nicaragua: A Response to Rural Credit Market Exclusion." *Development Policy Review* 17 (1999).

Kaltwasser, Rovira. "Toward Post-Neoliberalism in Latin America." *Latin America Research Review* 46, no. 2 (2001): 225–234.

Katz, Claudio. "Is South America's 'Progressive Cycle' At an End." *Socialist Project*. March 9, 2016.

Keane, John. *The Life and Death of Democracy*. London: Simon and Schuster, 2009.

Keck, Margaret, and Kathryn Sikkink. *Activists Beyond Borders: Advocacy Networks in International Politics*. Ithaca, NY: Cornell University, 1998.

Kellner, Douglas. "Theorizing Globalization." *Sociological Theory* 20, no. 3 (2002): 285–503.

Koerner, Lucas. "Venezuela Ramps up Anti-Crime Offensive, Targets Hoarding and Contraband." *Venezuelanalysis*, August 10, 2015. https://venezuelanalysis.com/news/11468.

Koerner, Lucas, and Rachael Boothroyd Rojas. "Venezuela: Commune Leader Blocked from Running for Mayor." *Green Left*, December 1, 2017. https://www.greenleft.org.au/content/ venezuela-commune-leader-blocked-running-mayor.

Korten, David C. *When Corporations Rule the World: Second Edition*. San Francisco, CA: Kumarian Press, 2001.

Kosuth, Dennis. "Hungary 1956: Revolution in a Workers' State." *Internationalist Socialist Review* 51 (2007).

Kowalewski, Zbigniew Marcin. "Give Us Back Our Factories! Between Resisting Exploitation and the Struggle for Worker's Power in Poland, 1944–1981." In *Ours to Master and to Own: Workers' Control from the Commune to the Present*. Eds. Immanuel Ness and Dario Azzellini. Chicago: Haymarket Books, 2011.

Krauss, Clifford. "Oil Prices: What's Behind the Drop? Simple Economics." *New York Times*, March 30, 2016. https://www.nytimes.com/2015/01/13/business/energy-environment/oil-prices.html.

La Botz, Dan. "The New Movement for Global Justice." *Against the Current* 88 (September– October 2000).

LaClase.info. "Maduro Entrega Seis Meses de Privilegios Fiscales a Los Empresarios Importadores." *LaClase.info*, January, 2020. http://laclase.info/content/maduro-entrega-seis-meses-de-privilegios-fiscales-a-los-empresarios-importadores/.

Laclau, Ernesto. *On Populist Reason*. London: Verso, 2005.

Laclau, Ernesto, and Chantal Mouffe. *Hegemony and Socialist Strategy: Towards a Radical Democratic Politics*. London: Verso, 1985.

La Iguana. "3800 More Toilet Paper Packs Found Hoarded." *Venezuelanalysis*, October 22, 2013. https://venezuelanalysis.com/news/10109.

Lander, Edgardo. "El Estado y Los Tensiones de la Participacion Popular en Venezuela." *Observatorio Social de America Latina* 8, no. 22 (2007).

Lander, Edgardo. "Venezuela: Un Barril de Polvora." *Nueva Sociedad* 269 (2017).

Lather, Patty. *Getting Smart: Feminist Research and Pedagogy Within/in the Postmodern*. New York: Routledge, 1991.

Laxer, James. *Democracy*. Toronto: Groundwood Books, 2009).

Le Blanc, Paul. "What Do Socialists Say About Democracy?" *International Socialist Review* 74 (2009).

Lee, Caroline. *Do-It-Yourself Democracy: The Rise of the Public Engagement Industry*. Oxford, UK: Oxford University Press, 2015.

Lehmann, David. *Democracy and Development in Latin America: Economics, Politics and Religion in the Post-War Period*. Philadelphia, PA: Temple University Press, 1992.

Lenski, Gerhard. *Power and Privilege*. New York: McGraw-Hill, 1966.

Lerner, Josh. "Communal Councils in Venezuela: Can 200 Families Revolutionize Democracy?" *Z Magazine*, March 6, 2007.

Lewit, David. "Porto Alegre's Budget of, by, and for the People." *Yesmagazine.org*, December 31, 2002. https://www.yesmagazine.org/issues/what-would-democracy-look-like/562.

Ley Organica del Poder Popular. 2010. *Gazeta Oficial* 6.011, 21 December 2010:7.

Londoño, Ernesto, and Nicholas Casey. "El Gobierno de Trump discutió un posible golpe de Estado con Militares Rebeldes en Venezuela." *The New York Times*, September 8, 2018. https://www.nytimes.com/es/2018/09/08/espanol/trump-golpe-de-estado-maduro.html.

Lopez Maya, Margarita. "Populism, 21st Century Socialism and Corruption in Venezuela." *Thesis Eleven* 149 (2018): 67–83.

Lopez, Virginia. "Venezuela's Economic Crisis Worsens as Oil Prices Fall." *Al Jazeera*, January 8, 2016. http://www.aljazeera.com/news/2016/01/venezuela-economic-crisis-worsens-oil-prices-fall-160108105010345.html.

Luzardo, Bernardo. "Allanaron Sede del Movimiento Marea Socialista." *Globovision*, October 6, 2016. https://www.globovision.com/article/allanaron-sede-del-movimiento-marea-socialista.

Machado, Jesús, Betty Núñez, and Nanciely Arraíz. 2018. "Poder Popular: Una Mirada Desde Las Bases." In *Venezuela Desde Adentro: Ocho Investigaciones para un Debate Necesario*. Eds. Karin Gabbart and Alexandra Martínez. Quito, Ecuador: Fundación Rosa Luxemburg Oficina Región Andina.

Manuare, Juan, and Carlos E. Juarena. "Venezuela: A Balance Sheet of 2016 and Perspectives for 2017." *In Defence of Marxism*, February 27, 2017. https://www.marxist.com/venezuela-a-balance-sheet-of-2016-and-perspectives-for-2017.htm.

Martin, Jorge. 2015. "The Transition to Socialism in Venezuela: What Is to be Done?." *In Defense of Marxism*, March 5, 2015. http://www.marxist.com/the-transition-to-socialism-in-venezuela-what-is-to-be-done.htm.

———. "Venezuela—A Last Warning." *In Defense of Marxism*, May 19, 2016. http://www.marxist.com/venezuela-last-warning.htm.

———. "Chavistas March Against Imperialism: What Is the Next Step in Trump's Coup?" *Venezuelanalysis*, February 19, 2019. https://venezuelanalysis.com/analysis/14311.

Martinez Carlos, Michael Fox, and Jojo Farrell. *Venezuela Speaks! Voices from the Grassroots*. Oakland, CA: PM Press, 2010.

Marx, Karl, and Friedrich Engels. *The Communist Manifesto*. Chicago: Haymarket Books, 1848, 2005.

———. *The Marx and Engles Reader*. Second edition. Ed. Robert C. Tucker. New York, London: W. W. Norton & Company, 1978.

Marcetic, Branko. "Sanctions Are Murder." *Jacobin Magazine*, May 6, 2019. https://jacobinmag.com/2019/05/venezuela-sanctions-trump-intervention/.

Mason, Jeff, and Roberta Rampton. "U.S. Declares Venezuela a National Security Threat, Sanctions Top Officials." *Reuters*, March 9, 2015. https://www.reuters.com/article/us-usa-venezuela-idUSKBN0M51NS20150310.

Maupin, Caleb T. "US-Led Economic War, Not Socialism, Is Tearing Venezuela Apart." *Mint News Press*, July 12, 2016. https://www.mintpressnews.com/us-led-economic-war-not-socialism-tearing-venezuela-apart/218335/.

Mazzeo, Miguel. *El Sueño de una Cosa: Introducción al Poder Popular*. Caracas, Venezuela: El Perro y la Rana, 2007.

Mazzeo, Miguel, and Fernando Stratta. *Reflexiones sobre Poder Popular*. Buenos Aires, Argentina: Editorial El Colectivo, 2007.

McAdam, Doug. *Political Process and the Development of Black Insurgency, 1930–1970*. Chicago: University of Chicago, 1982.

McCaughan, Michael. *The Battle for Venezuela*. New York: Seven Stories Press, 2005.

McMichael, Philip. *Development and Social Change: A Global Perspective*. Sixth Edition. Thousand Oaks, CA: Sage Publications, 2016.

Mills, Frederick B. "Chavista Transition to the Communal State." *Open Democracy*, July 22, 2015. https://www.opendemocracy.net/frederick-b-mills/chavista-theory-of-transition -towards-communal-state.

Mohan, Giles, Ed Brown, Bob Milward, and Alfred B. Zack-Williams. *Structural Adjustment: Theory, Practice and Impacts*. London: Routledge, 2000.

Montambeault, Francoise. "Learning to Be Better Democrats? The Role of Informal Practices in Brazilian Participatory Budgeting Experiences." In *New Institutions for Participatory Democracy in Latin America: Voices and Consequence*. Eds. Maxwell A. Cameron, Eric Hershberg, and Kenneth E. Sharpe. London: Palgrave MacMillan, 2012.

Montesquieu, Charles. *The Spirit of the Laws*. New York: Cosimo Classics, 1748, 2010.

Moreno Losada, Vanessa. "Provea: 45 Representantes del Chavismo Disidente Han Sido Agregados Por el Gobierno de Maduro." *Efecto Cocuyo*, November 6, 2018. https://efec-tococuyo.com/politica/provea-45-representantes-del-chavismo-disidente-han-sido-agredi-dos-por-el-gobierno-de-maduro/.

Mouffe, Chantal. *The Democratic Paradox*. London: Verso, 2000.

Muhr, Thomas. "TINA go home! ALBA and Re-theorizing Resistance to Global Capitalism." *Cosmos and History: The Journal of Natural and Social Philosophy* 6, no. 2 (2010): 27–54.

Music, Goran. "Yugoslavia: Workers' Self-Management as State Paradigm." In *Ours to Master and to Own: Workers' Control from the Commune to the Present*. Eds. Immanuel Ness and Dario Azzellini. Chicago: Haymarket Books, 2011.

Nacional Web. "Sindicalistas: En 2019 Recrudecerá Persecución para Impedir las Protestas." *El Nacional Web*, January 4, 2019. https://www.elnacional.com/economia/sindicalistas -2019-recrudecera-persecucion-para-impedir-las-protestas_265128/.

Nagy Hesse-Biber, Sharlene, ed. *Handbook of Feminist Research: Theory and Practice*. 2nd edition. New York: Sage Publications, 2012.

Ness, Immanuel, and Dario Azzellini. *Ours to Master and to Own: Workers' Control from the Commune to the Present*. Chicago: Haymarket Books, 2011.

Norris, Pippa. *Democratic Deficit: Critical Citizens Revisited*. Cambridge, UK: Cambridge University Press, 2011.

O'Donnell, Guillermo, and Phillipe Schmitter. *Transitions from Authoritarian Rule: Tentative Conclusions about Uncertain Democracies*. Baltimore: Johns Hopkins University Press, 1986.

Olivera, Oscar, and Tom Lewis. *Cochabamba! Water War in Bolivia*. New York: South End Press, 2008.

Ong, Aihwa. *Neoliberalism as Exception: Mutations in Citizenship and Sovereignty*. Durham, NC: Duke University Press, 2006.

OPEC Website. "Venezuela Facts and Figures." 2016. http://www.opec.org/opec_web/en/about_us/171.htm.

Pateman, Carole. *Participation and Democratic Theory*. Cambridge, UK: Cambridge University Press, 1970.

Patton, Mike. "The Three Countries with the Highest Inflation." *Forbes*, May 9, 2014. https://www.forbes.com/sites/mikepatton/2014/05/09/the-three-countries-with-the-highest -inflation/#6bfb61f2172e.

Pascua Marquina, Cira. "How to Get Venezuela's Economy Going Again: A Conversation with Luis Enrique Gavazut." *Venezuelanalysis*, January 3, 2019. https://venezuelanalysis .com/analysis/14203.

Pascual Marquina, Cira. "Working-Class Struggle in Venezuela: A Conversation with Leander Perez." *Venezuelanalysis*, February 21, 2020. https://venezuelanalysis.com/analysis/ 14792.

Pearson, Tamara. "Venezuelan Government Confronts Milk Hoarding." *Venezuelanalysis*, December 7, 2011. https://venezuelanalysis.com/news/6673#:~:text=Venezuelan%20 Government%20Confronts%20Milk%20Hoarding%20Since%20confronting%20 Italian,offensive%20to%20get%20hoarded%20milk%20to%20the%20people.

————. "Venezuela Guarimbas: 11 Things the Media Didn't Tell You." *Telesur*, February 11, 2015. http://www.telesurtv.net/english/analysis/Venezuelan-Guarimbas-11-Things-the -Media-Didnt-Tell-You-20150211-0025.html.

Perczynski, Piotr. "Active Citizenship and Associative Democracy." In *Democratic Innovation: Deliberation, Representation and Association.* Ed. Michael Saward. London and New York: Routledge, 2000.

Pogrebinschi, Thamy. "Participation as Representation: Democratic Policymaking in Brazil." In *New Institutions for Participatory Democracy in Latin America: Voices and Consequence.* Eds. Maxwell A. Cameron, Eric Hershberg, and Kenneth E. Sharpe. London: Palgrave MacMillan, 2012.

Politika UCAB. "CNE Niega a Vente Venezuela y Marea Socialista Inscribirse como Partidos." Politika UCAB, May 18, 2015. https://politikaucab.net/2015/05/18/cne-niega-a-vente -venezuela-y-marea-socialista-inscribirse-como-partidos/.

Polleta, Francesca. *Freedom Is an Endless Meeting: Democracy in American Social Movements.* Chicago: University of Chicago Press, 2002.

Pons, Corina. "Venezuela 2016 hits 800 percent, GDP shrinks 19 percent: document." *Reuters*, January 20, 2017. https://www.reuters.com/article/us-venezuela-economy-idUSK BN154244.

Putnam, Robert, and Robert Leonardi. *Making Democracy Work: Civic Traditions in Modern Italy.* Princeton, NJ: Princeton University Press, 1993.

Ragin, Charles. *The Comparative Method: Moving Beyond Qualitative and Quantitative Strategies.* Oakland: University of California Press, 1987.

Rajagopal, Balakrishnan. "The Role of Law in Counter-hegemonic Globalization and Global Legal Pluralism: Lessons from the Narmada Valley Struggle in India." *Leiden Journal of International Law* 18, no. 3(2005): 345–387.

Ranis, Peter. "Factories Without Bosses: Argentina's Experience with Worker-run Enterprises." *Labor: Studies in Working-Class History of the Americas* 3, no. 1 (2006).

Reardon, Juan. "Venezuelan National Assembly Passes People's Power 'Law of Communes.'" *Venezuelanalysis.com*, December 4, 2010. http://venezuelanalysis.com/news/5858.

Reygadas, Luis. "Latin America: Persistent Inequality and Recent Transformations." In *Latin America After Neoliberalism: Turning the Tide in the 21st Century.* Eds. Eric Hershberg and Fred Rosen. New York City: The New Press, 2007, 122.

Richards, Patricia. *Pobladoras, Indigenas, and the State: Conflicts over Women's Rights in Chile.* Princeton, NJ: Princeton University Press, 2004.

Robertson, Ewan. "Independent National Communard Council Created in Venezuela." *Venezuelaanalysis.com*, June 6, 2014. https://venezuelanalysis.com/news/10727.

Robinson, William I. *Latin America and Global Capitalism.* Baltimore: Johns Hopkins University Press, 2008.

————. "Latin America's Pink Tide: The Straightjacket of Global Capitalism." In *Latin America's Pink Tide: Breakthroughs and Shortcomings.* New York: Rowman & Littlefield, 2020.

Rojas, Rene. 2018. "The Latin American Left's Shifting Tides." *Catalyst* 2, no. 2 (2018): 7–71.

Romero, Cesar. "Evolucion de la violencia en el entorno minero del estado Bolivar (marzo de 2016–febrero de 20190." *Observatorio de Ecología Política de Venezuela.* May 26, 2020.

Sanchez, German. *Cuba and Venezuela: An Insight on Two Revolutions.* Old Chelsea, NY: Ocean Press, 2007.

Sanchez Uribarri, R. A. "Venezuela, Turning Further Left?" In *Leftovers.* Ed. Jorge Castenada and Marco Morales. New York: Routledge, 2008.

Schiavoni, Christina, and William Camacaro. "The Venezuelan Effort to Build a New Food and Agricultural System." *The Monthly Review*, July 1, 2009. http://monthlyreview .org/2009/07/01/the-venezuelan-effort-to-build-a-new-food-and-agriculture-system/.

Schutt, Russel K. *Investigating the Social World: The Process and Practice of Research.* Fifth edition. New York: Sage Publications, 2006.

Schumpeter, Joseph A. *Capitalism, Socialism, and Democracy.* New York: Harper & Brothers, 1942.

Selee, Andrew, and Enrique Peruzzotti. *Participatory Innovation and Representitive Democracy in Latin America*. Washington, DC: Woodrow Wilson Center Press, 2009.

Shefner, Jon. *The Illusion of Civil Society: Democratization and Community Mobilization in Low-Income Mexico*. University Park: Pennsylvania State University Press, 2008.

Sitrin, Marina, ed. *Horizontalism: Voices of Popular Power in Argentina*. Chico, CA: AK Press, 2006.

Skocpol, Theda. "Emerging Agendas and Recurrent Strategies." In *Vision and Method in Historical Sociology*. Ed. Theda Skocpol. Cambridge, UK: Cambridge University Press, 1984.

Skocpol, Theda, and Margaret Somers. 1980. "The Uses of Comparative History in Macrosocial Inquiry." *Comparative Studies in Society and History* 22, no. 2 (1980): 174–197.

Smilde, David, and Daniel Hellinger. *Participation, Politics and Culture in Venezuela's Bolivarian Democracy*. Durham, NC: Duke University Press, 2011.

Smith, Dorothy. *The Everyday World as Problematic: A Feminist Sociology*. Boston: Northeastern University Press, 1987.

———. *The Conceptual Practices of Power: A Feminist Sociology of Knowledge*. Boston: Northeastern University Press, 1990.

Smith, Jackie. *Social Movements for Global Democracy*. Baltimore: Johns Hopkins University Press, 2008.

Somma, Nicolás M. "Social Movements in Latin America: Mapping the Literature." In *The Oxford Handbook of the Sociology of Latin America*. Eds. Xóchitl Bada and Liliana Rivera-Sánchez. Oxford, UK: Oxford University Press, 2020.

Spetalnick, Matt, and Roberta Rampton. "Trump Freezes all Venezuelan Government Assets in Bid to Pressure Maduro." *Reuters*, August 5, 2019. https://www.reuters.com/article/us-venezuela-politics-usa-order-idUSKCN1UW03C.

Surgentes. 2019. "Ante la Invisibilization de las Muertes de Manifestantes de los Sectores Populares." *America Latina en Movimiento*, January 25, 2019. https://www.alainet.org/es/articulo/197779.

Tarrow, Sidney. *Power in Movement*. Cambridge, UK: Cambridge University Press, 1994.

Tarver, H. Michael, and Julia C. Frederick. *The History of Venezuela*. New York: Palgrave MacMillan, 2006.

Taylor, Marilyn. "Community Participation in the Real World: Opportunities and Pitfalls in New Governance Spaces." *Urban Societies* 44, no. 2 (2017): 297–317.

Tilly, Charles. *From Mobilization to Revolution*. Reading, PA: Addison-Wesley, 1978.

———. *European Revolutions 1492–1992*. Oxford/Cambridge, UK: Blackwell, 1993.

———. *Popular Contention in Great Britain, 1758–1834*. Cambridge, MA: Harvard University Press, 1995.

———. *Social Movements, 1768–2004*. Boulder, CO: Paradigm Publishers, 2004.

———. *Contentious Performances*. Cambridge, UK: Cambridge University Press, 2008.

Tilly, Charles, and Lesley Wood. *Social Movements 1768–2012*. Third edition. London: Paradigm Publishers, 2013.

Tinker Salas, Miguel. *Venezuela: What Everyone Needs to Know*. Oxford, UK: Oxford University Press, 2015.

Ulfelder, Jay. "Contenious Collective Action and the Breakdown of Authoritarian Regimes." *International Political Science Review* 26, no. 3 (2005): 311–334.

United Nations Human Rights Office of the High Commissioner. "Violaciones de los Derechos Humanos en la Republica Bolivariana de Venezuela: Una Espiral Descendente que no Parece Tener Fin." *Naciones Unidas Derechos Humanos Oficina Del Alto Comisionado*. June 2018.

United Nations Human Rights Office of the High Commissioner. "Venezuela Sanctions Harm Human Rights of Innocent People, UN Expert Warns." January 31, 2019. https://www.ohchr.org/en/NewsEvents/Pages/DisplayNews.aspx?NewsID=24131&LangID=E%20.

United Nations Human Rights Office of the High Commissioner. "Venezuela: Crisis de Refugiados y Migrantes: El Éxodo Mas Grade de la Historia Reciente de América Latina." May 2020.

Valesco, Alejandro. "A Call for Cooler Heads on Venezuela: How to Criticize Maduro While Opposing U.S. Regime Change." *In These Times*, March 11, 2019. http://inthesetimes.com/article/21789/venezuela-maduro-trump-barrios-intervention-sanctions-chavismo-guaido.

Vaz, Ricardo. "Venezuela: Popular Movements Secure Release of Detained Communards." *Venezuelanalysis*, April 24, 2019. https://venezuelanalysis.com/news/14441.

Wagner, Sarah. "Women and Venezuela's Bolivarian Revolution." In *Venezuela's Bolivarian Process*. Ed. Gregory Wilpert. *Venezuelaanalysis.com*, 2004.

Waitzkin, Howard, Rebeca Jasso-Aguilar, and Celia Iriat. "Privatization of Health Services in Less Developed Countries: An Empirical Response to the Proposals of the World Bank and Wharton School." *International Journal of Health Services* 37, no. 2 (2007).

Walker, Thomas. *Nicaragua Without Illusions*. Lanham, MD: Rowman & Littlefield, 1997.

Wallis, Victor. "Workers Control and Revolution." In *Ours to Master and to Own: Workers' Control from the Commune to the Present*. Eds. Immanuel Ness and Dario Azzellini. Chicago: Haymarket Books, 2011.

Weale, Albert. *Democracy*. Second edition. New York: Palgrave Macmillan, 2007.

Webber, Jeffery R. "What Is Hugo Chávez's Legacy?" *SocialistWorker.org*, March 8, 2013. http://socialistworker.org/2013/03/08/what-is-hugo-chavezs-legacy.

———. "Dual Powers, Class Compositions, and the Venezuelan People." *Historical Materialism* 23, no. 2 (2015): 189–227.

———. *The Last Day of Oppression and the First Day of the Same: The Politics and Economics of the New Latin American Left*. Chicago: Haymarket Books (2017).

———. "The Retreat of the Pink Tide in Latin America." *International Socialist Review* 110, April 5, 2018.

Webber, Jeffery R., and Susan Spronk. "Voices from Venezuela on Worker Control and Bureaucracy in the Bolivarian Revolution." *Venezuelaanalysis*, September 7, 2010. https://venezuelanalysis.com/analysis/5615.

———. "The Revolution Will Not Be Decreed: An Interview with Gonzalo Gomez." *Venezuelanalysis*, August 19, 2012. https://venezuelanalysis.com/analysis/7182.

Weinberg, Bill. "Forgotten Voices in Venezuelan Crisis." *Countervortex*, January 24, 2019. https://countervortex.org/blog/forgotten-voices-in-venezuela-crisis/#:~:text=Things%20are%20approaching%20a%20crisis%20point%20in%20the,thousands%20of%20supporters%20in%20Caracas%20on%20Jan.%2023.

Weisbrot, Mark. 2012. "Why the US Demonizes Venezuela's Democracy." *The Guardian*, October 3, 2012. https://www.theguardian.com/commentisfree/2012/oct/03/why-us-dcemonises-venezuelas-democracy.

Weisbrot, Mark, and Jeffrey Sachs. "Economic Sanctions as Collective Punishment: The Case of Venezuela." *Center for Economic and Policy Research*, April 2019.

Welle, Deutch. "ACNUR: 'Nos preocupa que se invisibilice la crisis de refugiados y migrantes de Venezuela." *Aporrea*, November 29, 2019. https://www.aporrea.org/ddhh/n349504.html.

Wilpert, G. *Venezuela's Bolivarian Process*. New York: Venezuelaanalysis Press, 2006.

———. *Changing Venezuela by Taking Power*. London: Verso 2007.

———. 2015. "The Roots of the Current Situation in Venezuela." *TeleSur*, November 22, 2015. https://www.telesurenglish.net/opinion/The-Roots-of-the-Current-Situation-in -Venezuela-20151122-0031.html.

Winn, Peter. *Weavers of Revolution: The Yarur Workers and Chile's Road to Socialism*. Oxford, UK: Oxford University Press, 1989.

Wong, Edward, and Nicholas Casey. "U.S. Targets Venezuela With Tough Oil Sanctions During Crisis of Power." *The New York Times*, January 28, 2019. https://www.nytimes .com/2019/01/28/us/politics/venezuela-sanctions-trump-oil.html.

Wood, Gordan. *The Radicalism of the American Revolution*. New York: Alfred A. Knopf, 1992.

Wyss, Jim. "Poll Shows Venezuela's Guiadó is Losing Popularity and Has Shrunk to Maduro Level." *Miami Herald*, December 4, 2019. https://www.miamiherald.com/news/nation -world/world/americas/article238040219.html.

Young, Iris. M. "Communication and the Other: Beyond Deliberative Democracy." In *Democracy and Difference: Contesting the Boundaries of the Political*. Ed. Seyla Benhabib. Princeton, NJ: Princeton University Press, 1996.

Zeguel, M. 2013. "El Poder Popular como perspectiva estratégica de construcción de la Izquierda libertaria." *Rebelión*, December 21, 2013. https://rebelion.org/el-poder-popular-como -perspectiva-estrategica-de-construccion-de-la-izquierda-libertaria/.

Zittel, Thomas, and Dieter Fuchs. *Participatory Democracy and Political Participation: Can Participatory Engineering Bring Citizens Back In?* New York: Routledge, 2007.

Zweifel, Thomas D. *Democratic Deficit: Institutions and Regulation in the European Union, Switzerland, and the United States in Comparative Perspective.* Lanham, MD: Lexington Books, 2002.

Index

About the Author

Anderson M. Bean is teaching assistant professor of sociology at North Carolina Agricultural and Technical State University.